Retheorizing Shakespeare through Presentist Readings

James O'Rourke

Routledge
Taylor & Francis Group
NEW YORK   LONDON

First published 2012
by Routledge
711 Third Avenue, New York, NY 10017

Simultaneously published in the UK
by Routledge
2 Park Square, Milton Park, Abingdon, Oxon OX14 4RN

*Routledge is an imprint of the Taylor & Francis Group,
an informa business*

© 2012 Taylor & Francis

The right of James O'Rourke to be identified as author of this work
has been asserted by him in accordance with sections 77 and 78 of the
Copyright, Designs and Patents Act 1988.

Typeset in Sabon by IBT Global.

Library of Congress Cataloging-in-Publication Data
O'Rourke, James L.
    Retheorizing Shakespeare through presentist readings / James O'Rourke.
        p. cm. — (Routledge studies in shakespeare ; v. 7)
    Includes bibliographical references and index.
    1. Shakespeare, William, 1564–1616—Criticism and interpretation.
2. Presentism (Literary analysis)   I. Title.
    PR2986.O76 2011
    822.3'3—dc23
    2011026131

ISBN13: 978-0-415-89703-7 (hbk)
ISBN13: 978-0-203-14519-7 (ebk)

Retheorizing Shakespeare through Presentist Readings

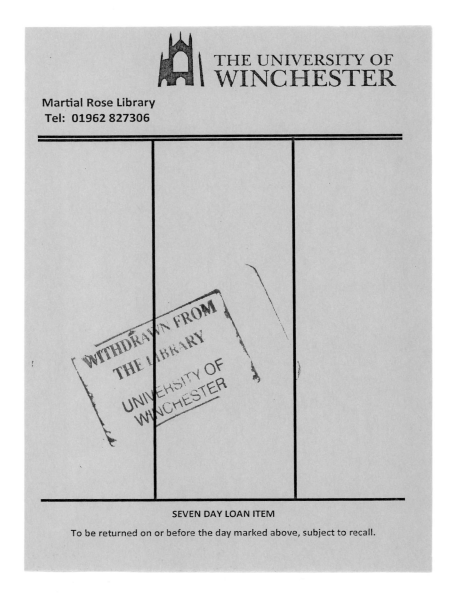

THE UNIVERSITY OF
WINCHESTER

Routledge Studies in Shakespeare

To Helen

Contents

Permissions

Frequently Cited Texts

Introduction
Retheorizing Shakespeare

For most of the twentieth century, Shakespeare was our contemporary. Jan
Kott found a cynical sensibility in him that spoke to a civilization living
in the shadow of the Bomb and the Holocaust, J. L. Styan discovered a
convergence between Shakespearean productions mounted by the Elizabethan original performance practices movement and Brecht's experiments
with alienation effects, and Brecht himself, when asked which authors of
the classical tradition were best suited to his style of "epic theatre," nomi-
nated Shakespeare.[1] But today, after a generation of Shakespeare studies
dominated by the new historicism and its offspring the new materialism,
the belief that we can share Shakespeare's world view has become not
only epistemologically dubious but ethically suspect. The assertion of an
epistemic gap between the early modern period and the present that was a
hallmark of the new historicism has been promoted to a moral imperative
in David Kastan's articulation of the principles of the new materialism.
When Kastan contends that we must recognize that "What value Shakespeare has for us" lies in "his difference from us," he argues for the "moral
relevance" of this concession in order to "ward off our narcissism" and
prevent the "premature imposition of present day interests and values" on
the alterity of the early modern world.[2]

The assertion of epistemic alterity has served, for both the new historicism and the new materialism, as a marker of professional objectivity.
Kastan's advocacy of a "post-theoretical moment" in Shakespeare studies
that would proceed "not by producing more theory but more facts" (*SAT*
31) indicates the increasingly positivist tendency of this historicist disposition, and it identifies the impediment to this positivism: "more theory."
When Kastan celebrates the post-theoretical era that has become possible
now that "the great age of theory is over" (31), we all understand what he
means by "theory": not a cultural materialism with roots in Marx, Foucault, or Williams but the deconstructive style of seventies theory that discovered truth in discontinuity, aberration, and abysses. Kastan's dismissal
of criticism that finds in "doublings and dislocations mere indeterminacy"
(181) echoes Stephen Greenblatt's disdain for the "*O altitudo*! of radical indeterminacy,"[3] an echo that marks the continuity between the new

historicist and the new materialist challenges to the principles and practices of the "great age of theory." Despite the ritual gestures of disaffiliation with the new historicism that now pervade Shakespeare studies, the swerve from formalism to historicism that took place in English and American literary studies a generation ago has never been reversed or even seriously compromised. Writing at the outset of this shift in 1979, Paul de Man observed the formation of a disciplinary consensus that years of "ascetic concentration on techniques" had left "the internal law and order of literature well policed," and so "our moral conscience" required that we turn to "the foreign affairs, the external politics, of literature."[4] As the center of gravity in English literary studies moved from Yale deconstruction of the Romantic period to the new historicist study of the English Renaissance, the new historicism provided early modern studies with the confidence to transcend both theoretical speculation and the ambiguities of close reading in order to focus on "the specific historical conditions that have determined the reading and writing of literature" (*SAT* 31). While de Man could write in 1979 that "Poetic writing is the most advanced and refined form of deconstruction" (*AR* 17), a subsequent generation of critical work devoted to knowing the past in its own terms has consigned the idea that the formal properties of literary language could offer a privileged vehicle of ideological critique to the status of false consciousness.

From an historicist perspective, Brecht's beliefs that his dramatic theory and practice could offer a presentist critique of ideology and at the same time could recover the performative conditions of the early modern stage, so that "an epic way of acting … seems to be most applicable … in works like Shakespeare's" (*BOT* 225), seem to represent only a naive failure to understand both the cultural specificity of early modernism and the relation between performativity and politics. In Kastan's narrative of progress, Brecht's presentist modernism can take its place alongside the "great age of theory" as a necessary stage in the construction of a mature materialism that has now "take[n] to heart and to mind the theoretical implications" of the work of its predecessors (*SAT* 31). But the new historicist/new materialist paradigm that dominates early modern literary studies has often been more opportunistic than rigorous in its adoption of critical principles of modernism and poststructuralism, with the result that current historicist practices are routinely based on a number of premises that were called into question both in the modernism of Brecht, Kott, and Walter Benjamin and in the age of poststructuralist theory. These premises include (1) the assertion of an epistemic gap between the past and the present; (2) the pursuit of synecdochal continuities between signifying particulars and a synchronic totality; (3) an admiration for a sublime aesthetic; (4) a belief in the separability of knowable "facts" from speculative "theory"; (5) the iteration of the principle of the intentional fallacy; and (6) the assumption that cultural context exerts a determinative role in the activities of reading and writing. A reliance on these premises has made it possible to dispatch Shakespeare's supposed contemporaneity to the realm of those transcendental subjects who lived before the great age of theory.

In the first chapter of this book, I will offer a more thorough account of how these premises structure historicist literary studies; in this introduction, I will sketch out my argument about the vulnerability of these premises and their problematic foundations. The often noted synecdochal structure of new historicist and new materialist narratives belies the regular invocation of Benjamin's work as an intellectual source of the new historicism.[5] Georg Lukacs's complaint that Benjamin's concept of allegory dissolves the necessary connection between the "individual" and the "typical"[6] indicates the fundamental clash between Benjamin's notion of the contingency of historical materialism and Lukacs's belief in totality. This conception of totality underlies the synecdochal narrative in which an anecdote or an object is contextualized in order to demonstrate its role in what Douglas Bruster calls the "ensemble of behavioral patterns, artifacts, ideas, and values" that show the "depth of difference between us and those sixteenth- and seventeenth-century persons who produced and consumed the texts that hold our attention even today."[7] Both the synecdochal continuity between the "individual" and the "typical" and the assertion of an epistemic gap between the past and the present are constitutive features of a Lukacsian historiography of synchronic totality and epistemic rupture; the new historicist dyad of the totalizing ensemble and the epistemic gap establishes a distance between early modernism and modernity that is as absolute as the gulf that separates Lukacs's worlds of the epic and the novel.[8]

The priority granted by Benjamin to allegory, a mode of representation that acknowledges its own artificiality, over the symbol, which promises the wholeness of an organic totality, and the corresponding distinction Benjamin makes between the tenuousness of the allegorical "trace" and the "aura" of the symbol constitute one of the most compelling twentieth century critiques of the poetics of the sublime.[9] A sublime poetics resurfaces, however, both in Greenblatt's celebration of a reception aesthetic of "resonance and wonder" (*LTC* 163) and in Kastan's espousal of a critical methodology of "'magic and positivism'" (*SAT* 18). The reified alterity of early modernism in new historicist studies is not the result of the positivist accumulation of facts, but is the inevitable effect of this sublime poetics. Greenblatt's notion of "absolutist theatricality" (*SN* 65), originally a model for the Elizabethan theatre, has metamorphosed into a conception of the early modern period itself as a sublime object of wonder: a vast, exotic alterity that becomes more fascinating as it becomes more Other. Greenblatt's description of the early modern theatrical spectator—"powerfully engaged by this visible presence and at the same time held at a respectful distance from it" (*SN* 64)—aptly describes the new historicist critic contemplating the early modern period. Brecht's description of the early modern, urban, public theatre characterizes this imaginary sublimity as anachronistic. Where Greenblatt argues that his model of "privileged visibility" simply acknowledges the generic "poetics of the theater" (*SN* 64), Brecht contends that the imposition of an aristotelian poetics of magnitude and inevitability upon the early modern theatre under the guise of the "'eternal laws of the theatre'" (*BOT* 161) is simply historically incorrect. The "naive surrealism"[10] of the Elizabethan theatre, Brecht argues, provided fertile ground for alienation effects that enabled both Shakespeare and his audience to establish a critical distance on theatrical and cultural norms and conventions (*BOT* 135). When we look back to the terms of twentieth century debates over Marxist poetics, we can see that the new historicism and the new materialism have placed themselves on the Lukacsian, antimodernist side of those debates.

Perhaps the least controversial principle of the new materialism has been its iteration of the premise of the "intentional fallacy," which Kastan describes as "the now standard theoretical claim about the limitations of authorial intention as a determinant of literary meaning" (*SAT* 28). Kastan's breezy assurance about the consensus that underlies this "standard theoretical claim" is based on a familiar critical history that runs from "The Intentional Fallacy" to "The Death of the Author,"[11] but these texts are actually broadly inconsistent both in their central arguments and in their assimilation into later critical practices. This imaginary consensus also elides some important discussions of the concept of intentionality in the poststructuralist era, including both Derrida's analysis of J. L. Austin's speech-act theory and Paul de Man's critique of the American New Critics. Derrida argues that Austin's performative conception of language shows that when language is considered as action, intentionality can be seen as the basis of its undecidability; "the structure of intentionality alone," Derrida contends, "can enable us to account for the differentiation between the 'locutionary,' 'illocutionary,' and 'perlocutionary' values of the 'same' marks or utterances."[12] De Man, too, identifies intentionality as the basis of the multiplicity of meanings that can inhabit the "same" words; he argues that the assertion of the "intentional fallacy" was the central error of the American New Criticism, an error that resulted from the failure of the New Critics to recognize the contradiction between a theory of organic form, in which works of art take on the qualities of natural objects for which "existence and essence coincide in them at all times," and the critical practice of close reading, which regularly produced a "plurality of significations" that "takes us into a discontinuous world of reflective irony and ambiguity."[13] Intentionality, de Man contends, does not limit or control this plurality; it produces it.

While the "standard theoretical claim" that marginalizes intentionality as an interpretive category assumes a classical conception of abundant intentionality, where a transcendental subject in full control of both illocutionary motive and perlocutionary effect produces a univocal message, both Derrida and de Man describe a performative concept of intentionality as the basis of the equivocality of language. When language is considered as action, it is the inflectional quality of intentionality that generates multiple possibilities within the same words and produces a discontinuity with pure iteration. This dual property of intentionality, its ability both to generate multiplicity and to assign differential values to the multiple possibilities that inhabit the same words, is ritually dismissed in historicist study as "mere" or "radical indeterminacy," a critical gesture that enables the assimilation of individual authors to the dominant vectors of their cultural moment as we have imagined them. Greenblatt's assertion that Shakespeare was only able to "explore," but not to "resist," the dominant relations of power in early modern England,[14] a crucial moment in the formation of the new historicist paradigm of subversion and containment, implicitly relies upon the concept of the "intentional fallacy" in order to elevate an absence of evidence—i. e., the impossibility of establishing a rule-governed protocol that would govern the ways in which a multiplicity of locutionary, illocutionary, and perlocutionary possibilities can inform the "same" words—into an evidence of absence, a proof of Shakespeare's inability to see and to critique the contradictions and inequities of power in his society as clearly and as actively as we do today. As the new historicist construction of the epistemic coherence of the early modern period draws upon a Lukacsian historiography, an anachronistic model of the theatre, and the organic poetics of the American New Criticism, it circumscribes the performative range of the early modern theatre.

In addition to outlining what I see as the errors and shortcuts that have informed the appropriation of the insights of the "great age of theory" in the new historicism and the new materialism, my opening chapter offers a theoretical foundation for Shakespearean "presentism," an emerging critical movement that has contested the retrospective focus of historicism in order to ground Shakespeare studies in the concerns of the present. The theoretical justification that I provide for Shakespearean presentism differs, however, from the current direction of this movement. As represented by the work of Hugh Grady, Terence Hawkes, and the contributors to the manifesto volume *Presentist Shakespeares*, presentism has forged "a committed engagement with the developments in critical and cultural theory that have taken place since the 1980s."[15] A focus on questions of agency has been a central theme of presentist work, and Grady draws a bright line between the activist commitments of British cultural materialism of the 1980s and the evolution of the American new historicism into a new, object-centered, materialism. But by adopting a critical legacy that reaches back no further than the 1980s, presentism, in its current configuration, has avoided any direct engagement with the deconstructive critique of performativity or with modernist poetics of defamiliarization (such as Brecht's model of alienation), and the result has been a flattening out of the conception of agency in presentist studies. To date, Shakespearean presentism has equated agency with a classical conception of abundant intentionality rather than with a contingent sense of performativity, and critical agency is more often located in the modern interpreter than in the immanent critical logic of the plays.[16]

In my readings of Shakespeare's plays, by contrast, Shakespeare's critical agency is located in a theatre that serves as the site for the contestation, rather than the iteration, of dominant cultural narratives. Brecht locates this subversive theatrical potential in the concept of "gest," the intersubjective relation between the producers (author, director, and actors) and the audience of a work. I have focused my readings of Shakespeare's plays on this fundamental Brechtian question: What is the "gest," the "particular attitudes . . . towards other men" (*BOT* 104), expressed by this work? Is it written, in condescension or in solidarity, "for scum who want the cockles of their hearts warmed," or does the author treat his audience "as thoroughly intelligent" and ask it to "come to grips with things"? (*BOT* 14, 23). Do the romantic comedies ratify the structural expectation of their genre, the premise that the happiest heterosexuals somehow deserve their good fortune? Do *The Merchant of Venice* and *Othello* congratulate racism for its ability to discern alien species trying to pass in human form, or do they situate racism as a cultural formation? Does *Troilus and Cressida* really locate a moral catastrophe, in the middle of a world war, in a woman who has a change of object cathexis after she has been forcibly transferred from one tribe of men to another? Does King Lear have a good death? In addressing these questions, I have not accepted the premise that an epistemic abyss has rendered our own most sophisticated interpretive discourses, such as deconstruction, psychoanalysis, or performance theory, irrelevant to our understanding of the past. I have used all of these tools in order to show how Shakespeare engages a series of reified discourses of his own cultural moment—romantic comedy, antisemitism, European racism, courtly love, and the *ars moriendi* tradition—and turns their conventions inside out.

A presentism which rediscovers Shakespearean dissidence by treating Shakespeare as an active critic of his own culture is not a naive imposition of the present on the past but a recognition of what Brecht found in Shakespeare's works, a dominant gest in which their "attitude to their social function" involves the "representation of reality with a view to influencing it" (*BOT* 225). Brecht's confidence in Shakespeare's prescient modernity is borne out when the most innovative recent productions and adaptations of his plays—such as Gale Edwards' *Taming of the Shrew* or Nicholas Hytner's *Henry V*, Julie-Anne Robinson's *Wicked Bastard of Venus* or Trevor Nunn's *Merchant of Venice*—explode their "obvious" meanings and illuminate a surprisingly modern illocutionary logic. Such adventurous theatrical forays into Shakespearean interpretation should serve both to release Shakespearean criticism from a debilitating fear of anachronism and set a standard for our critical engagements with Shakespeare's uncanny modernity.

Brecht's conception of early modern theatricality inspired both criticism and performance. Working from Brechtian premises, Jan Kott's essay on

King Lear informed Peter Brook's innovative production of the play not through an account of technique but through an interrogation of the play's gest and a deconstruction of its traditional sublimity. Reading for Shakespearean gest today, however, requires breaching two of the most widely agreed principles of literary criticism—the taboo against epistemic crossings and the sanctity of the intentional fallacy. Since these strictures are only artificial effects of our current interpretive protocols, I have regularly violated both of these principles in my readings of the plays as I have sought to reimagine why these plays mattered to their original audiences and how they can matter to us today. In my second chapter, I look at the conditions of original performance of *The Taming of the Shrew* and *Twelfth Night* and at a modern, radical adaptation of *As You Like It* in order to show how Shakespeare's most popular romantic comedies regularly use the figure of the cross-dressed boy actor as a pivot that turns the comic plot into a zero-sum battle for power. In Chapter 3, I provide what Leah Marcus calls a "local reading" of *The Merchant of Venice* to illustrate the challenge posed to the antisemitism of an early modern London audience when it is pressed to take sides in a conflict between a stereotyped stage Jew and a subtle caricature of a homosexual Italian Catholic merchant. In Chapter 4, I describe how Shakespeare takes up the paradoxes of a revisionary literary tradition in order to undermine the masculinist ethos of heroic epic with a paradoxically proto-feminist theme from courtly love literature, the insistence that desire only achieves the moral quality of love when it is based on the uncoerced choice of both partners. In Chapter 5, I show how the basic question that *Othello* poses to its original audience—Is the title character a pathological type (a "black") who murders an innocent (i. e., "white") woman, or is he the victim of an irrational cultural prejudice?—stages a conflict between two Freudian narratives, the normative oedipal complex and the subversive critique of mass psychology. In my final chapter, I look at how Shakespeare uses the schematic form of the medieval morality in order to reengage the central concern of the *ars moriendi* tradition, the difficulty of achieving a "good death," in a cultural setting in which Protestant reformers were encouraging their followers to embrace the passage to the next world without the need for elaborate mourning rituals.

Throughout this book, I have tried to remain close to the facts of Shakespeare's texts by imagining the range of interplays that could take place between Shakespeare's words, the nonillusionist performance devices of the early modern stage, and the live audiences that shared the physical space of the theatre with Shakespeare's actors. I have assumed that those audiences came to the theatre to be surprised, challenged, and even disturbed, that Shakespeare delivered for them, and that he can still do so today.

1 Spectres of Intention
Epic Theatre and the Lessons of Theory

I NEW HISTORICISM AND THE POETICS OF THE SUBLIME

In *Retheorizing Shakespeare*, I argue (1) that the most sweeping change that has taken place in literary studies over the past generation, the displacement of close reading by historicist inquiry, has been founded on a shift from a poetics of irony to a poetics of the sublime; (2) that the modern theatrical models of these competing poetics are Bertolt Brecht's "epic theatre" (*BOT* 22) and Stephen Greenblatt's "absolutist theatricality" (*SN* 65); and (3) that the adoption of a performative model of close reading that incorporates the defamiliarizing techniques of Brecht's alienation-effect[1] and of poststructuralist theory is the most productive way to rediscover Shakespeare not simply as a site of cultural complexity but as an active cultural interrogator in his own right. While Greenblatt's conception of "absolutist theatricality" is ultimately based on an aristotelian poetics of magnitude and inevitability, the Brechtian technique of alienation, or "playing in quotation marks," contests the claims of aristotelian poetics to represent the "eternal laws of the theatre" (*BOT* 17, 161). Brecht's challenge to Aristotle begins at the level of representation and extends into a disagreement over the purpose of theatre. Aristotle draws upon the distinction between narrative and dramatic representation in order to argue for the superiority of dramatic representation that is based on the "natural instinct of imitation,"[2] but Brecht's decision to name his theatre *epische*, or "narrative," contests the natural grounding of mimesis by emphasizing the inflectional, rather than the iterative, properties of representation. In epic theatre, as mimesis is framed by narrative, the "laws of probability or necessity" (*Poetics* 12) revealed in aristotelian drama lose their aura of inevitability and are displayed as contingent constructions. In aesthetic theory, the name for the contingent, mimetic formation that Aristotle presents as natural, grand, and inevitable is the sublime. As Kant's articulation of the concept of the sublime shows, when an encounter between subjectivity and the totality of nature is framed by the synthetic concept of the sublime, it becomes possible to totalize alterity and thus provide self-knowledge for a subject who is able to recognize herself in her difference from a grand but finite Other.[3] Aristotle and Kant posit this recognition of natural laws as the summit of human awareness, but Brecht's demand that theatre should reveal the fabricated nature of representation is designed to fulfill Marx's injunction to the philosophers: the point is not simply to interpret the world, but to change it.[4]

A sublime poetics has been a central feature of both the new historicism and the new materialism in early modern studies. When Greenblatt supplements the positivist dimension of historicist research with a reception aesthetic of "resonance and wonder" (*LTC* 163), and when David Kastan locates a critical method for the new materialism at the "'crossroads of magic and positivism'" (*SAT* 18), this aesthetic of "wonder" and "magic" is derived from the discourse of the sublime. I would nominate as the inaugural sublime moment of the new historicism Greenblatt's influential assertion in "Invisible Bullets" that drama became the dominant literary genre of Elizabethan England because the "poetics of the theater" reflects a homology between the "privileged visibility" of the stage and the grounding of Tudor and Stuart royal authority in the "display of power at the center of society" (*SN* 64). Greenblatt's equation of a generic "poetics of the theater" with a dominating "absolutist theatricality" imagines the Elizabethan theatre as an effective site for the interpellation of receptive subjects. In Greenblatt's account, a generic imperative dictates a unified spectatorial response because "the theater . . . manifestly addresses its audience as a collectivity" (*SN* 4–5). Aristotle's confident description of the universal pleasures afforded by drama needs only a veneer of cultural specificity in order for Greenblatt to imagine an early modern audience as homogeneous as Aristotle's "man," where neither class, gender, age, nor personal temperament cause any spectator to respond any differently from any other. In the synchronic unities of the new historicism, the early moderns are unlike us, but they are all just like each other, and they are incapable of resisting the power of absolutist spectacle.

Brecht's conception of epic theatre clashes sharply with Greenblatt's notion of the "privileged visibility" of onstage action and the passivity of the audience in the early modern, urban, public theatre. Brecht describes the importance of "alienation effects" in the Elizabethan theatre (*BOT* 135), and he locates these effects in the simplest of devices. Walter Benjamin reports on a conversation in which he and Brecht agreed that both Brecht's alienation-effect and Benjamin's concept of allegory could be identified with "the crown worn crookedly on the king's head" in a Geneva theatre production (*AP* 94). Brecht has several terms (all pejorative) for what Greenblatt simply calls the "poetics of the theater" (*SN* 64). Brecht describes this totalizing mode of representation as the "theatre of hypnosis" or "aristotelian theatre," and he always places in quotation marks its claim to represent "'the eternal laws of the theatre'" (*BOT* 26, 60, 161). Where Greenblatt argues for the impossibility of resistance to the power of display in the Henriad because "we are, after all, in the theater, and our pleasure depends on there being no escape, and our applause ratifies our confinement" (*SN* 47), Brecht derides this "theatre of hypnosis," which he identifies with the bourgeois theatre, for homogenizing its audience into a "cowed, credulous, hypnotized mass" (*BOT* 188). Brecht's principle that "Individuals should not occupy much more space in books and above all not a different kind of space, than in reality" (*AP* 77) diminishes the magnitude of the "privileged visibility" that Greenblatt confers on both theatrical spectacle and royal display. The interpretive consequences of these different conceptions of theatrical scale are significant. In epic theatre, the critical faculties of the spectator are awakened; she is continually reminded that she simultaneously occupies two temporal frames, the fictive world of the play and the real world of the playhouse, and her ability to compare these worlds exposes both the theatre as a site of naked artifice and the conventions of real life as equally fabricated. But within the hypnotic realm of "absolutist theatricality," it is difficult to imagine that a significant portion of Shakespeare's audience might have been as skeptical of Machiavellian monarchs as we are today.

Greenblatt's assertion of the impossibility of subversion in the present (*SN* 65) is the most famous invocation of the legacy of Walter Benjamin in the new historicism, but Greenblatt's celebration of a sublime aesthetic of "resonance and wonder" blunts the critical edge of Benjamin's ambiguous account of aesthetic "aura." Despite Greenblatt's self-identification with "Benjamin, [and] the early rather than later Lukacs" (*LTC* 147), the aesthetic principles he adopts in the essay "Resonance and Wonder" have none of the reflexivity of the Benjaminian trace and all of the sanctity of the aura. Greenblatt's disaffiliation with the "later Lukacs" is also difficult to reconcile with his own critical legacy. It is in Lukacs's late work *The Meaning of Contemporary Realism*, published in 1957, that Lukacs denounces Benjamin's concept of allegory in favor of a more totalizing version of realism in which "each descriptive detail is both *individual* and *typical*"; "modern allegory," Lukacs complains, "denies the typical."[5] The seeming randomness of the data in Walter Cohen's famous list of new historicist exotica—"dreams, popular or aristocratic festivals, denunciations of witchcraft, sexual treatises, diaries and autobiographies, descriptions of clothing, reports of disease, birth and death records, accounts of insanity"[6]—illustrates the charm of new historicist method, where the ingenuity of the interpreter is tested by her ability to show how a seemingly marginal datum typifies the "early modern," but the presumption of synecdochal continuities between these random particulars and the synchronic unity of the early modern period betrays the influence of a Lukacsian historiography in the new historicism. The congruence of the "individual" and the "typical" is the hallmark of Lukacs's epic world, and it is the assumption that enables the ubiquitous rhetorical device of the new historicism and the new materialism, the synecdoche through which an anecdote or an object reveals the deep totality of its cultural context.

Although Kastan distances the new materialism from Greenblatt's model of "privileged visibility" (*SAT* 206), his defense of a critical methodology of "magic and positivism" (*SAT* 31) is equally reliant on a poetics of the sublime. Kastan borrows this paradoxical blend of "magic and positivism" from a dialogue between Benjamin and Theodor Adorno over the *Arcades* manuscript, and although Kastan claims to take Benjamin's side in this dispute, he misreads Benjamin's part in the exchange. When Adorno criticizes Benjamin for "the wide-eyed presentation of mere facts," Kastan casts his lot with Benjamin, expressing a preference for being "situated somewhere near the very 'crossroads of magic and positivism' that made Adorno so uncomfortable" (*SAT* 18). But it is Adorno, not Benjamin, who coins the phrase the "crossroads of magic and positivism" (*AP* 129), and Benjamin subtly objects to this characterization of his work. When Adorno complains that he finds it excessively literalminded that "the arcades are introduced with a reference to the narrowness of the pavements which impede the flaneur" (*AP* 127), Benjamin's reply is sly and slightly mocking; he counters that as for the "term, arcades . . . the bottomless bonhomie of its use cannot have escaped you. . . . It occurs like the picture of a rocky spring on a drinking cup" (*AP* 135). Adorno sees the arcade as a "mere fact" in Benjamin's essay, but Benjamin suggests that Adorno has fallen for a naturalist illusion; he has mistaken the density of the signifier for an empirical object.

Where Kastan asks for a critical method that transcends "theory" in favor of "more facts" (*SAT* 31), Benjamin's description of his rhetorical strategy in the *Arcades Project* shows that he was not a positivist who believed that facts construct their own signifying logic, nor did he think that they belonged to a fixed and remote past. He explains to Adorno that

> If a concept like the trace was to be given a convincing interpretation, it had to be introduced with complete naturalness at the empirical level. . . . precisely in order to receive in the decisive contexts its sudden illumination. This illumination is intended. The concept of the trace finds its philosophical determination in opposition to the concept of aura. (*AP* 135)

Benjamin addresses the central methodological concern of both the new historicism and the new materialism, the relation of a material singularity, an event or an object, to a larger signifying context, but he does not discover a synecdochal continuity between the individual and the typical. Where historicism asks the literary critic to relinquish her situatedness in the present in return for the promise of an encounter with the exotic alterity of the past, Benjamin instructs Adorno that whatever truth is to be derived from the traces of the past arrives through an intentional construct that dispels any sublime or magical aura: "This illumination is intended." Allegorical claims to truth do not present themselves as synecdoches of an organic totality; they are only markers of possibilities that need to be brought into being by an active intervention from the present.

II   THE "INTENTIONAL FALLACY"

A sublime poetics, based on mimesis, describes a subject-object relation, but Brecht's conception of epic theater grounds the theater in its intersubjectivity. The critical premise of the "intentional fallacy" is thus a significant impediment to a shift from an aristotelian to a Brechtian theatrical model. While the reception of Benjamin by the new historicism and the new materialism has shifted the balance of his work towards the organic poetics of Lukacs, Paul de Man's appropriation of Benjamin's concept of allegory serves as the basis for an incisive critique of the authority of the "intentional fallacy." De Man asserts that Benjaminian allegory, "a pure decision of the mind," and not the symbol, which is based "on the organic coherence of the synecdoche," is the exemplary mode of representation in Romantic literature (*BI* 192), and he identifies the mistaken overvaluation of the symbol with the New Critical valorization of organic form. This argument is given a patient, schematic grounding in "Form and Intent in the American New Criticism," where de Man first puts forward the disanalogy between a natural object like a stone, which can be identified simply as the sum of its physical properties, and a chair, which can only be understood through the use to which it will be put. Texts, de Man argues, fall into the domain of intentional objects; they are the effects of multiple and contradictory purposes, and can never achieve the organic unity of natural objects. In de Man's view, the New Critics were led into the error of asserting the intentional fallacy because of their failure to address the contradiction between the "plurality of significations" they discovered in their close readings and the premise of the organic unity of artworks (*BI* 28), and as a result of this unexamined contradiction Anglo-American formalism regularly lapses into a Romantic aesthetic that effaces any distinction between artworks and natural objects. When Greenblatt's defense of a reception aesthetic of "resonance and wonder" culminates in an equation between the admiration felt by Albrecht Durer for the *ingenia* of the makers of the loot that had been expropriated by Spanish explorers and the wonder produced by the contents of Renaissance wonder-cabinets—"nautilus shells, ostrich eggs" etc. (*LTC* 177)—the equation of natural and fabricated objects completes the arc of a sublime, organic aesthetic and produces an inherently neutering model for reading Shakespearean political drama.

De Man's rehabilitation of the concept of intentionality may seem like only a quirky deviation from what Kastan calls the "now standard theoretical claim about the limitations of authorial intention as a determinant of literary meaning" (*SAT* 28), but the underlying consensus for this "standard theoretical claim" is less secure than it appears. Wimsatt and Beardsley's argument in "The Intentional Fallacy" shares very little, at the level of critical principles, with Barthes' "The Death of the Author." What these texts do have in common is the sense that some entity—the literary text for Wimsatt and Beardsley, the reader for Barthes—needs to be set free from the dead hand of history, but neither the New Critics nor Barthes had much to say in these essays about the role of authorial intention in the production of literary texts. Wimsatt and Beardsley were primarily concerned with the relative value of what they called "internal and external evidence for the meaning of a poem,"[7] and they came to precisely the opposite conclusion to Kastan on this point. Where Kastan argues for the primacy of contextual evidence in literary interpretation because "both reading and writing are not unmediated activities but take place only and always in context" (*SAT* 31), Wimsatt and Beardsley argued against an overreliance on context because, they said, the invocation of authorial intention had become the vehicle of "Tillyardism," the use of broad contextual frameworks like the Elizabethan World Picture, to offer probabilistic contexts for the reading of literary texts. Barthes, too, saw the category of the author as a constraint, but not upon the ironic range of the text; for Barthes, it was the freedom and the pleasure of the reader that required liberation from an imaginary obligation to the past. In each case, a focus on the reception, rather than the production, of texts led to the marginalizing of intentionality as a vehicle of literary interpretation, but these conclusions were predicated not upon a reflective analysis of the relation of authors to language and culture, but upon the sense that an important freedom was at stake. The formalists who have followed the New Critics in decrying the "spectres of intention"[8] and the reader-response and performance critics who have adopted Barthesian principles have embraced those freedoms without reengaging the questions that inspired de Man's critique of the place of intentionality in the production of different modes of literary representation.

While the deconstructive critique of the role of intentionality in literary production has often been assimilated to a Barthesian conception of free play, a closer reading of that legacy shows how both Derrida and de Man use intentionality as a pivotal concept in the construction of a nuanced opposition between a poetics of performativity and a poetics of the sublime. When Derrida takes up de Man's analysis of the Kantian sublime, he finds a prising open of the relation between a singular "event" and its context. The challenge in thinking about "events," Derrida contends, is not how to account for the emergence of an event from its conditions of possibility; the real challenge is to imagine discontinuity, "how to think together the machine and the event, a machine-like repetition and that which happens" so that "the event" actually "interrupts the course of the possible."[9] De Man's deconstruction of the Kantian sublime theorizes this rupture as the intentional subversion of sublime figuration. Where Kant argues that the contemplation of the sublime enables us to see the world "as the poets do," as an architectonic form that reconciles the intuitive and the transcendental when it displays the ocean as "a clear mirror of water bounded only by the heaven," de Man responds that this is exactly what real poets do not do. "It is not the case," de Man insists, "that the heaven is a vault or that the horizon bounds the ocean like the walls of a building."[10] When poets introduce us to a "discontinuous world of reflective irony and ambiguity," de Man argues, they do so through the simultaneous production of "two texts,"[11] one that presents the phenomenal synthesis of perception and cognition, and another that disarticulates that synthesis. In Derrida's reading of de Man's essay on Kant, he grounds this disarticulation in a "pure performativity" that can only be produced by the active intervention of "a living being" standing in opposition to the self-evident power of the "natural": "Pure performativity implies the presence of a living being, and of a living being speaking one time only," Derrida contends, and he goes on to argue that "This foreclosure of the machine answers to the intentionality of intention itself. It is intentionality."[12] Intentionality, as Derrida describes it, is not the free act of an autonomous subject discovering her relation to a natural Other; rather, intentionality describes the reinflection of a reified constellation that has achieved the status of the natural.

Derrida's most extensive treatment of the concept of intentionality appears in his analysis of J. L. Austin's speech-act theory, where Derrida does not treat intentionality as a binary question of presence or absence, or even as a matter of quantification; rather, intentionality occupies a structural position in relation to language, one that is neither subordinate to nor subsumed within context. The irreducibility of this performative concept of intentionality is central to Derrida's position in his dialogue with John Searle, where Derrida argues that Searle is mistaken when he claims that Derrida's deconstruction of Austin's model of the "teleological jurisdiction of an entire field whose organizing center remains *intention*" (*LI* 15) implies a dismissal of the concept of intentionality. Although many of Derrida's closest readers follow Searle in believing that Derrida's critique of Austin simply disqualifies the concept of intentionality,[13] Derrida specifically corrects Searle's simplification of this point; he explains that

> Sarl [Searle] attributes to *Sec* ["Signature Event Context"] the following affirmation: intentionality is (supposedly) purely and simply "absent" from writing. . . . *Sec* has not simply effaced or denied intentionality, as Sarl claims. On the contrary, *Sec* insists on the fact that "the category of intention will not disappear, it will have its place." (*LI* 55, 58)

The form of intentionality that Derrida does efface in *Sec* is the "teleological" dimension of Austin's model, in which the abundant intentionality of a speaker can willfully guarantee the conversion of a univocal illocutionary motive into a singular perlocutionary effect. For Searle, who believes in this classical conception of intentionality, this is a denial of intentionality. For

Derrida, it is a displacement of a classical conception of intentionality into a performative model.

As the distinction between performative and teleological intentionality draws Derrida and Searle into a discussion of the relation between stage performance and what Searle calls "real life," Searle is nonplussed over Derrida's refusal to acknowledge the most basic facts about "real life." He seems genuinely puzzled at why Derrida objects to Austin's characterization of utterances "said by an actor on stage" as "*parasitic* upon normal use,"[14] and he patiently explains to the obtuse Derrida that "there could not be promises made by actors in a play if there were not the possibility of promises made in real life." Since the sort of empty citationality characteristic of stage performance, where an actor who says "I do" is not actually married, is "logically dependent" upon what Searle calls "serious discourse,"[15] it is therefore "perfectly straightforward" to Searle that there is a clear distinction between the efficacious performances of "real life" and their empty fictional representations. In "real life," "intention is the heart of meaning and communication" and "*a meaningful sentence is just a standing possibility of the corresponding (intentional) speech act*" of a "serious speaker" (207, 202). For Searle, intention simply abolishes overdetermination and establishes the natural grounding of "real life."

Searle's articulation of the principles of classical speech-act theory is grounded on a distinction between mention and use, or mechanical citation and purposive iteration, but Derrida unsettles this distinction when he asks of Austin and Searle, "if what they call the 'standard,' 'fulfilled,' 'normal,' 'serious,' 'literal,' etc. is *always capable* of being affected by the non-standard, the 'void,' the 'abnormal,' the 'nonserious,' the 'parasitical,' what does that tell us about the former?" (*LI* 89). By reinflecting the words that Searle takes so seriously, Derrida exploits the performative character of his own discourse and exemplifies his argument that it is not iteration but citation that has the power to create "events." As Derrida puts it in his essay on de Man and the sublime, the original originates in the displacement of iteration into citation: "One is thus inaugurating another word, a homonym that must be put forward cautiously within quotation marks. . . . The quotation marks signal in this case that one is citing only oneself . . . in a gesture that is as inaugural as it is arbitrary."[16] Derrida's reframing of the "standard," the "fulfilled," and the "normal" within quotation marks produces a Brechtian alienation-effect; by collapsing the distance between the empty promises of the stage and the arbitrariness and the fragility of "serious discourse," Derrida's performative model of discourse shows how the nonserious, or the fictional, is not outside, secondary to, or parasitic upon the spontaneity of "real life," but is the very condition of its existence.

While Searle confidently names "promises made in real life" as the condition of possibility of "promises made by actors on the stage," Derrida notes that when it comes to the conditions of possibility of those ordinary, "serious" promises, Searle has nothing to say. For the serious Searle, "real life" is simply itself; existence and essence naturally coincide. In the (mostly) serious essay "Signature Event Context," Derrida outlines the premises that enable classical speech-act theory to equate ordinary speech with successful perlocution: "signature," a "free consciousness present to the totality of the operation"; "event," an "absolutely meaningful speech [*vouloir-dire*] master of itself"; and "context," "an exhaustively definable context" (*LI* 15). In his response to Searle in *Limited Inc*, Derrida expands on his thesis that none of these terms delivers on the promise of its concept. No consciousness is fully present to itself, no speech-act can guarantee the conversion of a univocal illocutionary motive into a singular perlocutionary effect, and there is no principle that can regulate when "context" reaches its "certain or saturated" limit (*LI* 3). The vulnerability of these concepts explains why Austin was never able to establish a categorical distinction between performatives and constatives. For Derrida, the great accomplishment of Austin's work is to show the interdependence and the mobility of these terms, in which the place of intentionality is irreducible: the "structure of intentionality alone can enable us to account for the differentiation between the 'locutionary,' 'illocutionary,' and 'perlocutionary' values of the 'same' marks or utterances" (*LI* 58). As Derrida and de Man show through the opposition between performativity and the sublime, the indeterminacy of language is neither a negation of intentionality nor a reflection of the purposelessness of the natural world; the multiplicity of discursive values that inhabit the "same" words reflects the range of interpretive possibilities that are available to purposive subjects. When Greenblatt negates this "radical indeterminacy" by invoking the power of an "absolutist theatricality" to effectively produce a single message for both elite and plebeian spectators, he guarantees perlocutionary success by unifying the realm of intentionality in a unitary collective subject: "we are, after all, in the theater, and our pleasure depends on there being no escape, and our applause ratifies our confinement" (*SN* 95, 65, 47). But as Derrida argues, this guarantee is only a fictional representation of real life, where the gaps and overdeterminations in every set of signatures, events, and contexts make the potential failure of every speech-act an omnipresent possibility.

III FORMALISM AND INTENTIONALITY

The irreducibility of performativity in language, and the irreducibility of intentionality in performativity, are insights from the "great age of theory" that have been marginalized not only in historicist and materialist poetics but also in the formalist response to historicism. A resistance to the predictability imposed on literary texts by a historicist machinery is regularly framed in terms that privilege the autonomy of literary language, but this formalist resistance is often enervated by a reliance on Kantian aesthetic values that offer an artificial choice between the aesthetic and the political.

An artificial distinction between "close reading" and "history" informs a series of recent books and essays by major critical figures from the 1980s— Catherine Belsey, Marjorie Garber, Ellen Rooney, and Jane Gallop—who argue that the historicist focus of recent literary criticism has led to a loss of attention to the intrinsic properties of literary texts. This argument is carried out in a formalist rhetoric that is both self-conscious and familiar; Belsey champions "undecidability" and "the opacity of the signifiers," while Garber looks for "counterintuitive interpretation" that is "transgressive" and that produces "a distance from the continuity of the familiar."[17] Even more plainly and provocatively, Jane Gallop asks for a return to "close reading," and even she is trumped by Ellen Rooney's defense of just plain "reading."[18] The vocabulary of poststructuralism reaches back into earlier twentieth century formalisms when Garber's plea for literary critics to focus on "questions about the *way* something means, rather than *what* it means" (12) recalls Roman Jakobson's opposition between the poetic and referential functions of language, and when Rooney echoes Cleanth Brooks in disparaging "reading-as-paraphrase" (26). But if close reading is to reclaim its centrality in literary studies, close readings that are responsive to the cultural and political interests of literary texts will need not only to disaffiliate from the organic poetics of the New Criticism; they will also have to transcend the covert synthesis of Saussurean linguistics and Kantian aesthetics through which intentionality fades into an agentless *langue* or aesthetic disinterestedness. The heightened undecidability of literary texts does not derive from a lack of intentionality but from its excess, from the production of multiple performative logics that inhabit the "same" words of a single text. These performative logics (locutionary, illocutionary, perlocutionary) take us into the realm of purposive speech-acts, where reassuring constatives are likely to undergo wilful subversions of iterative predictability when we ask questions like: What are the politics of *Henry V*? Of *King Lear*? What do *The Merchant of Venice* and *Othello* have to say about irrational cultural prejudices? How does *Troilus and Cressida* tease out the frictions between conceptions of love, sex, and marriage? As the latter question, which would have been deeply familiar to Andreas Capellanus, shows, our own queries may reflect medieval and early modern discourses that treat these questions just as meticulously as we do. And when we find that the central concerns of early modern texts become most accessible to us in terms of our own devising (e. g., marxism, feminism, psychoanalysis), this should not enable the assumption that the layers of overdetermination that we recognize in these discourses were inaccessible to the original producers and consumers of these works.

De Man's critique of the contradiction within New Critical poetics between the subjective concept of irony and an organic poetics of the symbol suggests that the most significant division in Anglo-American literary criticism is not between formalist methods that focus on the internal workings of literary texts versus historicist approaches that rely on evidence that is external to the text; the more fundamental opposition lies between a performative concept of language that is able to put the overdeterminations of "real life" into quotation marks and the Romantic aesthetic that valorizes the natural and reaches its apotheosis in the inevitability and self-sufficiency of the sublime. While the anti-intentionalist critique that identifies intentionality with the production of "unitary meaning"[19] presumes that intentionality can be identified with unambiguous, declarative statements, de Man's description of intentionality as the entry point into "a discontinuous world of reflective irony and ambiguity" (*BI* 28) suggests an antithesis, and not an identity, between intentionality and a constative rhetorical mode. It is only because a text is an intentional construct and not a natural object that it opens itself to discontinuities between interpretive possibilities. When Greenblatt and Kastan deride as "mere" or "radical indeterminacy" the classic deconstructive aporia in which the necessity of interpretive choice cannot be justified by a saturated context, they dismiss a truly performative concept of intentionality, one that recognizes that the same words can sustain a multiplicity of illocutionary and perlocutionary logics, in favor of a more "serious" logic that grants discursive formations the stability and self-identity of the natural world.

In the later stages of de Man's exploration of the potential relevance of speech-act theory to formalist poetics, he contends that as criticism begins to move from an account of the organization of tropes and themes in a text to an account of its illocutionary logic, it is forced to recognize the double meaning of the term "rhetoric"; rhetoric involves both the study "of tropes and of figures" and the study of language as action, as an art of persuasion (*AR* 6–8). Twentieth century formalisms, including deconstruction, have not devoted equal attention to these two dimensions of rhetoric. Formalist close reading typically focuses on what Jakobson calls poetic grammar, the arrangement of tropes and themes that forms the narrative coherence of a text, a focus that allows the authority of the "intentional fallacy" and the premise of aesthetic disinterestedness to deflect attention away from questions of illocutionary purpose. As a result, we now have an array of reasonably sophisticated techniques for the analysis of poetic grammar, but our means of assessing the conversions of the locutionary, illocutionary, and perlocutionary values of words remain comparatively haphazard. A poetics of the sublime provides aesthetic cover for this state of affairs by declaring questions of intentionality to be out of bounds, but the declaration of "intentional fallacy" precludes consideration of the ineluctably performative dimension of language. As Austin shows, understanding the locutionary rules of a statement without recognizing its illocutionary intent constitutes a complete failure to understand it as a speech-act. If someone says, "I would not do that if I were you," it is very much worth knowing whether this is, in illocutionary terms, a friendly caution or a threat. If someone writes a play about monarchy, ethnic conflict, sexual jealousy, or death, it will probably be worth asking why he did so.

IV CONTEXT AND INTENTIONALITY: *KING LEAR*

When Kastan argues that "It makes little sense . . . for literary interpretation to assume as its primary task the recovery of an authorial intention"
because the lesson of "theory" is that "reading and writing are not unmediated activities but take place only and always in context" (*SAT* 39, 31),
he elevates one piece of the Derridean circuit of signification (context) into
a determinative role and casts another (signature) aside. But the reliance
on context, as Wimsatt and Beardsley objected, privileges the probabilities
of historical narratives over the often contradictory details of close reading. Derrida's observation that only the "structure of intentionality" can
account for the multiple performative logics that inhabit the same words
reconciles intentionality and fictionality in the act of close reading, an act
which consists of the discrimination of multiple interpretive possibilities
in the "same" words that constitute a text. At the same time, Derrida sub-
verts the positivist confidence that informs Kastan's opposition between
"facts" and "theory." "Facts," however seriously they present themselves,
always leave room for inflection, and their contingency is illustrated by the
disparities of interpretive results that, despite a shared positivist rhetoric,
divide the new materialism of Kastan and Bruster from the "neohistori-
cism" of critics like Robin Headlam Wells and Judy Kronenfeld. While the
new materialism typically looks at Shakespeare from the left, "neohistori-
cism" employs a similarly positivist critical vocabulary to restore a more
traditional, Tillyardian bard. Kastan's attempt to overcome an epistemic
gulf by rhetorical fiat in his declaration that although "history can no longer pretend to recover the past 'as it actually was' . . . it need not, therefore, abandon the desire for definitive and usable historical knowledge"
(*SAT* 41) finds an enthusiastic echo in Wells's argument that empiricism
trumps hermeneutics as a critical method because hermeneutics, by definition, can only discover what it looks for. Wells offers empiricism as a
healthy corrective to "theory," arguing that "Despite the inadmissibility
of empiricist claims to complete scientific objectivity, accurate knowledge
of the past is arguably still the best means of providing a perspective on
the present."[20] The slippage in terms is similar in both Kastan and Wells;
the "desire" for "definitive" or "accurate" historical knowledge somehow
enables positivist inquiry to arrive at truths that are immune to the "mere
indeterminacy" of "theory" (*SAT* 181). Wells's compilation of the "facts"
of early modern culture leads to readings of Shakespeare's plays that would
amuse or appall a new historicist or new materialist sensibility. Finding
little evidence to support Greenblatt's view of Henry V as (in Wells's words)
a "Machiavellian juggler and conniving hypocrite," Wells finds it clear that
Henry's "piety seems indisputable, and his honour bright" (32). In the case
of *Othello*, Wells argues that the use of a "black man of Islamic origins" to
"suggest the inherently barbaric nature of pre-civilized heroic values" isn't
racist; it's simply "dramaturgical shorthand" (113). The premise that these

conclusions simply represent "facts" from the past rather than reconstructions of the illocutionary logic of texts is, to say the least, a tendentious use of constative rhetoric.

A shared trust in the truth value of "facts" does not prevent sharply divergent new materialist and neohistoricist readings of the governing performative logic of *King Lear*. Although Kastan insists that "the past . . . *existed* independent of any of our representations; and that existence imposes an obligation" upon us (*SAT* 41), a clearly presentist moral imperative colors the conclusion to his own reading of *Lear* when, despite Kastan's admonitions to the contrary, our moral obligation to the past gives way to the ethical demands of the present:

> As "houseless poverty" is again visible both as a social fact and a political issue, Edgar's counterfeiting may well remind even the bourgeois audience of our modern theatre of the reality of human misery that waits outside and remind us as well that perhaps it need not be so. (*SAT* 164)

This egalitarian reading of *Lear* is not only presentist in its sense of moral purpose but, Kronenfeld argues, thoroughly anachronistic. Kronenfeld's neohistoricist booklength study of *Lear* seeks to demonstrate that the play had no such resonance for its original audience, that readings which discover in it a protest against social inequity are guilty of "poststructuralist historicism," and that *Lear* represents Shakespeare's endorsement of "the common Christian culture" that surrounded him, "an organic, hierarchical state in which all are linked together in brotherly love."[21] Kronenfeld's documentation of her case is voluminous, but Hugh Grady is nevertheless dissatisfied with her conclusion. Characterizing Kronenfeld's work as "a return to Tillyardism," Grady objects that

> Of course there was an established discourse of alms-giving at the time of the play, and the play *can* be assimilated to it. The question remains, however: why should we read these passages as simply affirming traditional ideologies which are everywhere put in question within this text?[22]

Grady accepts the existence of all of Kronenfeld's contextual facts, but he contests their bearing on the illocutionary logic of the play. Where Kronenfeld sees the appearance of the same terms—"distribution," "excess," and "enough"—in the play and in common usage in homiletic texts that defined and delimited the charitable obligations of the rich as evidence that Shakespeare meant to ratify a "common Christian culture" that embraced Anglicans, Puritans, and Anabaptists alike, Grady sees in *Lear* a different illocutionary logic—one that, rather than "affirming" that hegemony, is able to "put [it] in question . . . everywhere" in the text. When one critic can believe that the use of similar terms in both homiletic texts and in *King Lear* shows that a fully saturated context establishes Shakespeare's Christian message while another finds that *Lear* questions that message "everywhere," Derrida's conclusion is that we have nowhere to look to adjudicate the potentially different performative values of these same words, but to intentionality.

V   ILLOCUTIONARY LOGIC AND PERFORMATIVITY: *OTHELLO*

As Kastan obliquely registers in his reading of *King Lear*, the task of converting the poetic grammar of a text into its illocutionary design involves a movement to a higher level of uncertainty and opacity. When it comes to the class politics of *Lear*, Kastan judges that "It is difficult, of course, to gauge the politics *of* the play"—i.e., its governing illocutionary logic—"as opposed to the politics *in* the play" (*SAT* 164; Kastan's italics). Kastan recognizes that there may well be a political logic "*of*" *Lear*, but he suggests that the difficulty of overcoming the indeterminacy of that intentional formation makes it an optional topic of commentary. When Kastan employs the class politics mimetically depicted "*in*" *Lear* to provoke a modern audience to think about the class politics of our own time while remaining uncertain about the original politics "*of*" the play, his appropriation of perlocutionary consequence and deflection of illocutionary intent maintains the priority of context over intentionality, while shifting the relevant context to the present. This displacement, which is a common new historicist maneuver, enables our own perlocutionary autonomy while denying it to the past. Karen Newman offers a detailed enactment of such an elision when she begins a brief epilogue to her reading of *Othello* with a question that seems to require a direct response to a question of intentionality: "Was Shakespeare a racist who condoned the negative image of blacks in his culture?" Newman does not, however, attempt to answer this question; instead, she immediately poses a second question: "Is Desdemona somehow guilty in her stubborn defense of Cassio and her admiring remark, 'Ludovico is a proper man'?"[23] Asking about a fictional character's guilt is not exactly the same as asking about an author's racism; the first question directly engages the category of authorial intention, but in the second question, it is not clear who might consider Desdemona guilty, Shakespeare or his audience. Intention and context remain in tension as Newman dismisses what she describes as a "formalist" objection to her questions, one that would "raise the spectres of intention" on behalf of artistic transcendence; responding to this hypothetical objection, Newman emphasizes the importance of context, insisting that "even highly formalist readings are political, inscribed in the discourse both of the period in which the work was produced and that in which it is consumed" (93). But the appeal to context brings us no closer to addressing the question of intentionality, the question of Shakespeare's possible racism. Although Newman identifies "formalism" as the culprit that attributes a spectral quality to intentionality, she never overcomes that spectre; instead, the conclusion of her essay strikes a tactful balance between the claims of literature and history, one that leaves the "spectres of intention" undisturbed as it offers a perfectly equivocal account of Shakespeare's perceptions of race:

> *Shakespeare* was certainly subject to the racist, sexist, and colonialist discourses of his time; but *by making* the black Othello a hero, and *by making* Desdemona's love for Othello and her transgression of her society's norms for women in choosing him sympathetic, *Shakespeare's play* stands in a contestatory relation to the hegemonic ideologies of race and gender in early modern England. . . . *Shakespeare's representation* of her as at once virtuous and desiring, and of her choice in love as heroic rather than demonic, *dislocates* the conventional ideology of gender the play also *enacts*. (93; my italics)

Newman exonerates Desdemona, but she only partly exculpates Shakespeare; while Desdemona is herself "heroic," the narrative agent that finally succeeds in contesting "hegemonic ideologies" and "making black Othello a hero" is, in a syntactic deferral, not "Shakespeare" but a disinterested aesthetic object, "Shakespeare's play." And when the subject becomes slightly more human than structural ("Shakespeare's representation of her"), the verbs become more equivocal; "Shakespeare's representation" of Desdemona equally "dislocates" and "enacts" racist ideology. While the careful balances of her prose suggest that Newman wishes to exempt Shakespeare from a blunt accusation of racism, neutrality, as Marx and Greenblatt suggest, always aligns itself with hegemony.[24]

   While Newman honors the principle of the "intentional fallacy" in her description of *Othello* as an equivocal object, she claims abundant intentionality for her own critical act when she deflects the constative, true/false structure of her initial query ("Was Shakespeare a racist?") into a consideration of the perlocutionary effect of the play's reception history and argues for a deliberate appropriation of that effect:

> The task of a political criticism is not merely to expose or demystify the ideological discourses that organize literary texts but to *reconstitute* those texts, to reread canonical texts in noncanonical ways that reveal the contingency of so-called canonical readings, that disturb conventional interpretations and discover them as partisan, constructed, made rather than given, natural, and inevitable. (93; Newman's italics)

As this agenda for political criticism focuses on questions of perlocutionary consequence, it offers an ambiguous account of authorial intention. In the equivocation between the "displacement" and the "enactment" of "hegemonic ideologies of race and gender," Newman's reading of *Othello* leaves open the questions with which it begins: If we find in *Othello* a critical force that illuminates the intellectual paucity of racism, are we working against the reception history of the play or against the text itself? Are "canonical texts" inscribed by the "ideological discourses" of their moments of origin, or after the fact by "conventional interpretations"? Do Shakespeare's intentions correspond to "canonical readings"? Was Shakespeare a racist?

Newman's description of two contradictory logics in *Othello*, one that "dislocates" and another that "enacts" a "canonical reading," corresponds to de Man's "two texts" principle, but Newman's assertion of an equivalence between these two structures differs from the sequential relation described by de Man. De Man outlines the basic principles of deconstructive reading when he advises that "The commentator should persist as long as possible in the canonical reading and should begin to swerve away from it only when he encounters difficulties which the methodological and substantial assertions of the system are no longer able to master." These "difficulties," de Man insists, are legitimate when they "arise from resistances encountered in the text itself . . . and not from preconceptions imported from elsewhere."[25] De Man's premise that the subversive reading of a text is sequentially structured so that it occurs after, and undoes, the canonical reading is based on an Althusserian conception of ideology. The canonical (racist) reading of *Othello* is obvious, but it is neither natural nor inevitable. Its obviousness is the sign of an ideological effect; it is the function of ideology, Althusser argues, that it "imposes . . . obviousnesses as obviousnesses, which we cannot *fail to recognize* and before which we have the inevitable and natural reaction of crying out (aloud or in the 'still, small voice of conscience'): 'That's obvious! That's right! That's true!'"[26] If the text of *Othello* simultaneously supports both an obvious racism and a contrary logic, the contradiction emerges as a resistance to the ideologically obvious. The gateway into this "discontinuous world of reflective irony and ambiguity" (*BI* 28), de Man argues, is intentionality.

Leah Marcus is less tactful than Newman, and more willing to grasp the nettle of intention, in suggesting that a study of the two early editions of *Othello*, the 1622 Quarto and the 1623 Folio, indicate a clear and unequivocal racist intent in the play's revisions. Marcus tends to accept the prevailing view, which I see no reason to contest, that the shorter Quarto is probably the earlier text, and she shows that as Q is revised into F, Shakespeare heightened the "racial virulence" of the play's imagery.[27] The "grosse claspes of a Lasciuious Moore," a "name that was as fresh / As Dian's Visage" made into something "begrim'd and black / As mine own face," and the Willow Song exist only in the Folio. Marcus argues, compellingly, that this amplified racist imagery intensifies the association between "black skin" and "hypersexuality [and] predation upon white womanhood," while the Willow Song solicits sympathy for "a miniature culture of female domesticity and intimacy" that Othello will destroy (32, 28). As the Folio revisions "ratchet up racial conflict to—and some would say past—the limits of human endurance," Marcus concludes, "Shakespeare as a reviser was, in effect, himself written by shifting contemporary attitudes towards race" (33). While there is no doubt that the racist imagery of the Folio *Othello* is more virulent than that of the Quarto, there is still ample reason to question the premise that the increased volume of racist imagery in the Folio text functions as an endorsement of the cultural logic of racism. Marcus suggests that Roderigo's expression of disgust at the "Lasciuious Moore" extends Iago's personal racism into a "community view" (25), but the vulgar xenophobia of Iago and Roderigo is quickly contradicted by the more benign view of Othello in the Venetian Senate. As the Willow Song generates sympathy for an endangered femininity, the playhouse pits that fragility not just against Othello but against masculinity in general; a scene with only two women's (or boys') voices interrupts the acoustic environment created by the dominant, deeper voices of the mature male actors that pervade the theatre throughout the play. While the visual signifier of skin color implies that race is at the root of the tragic narrative that is enveloping the play's characters, the Willow Song participates in an aural fabric which suggests that the impending catastrophe is based on an intractable conflict of genders.

Marcus contends that Othello himself consolidates an irresistible stigmatization of his skin color as he internalizes the racism of Venetian culture ("begrimed and black / As mine own face" [3.3.392–93]), but Brecht would suggest that it all depends on how the character is played. Does the actor "go into a trance and take the audience with [him]" (*BOT* 26), creating a hypnotic aura as he acquires the elemental force of a natural phenomenon? Or does he divide himself, playing the role "in quotation marks" (*BOT* 17), like someone "who is astounded" at "the conduct of the man he is playing," who believes that "not only the occurrence of the incidents" but his own conduct "must be weighed up by him and [its] peculiarities understood; none can be taken as given, as something that 'was bound to turn out that way,' that was 'only to be expected from a character like that'" (*BOT* 137). Naturalist theatre offers little space for such reflection, leaving Hugh Quarshie, a black Royal Shakespeare Company actor, to warn against the dangers of black actors playing Othello and "making racial stereotypes seem legitimate and even true." Quarshie argues that "When a black actor plays a role written for a white actor in black make-up for a predominantly white audience," he risks reinforcing the stereotype that "black men . . . are over-emotional, excitable and unstable."[28] Quarshie's concerns have been abundantly realized in modern stage and film productions of *Othello*, where a compelling naturalistic portrayal of obsessive jealousy by an actor with black skin easily activates the "dramaturgical shorthand" of racist stereotypes, but this does not necessarily tell us what happened in Shakespeare's Globe when Richard Burbage personated a Moor and asked if the reason his life had come to catastrophe is "Haply for I am black"? (3.3.267). It would take only the slightest degree of acknowledgment of the presence of the audience—a gest that, in Brecht's view, would be unexceptional in the atmosphere of "naive surrealism"[29] of the early modern theatre—for Burbage to provoke the Globe spectators to ponder that question along with him, and thus dispel both the hypnotic aura of naturalism and the exotic aura of the Moor.

Addressing not merely the racist politics *in*, but the racial politics *of* *Othello* (Was Shakespeare a racist?) seems to require a willful conflation of locutionary, illocutionary, and perlocutionary values. Where Newman and Quarshie focus on the perlocutionary effects of modern interpretive practices, Marcus assumes an identity of locutionary and illocutionary values, as if the sheer volume of racist imagery in the play is proof of racist intent, but the recent performance history of the play shows how easily the virulence of racist expression can be turned against itself. When Anthony Sher played Iago, he grunted and scratched like a gorilla over the prostrate body of Othello during his epileptic fit, and this unfettered expression of racism by a psychopathic character made it impossible to identify him as a spokesperson for a "community view."[30] The interpretive dilemma here is that, in the endlessly cited example from Gilbert Ryle, a constriction of the eyelid, a wink, and a parody of a wink are the same gesture. Austin's precept that a speech-act can only be understood in its "total context" is exploded by Derrida's deconstruction of the concept of the "total context." We are left with only degrees of plausibility in trying to show how three indeterminate variables, signature/intent, event/speech-act, and context, produce and offer access to each other.

If we were to look for any plausible logic through which the exacerbated racist imagery of the Folio *Othello* could serve any purpose other than the promotion of racist stereotypes, two instances from American popular culture might provide some illumination. The blues song "What Did I Do to be So Black and Blue," written by Fats Waller and Andy Razaf in 1929, contains lines that translate Othello's self-hatred into a modern idiom: "I'm white inside / But that don't help my case / Cause I can't hide / What is in my face," and "My only sin / Is in my skin." When the words that sit on the page as inert, obvious racism are performed by black singers like Louis Armstrong and Ethel Waters, the division between the racist message and the performative event produces a classic alienation effect; the written text articulates an association between black skin and fallenness, but the performative event contests that articulation through an iteration that occurs simultaneously "in quotation marks."[31] The presumption that *Othello* more powerfully enacts, rather than displaces, its expression of racism depends upon the assumption that its dominant performative texture is as a naturalist representation rather than as a self-conscious interaction between a performer and an audience.

A second modern instance of the volatility of iteration in the treatment of cultural stereotypes occurred in the production and the abandonment of the American television show *Chappelle's Show*. Dave Chappelle shut down his comedy show in 2005, he told *Time* magazine, when "he wondered if . . . he had gone from sending up stereotypes to merely reinforcing them." This perplexity was inexplicable to his coworkers; one of the writers on the show told *Time* that "There was this confusing contradictory thing: he was calling his own writing racist."[32] Where Chappelle's coworker simply subscribed to a classical conception of abundant intentionality (If Dave is black, how can he be racist?), the problem of representation that perplexed Chappelle, and that has to be engaged in moving from the Quarto to the Folio *Othello*, resulted from Chappelle's attempt to enact a more complex performative logic than that of his generational predecessor on American television, *The Cosby Show*. If *The Cosby Show* is viewed in illocutionary terms as an act of persuasion rather than as a mimetic representation of "real life," its purpose is clearly to stress a common, "human" essence that bridges the American racial divide. Chappelle's more acerbic comedy is based on compelling an audience to recognize everything that is omitted in the benign *Cosby* world. As Chappelle regularly puts the n-word and other stereotypes into scare quotes, he performs the function of Brechtian alienation, citing and "dislocating our stock associations" (*BOT* 11). This parodic discourse mimics Marx's critique of the commodity-fetish, denaturalizing the reified forms in which stereotypes appear in "real life" without the history that has produced them. Reification provides the obvious language of ideology as it hardens the constructed associations between signifiers and signifieds, and allows terms like "black," "n*****," "queer," "Jew," "man," "woman," "love," and "king" to acquire the status of natural entities. When this overdetermination is subsumed within concepts that give real life its ordinary, natural texture, language acquires its power over the lives of subjects; as Marx says of the commodity-fetish, "man's own deed becomes an alien power opposed to him, which enslaves him instead of being controlled by him."[33] When aristotelian theatre convinces an audience that it presents a simulacrum of reality, it reinforces this process of reification; when epic theatre puts a simulacrum of what we think of as real life into quotations, it illuminates the ideological character of everyday speech.

VI SUBVERSION, CONTAINMENT, AND EPIC THEATRE: *HENRY V*

While the public space occupied by theatre inevitably implicates it in the political life of its culture, Brecht and Greenblatt offer very different accounts of what happens at the intersection of theatre and politics. As Greenblatt's analysis of the early modern theatre conveys the wonder of "absolutist theatricality," he confers an aura of inevitability over that aesthetic force. Greenblatt's judgment that "even today," when the political themes of the Henriad no longer matter, "it is not at all clear that *Henry V* can be successfully performed as subversive" (*SN* 63) is an aesthetic judgment; if the dramatic power of the play depends upon its ability to inspire wonder, then an ironic *Henry V* is not only a subversion of Tudor politics but a denial of the "poetics of the theater" (*SN* 64). Greenblatt includes not only the early moderns but ourselves in a rapturous collectivity when he contends that "we are, after all, in the theater, and our pleasure depends upon there being no escape, and our applause ratifies our confinement" (*SN* 47), but where Greenblatt argues that the absolutist display of *Henry V* produces a complex effect of identification that causes even plebeian spectators to forget their class interest when they are "dazzled by their own imaginary identification with the conqueror" (*SN* 63), Brecht objects that this model of aspirational identification is not the aesthetic of the early modern, urban, public theatre. Brecht contends that we are anachronistic when "We grasp the old works by a comparatively new method—empathy—on which they rely little" (*BOT* 182–83). Brecht recognizes that "plays of the aristotelian type . . . flatten out class conflicts," but he argues that this is only the poetics of the bourgeois, fourth wall theatre, whereas "epic theatre," an older and more interactive performance style, "divides its audience" (*BOT* 60); "such productions split the audience into at least two mutually hostile social groups, and thus put a stop to any common experience of art" (*BOT* 132). Brecht's experiments in epic theatre were not targeted to an intellectual elite; he notes that when "the workers" were presented with sophisticated alienation effects, they "fell in with the most complicated assumptions without fuss" (*BOT* 62), but the same devices were more likely to encounter objections from "those who profited by the circumstances in question" (*BOT* 75). "Artistic appreciation," Brecht concludes, "depends on one's political attitude" (*BOT* 132).

While J. L. Styan's chronicle of the "Shakespeare Revolution" concludes with the observation that the original performance practices movement of the twentieth century discovered a natural convergence with Brechtian principles,[34] Brecht consistently argued that the use of alienation effects in the modern theatre should have the presentist agenda of illuminating contemporary social processes. Nicholas Hytner's 2003 production of *Henry V* at the National Theatre provided a compelling instance of the use of modern alienation effects in Shakespearean production, and it also offered a test case of Greenblatt's thesis about the impossibility of a subversive *Henry*. The setting for Hytner's *Henry* was updated to the present, creating obvious analogies to the Anglo-American war in Iraq; Adrian Lester played Henry as an alpha warrior, and the production adopted the Brechtian device of framing Henry's major speeches ("Once more unto the breach," "we happy few, we band of brothers") on large television screens mounted over the stage.[35] The premise behind the screens was that embedded reporters had followed Henry into battle, and were transmitting his speeches to a television audience. When Henry spoke directly into a handheld news camera and his image simultaneously appeared above him on a screen with a CNN logo, the illocutionary intent behind intimacies like "he today that sheds his blood with me / Shall be my brother" (4.3.61–62) became all too palpable. As the screen images produced a mediated dialogue between Henry and the theater audience, they offered a perfect alienation effect; Henry's character lost any sense of privileged scale, and he was located in the liminal space of the epic actor. As Brecht explains, when "the illusion of a fourth wall" is removed, the actor is no longer immersed in a separate world; now he is positioned "between the spectator and the event" (*BOT* 58), and his recognition of the audience is not limited to the mere fact of their existence: "He does not address himself to everybody alike; he allows the existing divisions within the audience to continue, in fact he widens them. He has friends and enemies in the audience; he is friendly to one group and hostile to the other" (*BOT* 143). In this production, the alienation of Henry's character did not depend upon the actor consciously standing apart from his role; rather, the distancing of this character emerged as a structural feature of the text. Henry's campfire dialogue with Williams, Bates, and Court reflected his position as the figure who is compelled to justify the action of the play to skeptical interlocutors, and his bitter remarks about the "vacant mind" and "gross brain" (4.1. 251, 264) of his soldiers reflected his understanding of the divisions within his body politic. In this production, when Henry offers "That he that hath no stomach to this fight, / Let him depart" (4.3. 35), he acknowledges that these divisions render every one of his speech-acts subject to failure.

Reviews of the production showed that Hytner successfully produced the Brechtian effect of dividing his audience along ideological lines. Critics felt compelled not only to assess the production but to issue preemptive challenges to the ways in which it would be misrepresented by their ideological adversaries. Charles Spencer in the *Daily Telegraph* wrote that "Traditionalists may bridle, but this is emphatically a *Henry V* for our times, and one of the most persuasive, and gripping, modern dress productions of Shakespeare I have ever seen. . . . Rarely has Shakespeare seemed more palpably to be our contemporary, echoing our own doubts, hopes and fears." Mark Steyn at the *New Criterion* did more than bridle; he trashed the production as "a kind of doctrinaire counter-tribalism that Shakespeare would have found incredibly tedious . . . precisely targeted at their niche demographic—the smug Guardian-reading Bush-despising NGO-adoring middle-class metropolitan theatregoer."[36] Behind the partisan invective, Spencer and Steyn share one assumption: Each knows what Shakespeare would think of this treatment of his work. The impossibility of establishing a rule-governed protocol that would adjudicate the competing claims of Spencer's Shakespeare, our skeptical contemporary, and Steyn's more conservative Shakespeare who would have perceived antimilitarism simply as a deplorable lack of patriotism has led to the declaration of the "intentional fallacy," but this critical protocol simply marginalizes interpretive questions that lie at the heart of the performative logic of Shakespeare's plays.

A similar disagreement, framed at the level of fact, divides Brecht and Robert Weimann in their assessments of the performative character of the early modern public theatre. When Brecht describes an Elizabethan theatre that "achieved results with alienation effects" (*BOT* 135) by employing "narrative" rather than "empathy" as the "soul of drama" (*BOT* 183), he bases this judgment not on a verifiable record of actual devices used in early modern productions but on a perceived affinity between Shakespeare's texts and what little is known of the techniques of a nonillusionist performance tradition. As Brecht imagines Shakespeare's actors standing apart from their roles, he sees actors and audiences joined in a critical exercise of viewing "the human social incidents" portrayed on stage as "something striking, something that calls for explanation, not to be taken for granted, not just natural" (*BOT* 125). At the conclusion of Weimann's exhaustive review of the influence of early English performance traditions on Shakespearean drama, he disagrees sharply with Brecht's hypothesis. Weimann contends that "Shakespeare's comedy is older than the Elizabethan age; and it points to a state of society, or, more likely, to a vision of Utopia that precedes any *Entzweiung* or alienation between the self and the social."[37] Weimann's disagreement with Brecht over the degree of alienation experienced by the members of Shakespeare's audience is not the result of access to more information on Weimann's part about early modern original performance practices or their reception; it is based entirely on a more "utopian" vision of the fundamental relation between "the self and the social." This is not a disagreement that can be resolved by dispensing with "theory" and appealing to the "facts" of the early modern period.

VII   SHAKESPEARE IN THE PRESENT

Two recent strands of Shakespeare criticism, a new performance criticism led by W. B. Worthen and Barbara Hodgdon, and a self-nominated "presentist" critical practice advanced by Terence Hawkes and Hugh Grady, have rejected the dominant retrospective focus of historicism and have sought to reorient Shakespeare studies towards the present, rather than the past. The new performance critics make aggressive use of a Derridean vocabulary in distinguishing their work from that of previous Shakespeare performance criticism, but the critical paradigm established by Worthen and Hodgdon depends upon a reified opposition between textuality and performance that belies Derrida's articulation of the irreducible performativity of texts. J. L. Styan comes in for particular censure from the new Shakespearean performance critics for his approval of the use of original performance practices as a means of recovering the original meanings and effects of Shakespeare's words; for the new performance critics, Styan's conception of "an intending author" betrays an "essentializing rhetoric" that makes him a "card-carrying essentialist" with a "logocentric idea of theatre."[38] The invocation of the intentional fallacy pervades the work of Worthen, Hodgdon, and the contributors to two recent essay collections (*Shakespeare, Theory and Performance* and *A Companion to Shakespeare and Performance*) when they protest that performance practices based on "attempting to discern Shakespeare's intentions"[39] inevitably compromise the freedom of modern directors and actors. But Worthen's complaint that the concept of "an intending author" makes "the modern stage" into "a site where meanings are found rather than made" and James Bulman's lament over the fate of theater practitioners who become "*interpreters* rather than *makers* of meaning"[40] are grounded in a classical concept of perlocutionary autonomy that owes more to Austin and Searle than it does to Derrida. Worthen and Bulman demand for the modern interpreter the autonomy of a free consciousness that controls the full range of implications of its speech-acts and "makes" the meanings it chooses, without contextual preconditions. A Derridean concept of performativity emphasizes the differences that emerge in every iteration, but it never gives any event in an iterative chain the status of a self-made origin.

When Hodgdon identifies intentionality as the foundational concept that makes texts into "repositories of unitary meaning" and calls for our liberation from "fidelity to a textual Shakespeare,"[41] the premise that the intentional fallacy stands in the way of our freedom depends upon two errors; the first is a simplified equation of intentionality with unequivocality, and the second is a reified opposition between textuality and performance, as if texts themselves do not reach towards their highest order of coherence in their performative logic—in the politics "of" *Lear,* rather than in the politics "in" *Lear.* Worthen grants a "potentially disruptive, 'performative' force" to performance only when it escapes the constraints of "the dramatic text," which he believes is mired in "the ideology of print" with its "emphasis on regularity and reproducibility."[42] Worthen thus reserves his highest praise for productions in which "the text disappears"; he congratulates Anthony Sher for finding a way to play the Fool in *Lear* that "act[s] against the grain—of the self, of the text, of 'Shakespeare'" and achieves an "economy of production [that] finally excludes 'Shakespeare' altogether."[43] In the scare quotes that Worthen is repeatedly compelled to put around "Shakespeare," he demonstrates the dependence of claims of perlocutionary autonomy—of "making" meaning in the present—upon the elision of the structural place of intentionality in performativity, an elision that collapses the difference between a "living being" capable of producing a disruptive "event"[44] and the postmortem construction of a canonical reception history. In demanding its freedom from a reified, canonical reception history of "Shakespeare" while recognizing no distinction between that fictional figure and the empirical

Shakespeare (b. 1564–d. 1616), the new performance criticism has embraced a vision of "Shakespeare" studies without Shakespeare.

Hugh Grady casts a wide net over the emerging presentist movement in Shakespeare studies, identifying it with "an array of critical practices that consciously situate themselves in the 'now' or present of our own day," and Grady includes within the assemblage of presentist methodologies "the older new historicism, cultural materialism, feminism, gay and queer criticism, post-colonial criticism and performance studies."[45] This movement has offered a critique, carried out in the registers of both fact and value, of the historicist project of defining early modernism in its own terms. On the one hand, presentist critics note the impossibility of overcoming one's own situatedness in the present and of knowing the past in the way that an early modern subject would inhabit its "ensemble of behavioral patterns, ideas and values,"[46] but the stronger pole of the presentist argument lies in the argument that the moral value of studying the literature of the past depends upon our ability to bring its concerns forward into our present moment. Terence Hawkes's dictum that "History is far too important to be left to scholars who believe themselves able to make contact with a past unshaped by their own concerns"[47] succinctly joins the epistemological and the ethical premises of the presentist movement in Shakespeare studies, and illustrates the commitment of presentism not only to interpret history, but to change it.

This critical presentism embraces a continuity with the British cultural materialism of the 1980s, and sets itself in opposition to the evolution of the American new historicism into a new materialism focused on the early modern object. Grady equates the recent fascination with early modern objects with the "antiquarianism" of the old historicism. Echoing Marx's criticism of the "reactionary character" of all "so-called *objective* historiography," Grady detects in the new materialism a confusion between the "concrete" and the merely "empirical" that produces "examples of commodity-fetishism more often than critiques of it."[48] Hawkes's work perpetuates the focus in British cultural materialism on the hegemonic reception history of Shakespeare; as Hawkes looks for ways to disrupt this history, he treats the plays as part of an imperial project that needs to be unraveled by the critical energy of the modern reader. When Ewan Fernie looks back past the 1980s, he finds only the debilitating force of the "masters of suspicion"—Freud, Althusser, Foucault, and Derrida—who have, Fernie argues, produced an "agency-aversive phase" of literary criticism.[49] Fernie recuperates agency through the Shakespearean text when he discovers a compelling representation of "fierce agency" in Henry's "impossible, emphatic victory" at Agincourt, an achievement that, Fernie argues, "contravenes the sort of maimed and spectral agency" that is "'always already' preempted and disarmed by culture, ideology, difference."[50]

In its resistance to a perceived enervating model of agency in the new historicism, Shakespearean presentism, in its current form, has come to rely on a classical conception of abundant intentionality rather than on a contingent sense of performativity. Despite Hawkes' frequent use of Derridean terminology, his assumption that he reads against the grain of the Shakespearean text whenever he reads against its reception history locates a plenitude of perlocutionary autonomy in the act of critical appropriation and disregards the value of close reading. As Grady's recurring identifications of the critical potential of Shakespeare's works with the concept of utopia orient the words of the plays towards a more perfect world than the one being enacted on stage, the plays function more as programmatic reading texts for vanguard interpreters than as live, multivalent, dramatic events. Fernie's equation of agency in Shakespeare with unequivocal action leads to sharply straitened readings of the most problematic actions in the plays. In a characteristic reading, Fernie recontains the potentially disturbing force of the encounter between Henry and Katherine in the final scene of *Henry V*, where Fernie argues that "Inasmuch as a powerful man is harassing a subjugated female, it's offensive. But, once again, isn't Henry's forcefulness, his wilfulness, attractive as well?"[51] Fernie's admiration of Henry's "fierce agency" echoes, in a somewhat more naive way, Greenblatt's perception of the irresistible force of Henry's political charisma, but Hytner's *Henry* showed just how much theatrical power could be generated from undermining Henry's appeal. When Felicité du Jeu's Katherine responded to Henry's advances in a flat, affectless manner, she produced a bluntly compelling effect in her dismissive delivery of the line "Dat is as it shall please *de roi mon pere*" (5.2.229), where her passive resistance cast Henry's wilfulness as sheer bullying.

VIII   SHAKESPEAREAN GEST

In its seamless blend of naturalism and alienation effects, Hytner's *Henry V* contradicted the canonical performance history of the play, enshrined in the films by Olivier and Branagh, that celebrates Henry's charisma. Nonetheless, Hytner's production was clearly presented as a close reading of the play and not as a willful, modernist revision of it. In Brecht's terms, Hytner's choice to deprive an audience of a romantic ending to *Henry V* does not necessarily violate the "eternal laws of the theatre" by robbing the theatre of emotion. Brecht insists that epic theatre does not renounce emotion, it only relegates one form of emotion, empathy, to a "subsidiary" (*BOT* 173) position and thus makes it possible to activate another source of emotion, the "sense of justice" and "righteous anger" (*BOT* 227) that informed Katherine's contempt for Henry in Hytner's production. This emotion that belongs to epic theatre is excluded from the conditions of possibility of the Shakespearean text in Greenblatt's argument that Shakespeare was able to "explore," but not to "resist," the "relations of power" (*RSF* 256) in early modern England. Greenblatt employs a form of the intentional fallacy, a circumscription of intention which allows disinterested reflection but not active resistance, to construct a Shakespeare who will always fail the test of Brechtian Realism. As Brecht argues, Realism is not the same thing as mimesis. "The mere reproduction of reality does not give an impression of truth" (*BOT* 11), Brecht warns; "*Realist* means laying bare society's causal network / showing up the dominant viewpoint as the viewpoint of the dominators" (*BOT* 109). Brecht was not always consistent in his judgment of whether Shakespeare was a true Realist. In his dismissals of Shakespeare's work as theatre for "barbarians" or "cannibals," Brecht focuses on how the plays are centered on "great solitary figures" with "Human sacrifices all around" (*BOT* 189), which would suggest an aristotelian aesthetic of empathy for a singular tragic hero. But when Brecht was asked what types of classical works lent themselves to epic acting, the first instance he offered was Shakespeare:

> An epic way of acting . . . seems to be most easily applicable, i. e., to hold most promise of results, in works like Shakespeare's. . . . It depends on their attitude to their social function: representation of reality with a view to influencing it. (*BOT* 225)

The relevance of epic conventions to a work, Brecht suggests, depends not only upon its representational style but also upon something at the core of the work: its "attitude" towards its social function. This "attitude" resides in an active sense of intentionality that, in Shakespeare's case, indicates to Brecht a desire to "influence" reality and not simply to "explore" it.

"Attitude" is the quality that determines what Brecht calls "gest," a central term in his dramatic theory that is elusive of definition because of the reciprocity between its role in spontaneous social intercourse and its self-conscious use in theatrical action. Brecht is emphatic in saying that gest cannot be equated with "gesticulation" or stylized gestures; instead, it refers to any means of conveying "particular attitudes . . . towards other men" (*BOT* 104). When gest is brought forward in the theatre, it foregrounds the spontaneous texture of everyday life, the "social gest" that defines the "mimetic and gestural expression of the social relationships prevailing between people of a given period" (*BOT* 139). While social gest ordinarily passes as a natural form of expression, it is the function of the alienation effect to make gest visible, knowable, and subject to change: "The object of the A-effect is to alienate the social gest underlying every incident" (*BOT* 139). Theatre thus takes up a privileged position in producing alienation effects, both through the range of its signifying systems (text, voice, movement, spectacle) and through the immediacy with which human bodies can reinflect the spontaneous gestures of everyday life.

By contradicting the aristotelian focus on immutable natural laws, epic theatre conveys an unlimited prospect for changing reality. Because of Shakespeare's cultural centrality, this potential is immediately apparent in innovative productions of his work; the first effect created by a production like Hytner's *Henry V* is a sense of just how thoroughly an evanescent theatrical event can displace the monumental weight of a canonical performance history. The transformative potential of such productions has attracted the notice of critics in Romanticism studies, who cite "anachronistic stagings of Shakespeare"[52] as a model for presentist literary studies. But a presentist criticism that seeks to engage in a real dialogue with the past cannot accept the term "anachronistic," with its implicit opposition between ingenious, revisionary formalism and objective, positivist historicism, at face value. According to Brecht's theatrical history, it would actually be the imposition of the "eternal," aristotelian "laws of the theatre" upon early modern plays that constitutes the true anachronism. When presentist, counterhegemonic Shakespearean productions are described as "anachronistic," this term suggests that ironic productions of the plays uncover signifying possibilities that were unavailable to their original producers and consumers, and it implies a tautology between irony and modernity, an assumption that owes more to historiographic principles that simplify the past than it does to historical realities. Identifying ironic or subversive productions or readings of Shakespeare's plays as anachronistic depends upon a progressive model of history, one that presumes that we can survey the epistemic borders of the past and know it as a coherent foreign culture whose inhabitants cannot speak our language, and who would be bewildered by what we claim to know about them. The influence of anthropological method on the new historicism has allowed us to think about authors as cultural practitioners, but not as interpreters. Although Geertz describes the Balinese cockfight as "a story they tell themselves about themselves,"[53] no individual Balinese has access to the metanarrative level of this practice, where its history can be unfolded and interrogated; that critical distance is the privilege of the anthropologist and her reader.

As de Man argues, when we engage strong texts of the past it is always possible to encounter "a consciousness which is itself engaged in an act of total interpretation" (*BI* 31), where "total interpretation" reshapes the reified materials of culture. Confronted with this act of "total interpretation," our own act of reading a text becomes an exercise in discerning intentionality; it requires "trying to come closer to being as rigorous a reader as the author had to be in order to write the sentence in the first place" (*AR* 17). Perhaps only de Man's aura of theoretical invincibility made it possible for such statements to escape derision as anything other than pure naivete, but that escape came at a price; these plain and unequivocal statements, which, if taken seriously, would install intentionality as a central principle of critical reading, are generally ignored even among de Man's closest readers, and the "now standard theoretical claim about the limitations of authorial intention as a determinant of literary meaning" (*SAT* 28) flourishes unchallenged.

When Richard Halpern describes the early to mid-twentieth century reception of Shakespeare by modernists like Jan Kott, Benjamin, and Brecht, he characterizes the "modernist practice of historical allegory" as "anachronism raised to the level of policy."[54] The idea of an ironic, presciently modern Shakespeare did not seem strained to the mid-twentieth century presentism practiced by Kott, Benjamin, and Brecht, who found a contemporaneity both in Shakespeare's authorship and in the ostentatious performativity of the premodern stage. The underlying gest behind Kott's equation of the Dover beach scene in *King Lear* with the demotic form of "clown theatre" (*SC* 141) is articulated by Benjamin when he describes the purpose of epic theatre as the transformation of sublimity into a conversation:

> The aims of the epic theater can be defined [as] . . . the filling in of the orchestra pit. The abyss which separated the players from the audience as it does the dead from the living; the abyss whose silence in a play heightens the sublimity . . . has steadily decreased in significance. The stage . . . has become a dais. The didactic play and the epic theater are attempts to sit down at a dais.[55]

The precondition for a conversation with the past, Benjamin suggests, is the dispelling of the aura of the sublime. The spooky rhetoric of embracing "a desire to speak with the dead" (*SN* 1) cultivates this aura even as it purports to disclaim it, but a real dialogue with the past requires the disavowal of any such mystifying sublimity. Just as the early modern theatre discarded the illusion of a fourth wall and foregrounded its own performativity, our ability to speak with, and not simply about, the past would mean that we knowingly bring our own situatedness (as feminists, marxists, deconstructionists, etc.) to the conference table, and recognize that our side of our dialogue with the past will necessarily proceed from the self-conscious use of our own critical and discursive resources.

In my readings of Shakespeare's plays, I have freely used the critical resources of the present in order to explore their themes, but I have also sought to be historically responsible at the most fundamental level of reading by basing my readings on the fit between the texts of Shakespeare's plays and the nonillusionist performance devices of the early modern theatre. Where aristotelian theatre offers the paradoxical appeal of an identification that "forbid[s] . . . deep intimacy" (*SN* 65), the performance space of the early modern, urban, public theatre offered a familiarity that allowed for a wide range of interactions between performers and audiences. Reading Shakespeare for his Brechtian "gest" requires a continual attention to the intersubjective effects that were available in the early modern, urban theatre. For example, as modern experiments with replica theatres have shown, an immediate intersubjectivity consistently informs the theatrical dynamic of soliloquies and asides in Shakespeare's theatre. When Petruchio, *solus*, announces that "This is a way to kill a wife with kindness," or Shylock says in an aside that "I hate him for he is a Christian," these statements are, in illocutionary terms, direct challenges to the audience, and they do not shrink from causing offense to women or to Christians. When the boy actor in *Shrew* looked out into the Theatre and addressed its women members as "unable worms," this was a deliberate provocation, and we would do well to keep in mind Brecht's description of the epic speaker: "He has friends and enemies in the audience; he is friendly to one group and hostile to the other" (*BOT* 143). The premise that Shakespeare's plays claimed the authority to articulate the shared beliefs of his audiences reduces Shakespeare to nothing but what classical speech-act theory calls a serious speaker, one who is effectively oblivious to the performativity of performance.

Throughout this book, I have tried to address Catherine Belsey's question—"Why Shakespeare?"—by treating Shakespeare as an interpreter who actively interrogates densely reified cultural formations that deal with affect and power, and that have demonstrated a surprisingly tenacious grip on the public and private lives of modern subjects. Shakespeare's texts are so unusually responsive to close reading because they so nimbly crisscross the line where language can either take on an alien force that is able to possess its speakers, or else that force can be turned against itself, knocked a little crooked, and remade into a vehicle through which we come to understand that the world we live in is, for the most part, the one that we have made. To engage Shakespeare's texts as allegories, and not as synecdoches, of their historical moment requires acts of interpretation aimed at recovering, reviewing, and never underestimating Shakespeare's own acts of total interpretation.

2 Boys Will Be Boys
Subtexts and Afterthoughts in the Comedies

The Taming of the Shrew, As You Like It, and *Twelfth Night* all tease their audiences with the perfect symmetry of comic form, and then mock the expectations that they have created. After a prolonged ritual of gender norming, *Taming* summarizes its point in a lecture delivered by a boy actor who addresses the women in his audience as "unable worms" (5.2.173), an insult that is followed by a celebratory kiss between the boy actor/woman character and her husband, and an expression of doubt from a minor character who wonders whether the action of the play truly matches the neatness of its explication: "'Tis a wonder, by your leave, she will be tamed so" (5.2.193). *As You Like It* sends a perfectly constructed erotic hierarchy of four clearly ranked couples off to the altar, and then allows the boy actor to ask the audience to imagine something completely different: "If I were a woman" (*Epi.* 14). *Twelfth Night* pairs off its main characters with such structural precision and absence of individual motivation that both a fiancé and a fiancée persist, to the end of the play, in calling their prospective spouses by the same fictional name, Cesario, but the perfect resolution is so fragile that it runs off into seemingly random events: a secondary character threatens to ruin everyone's life, the clown sings a song, and the show is over. In each of these plays, as a recognizable comic plot approaches closure, it undermines its generic promise, that it is possible to imagine a world in which the happiest people somehow deserve their good fortune. Working in the sunniest of genres, Shakespeare plunges his comic characters into zero-sum games in which the best one can hope for is an uncertain ending, and so that is what we get.

The Taming of the Shrew can be read and performed either as a misogynist play that legitimates its misogyny through humor and erotic friction, or else as a play in which the bond between love and marriage is so stressed by a flagrant display of inequality that it becomes incredible either that marriage represents a happy ending for Katherine or that the world "love" describes her relationship to Petruchio. That such different values can be articulated through the same words is borne out in the play's performance history. Alongside a dominant performance tradition in which Katherine becomes the willing spokesperson for the natural intimacy of two complementary genders, a minority treatment of the play finds an immanent critique of its misogyny in the very fulsomeness of its expression. Orthodox productions of *Taming* generally adopt naturalist performance values; it is difficult to imagine a more solemnly literalminded *Taming* than Jonathan Miller's 1980 production for BBC-TV, and although the 1966 Franco Zeffirelli film often seems to treat Richard Burton and Elizabeth Taylor like Punch and Judy puppets, the casting of a married couple with a high tabloid profile grounded the film in a real life romantic bond. If Burton and Taylor could be so tumultuously in love, why not Katherine and Petruchio? Both Zeffirelli and Miller, in keeping with a naturalist ethos, dispensed with the Induction, while productions that seek to give the play a reflexive structure of representation and a subversive, feminist perspective tend to include the Induction. Two of the most innovative *Tamings* of the past generation, directed for the Royal Shakespeare Company by Michael Bogdanov and Gale Edwards, embellished the Induction frame. Bogdanov began the play with his Petruchio-actor impersonating a drunken lout in the pit who metamorphosed first into Sly and then into Petruchio, while Edwards returned to the Induction setting at the play's conclusion in order to transform Petruchio back into a Sly figure who saw his fantasy turn into a nightmare as Katherine gave her final speech in abject resignation.[1]

The reception history of this divided performance tradition has its own conventions. Conservative productions such as Miller's are described as authentic vehicles of the values, if not the techniques, of the play's original conception, while the Bogdanov/Edwards approach is said to constitute "director's theatre," a willful appropriation of Shakespearean material for modern ends. Even Edwards agreed that she had reshaped the play to her own sensibility, while Miller expressed supreme confidence that he had fulfilled the BBC mandate to deliver a "straightforward" rendering of the play as a reflection of its original conception.[2] The paradox that this recovery of historical authenticity required such a significant cut to the Folio text was attributed to the demands of the different media of theater and television. Miller's explanation that the Induction was "a stage device" that "sits rather uncomfortably in this very twentieth century medium of domestic viewing" was amplified by David Snodin, the script director for the production, who observed that the Induction "presents the play's characters as 'actors,' and we felt that this would hinder the attempt, in this production, to present them as real people in a real, and ultimately quite serious situation."[3] But as Derrida might ask, how securely can we believe in these "real people" and this "serious situation" if both the "real" and the "serious" need to be protected from the parasitic encroachment of mere "'actors'" by a radical excision of the text?[4]

Miller pronounces with great certainty that his "straightforward" presentation of *Taming* centers the play on "a belief held by the vast majority of Shakespeare's audience," an assurance based on a perception of the early modern London theatre audience as a unified collectivity whose beliefs were entirely different from our own: "Now we don't happen to think that . . . orderliness can only be preserved by deputing power to magistrates and sovereigns, fathers and husbands. But the fact that they did think like that," Miller insists, "is absolutely undeniable."[5] While the breadth of Miller's historical brushstrokes and the principles he describes as Elizabethan values ("orderliness," respect for authority, a hierarchic chain of being) demonstrate that Tillyardism is alive and well in products designed for the Anglo-American educational market, the affective argument made by Miller's production, that *Taming* celebrates "a sacramental view of the nature of marriage, whereby this couple had come to love each other,"[6] continues to inform the majority of productions of the play throughout the UK and North America. Nevertheless, Miller's certainty "that they did think like that" does not stand up very well to Pamela Allen Brown's wide-ranging account of sixteenth century English vernacular literature that celebrated the flyting skills of women who resisted boorish, mercenary suitors. Contrary to Miller's effortless absorption of the original women spectators of *Taming* into a homogeneous early modern "they," Brown contends that the stance taken by Bianca and the Widow, who register their disagreement with Katherine's closing lecture, reflects the common depiction of "jesting women . . . who mock any woman who makes herself a spectacle of submission." While modern feminist readings of the play may look for grounds of sympathy with Katherine's victimization, "Early modern women," Brown concludes, "were not likely to have made that mistake."[7]

Brown's observations about the gap between early modern women's potential resistance to *Taming* and the modern performance history of the play might seem to suggest a loss of feminist consciousness over the past four centuries, but I would propose that the reason for this gap is not a historical regression but a shift in performance techniques. Brown's judgment that the "one-sidedness" of *Taming* is "deliberately divisive" and that the play is "tailor-made to split spectators into factions" along gender lines (289–90) is a useful corrective to the presumption of the homogeneity of the Elizabethan audience, but when Brown describes "Kate as a figure who would annoy some women rather than inspire identification or sympathy" (299) because her final speech offers "the noxiousness of being lectured by a reincarnation of Griselda" (289), this text-centered account of Katherine as a submissive woman character underestimates the heightened annoyance factor of hearing the play's final lecture delivered by a boy actor. The shifting pronouns of Katherine's closing speech exploit the dissonant effects that result when the referentiality of the first person plural ("Why are our bodies soft, and weak, and smooth" [5.2.169]) is divided between the bodies of the boy actor and the woman spectator, and when direct, second person address ("you froward and unable worms" [173]) is delivered from a male body that disclaims alliance with "your" larval form. While a modern, straight-cast, fourth wall *Taming* displays a woman claiming to speak for all women and aspiring to the values she articulates, the transvestite early modern *Taming* allows an immature male to instruct adult women about their nature and their obligations.

The practices of replica theatres have shown that a speech of the length and the public rhetorical style of Katherine's final address quickly turns from its ostensible recipients, Bianca and the Widow, to become a *platea* address to the audience. The exhortation, "Fie, fie, unknit that threat'ning, unkind brow, / And dart not scornful glances from those eyes" (5.2.140–41), speaks not only to the expressed opposition of the women characters onstage but to the presumed resistance of women in the audience. When the identification of a husband as "thy lord, thy king, thy governor" (142) is amplified into "thy lord, thy life, thy keeper, / Thy head, thy sovereign" (150–51), the expansion of the series registers the attempt by the boy speaker to assert mastery over an antagonistic force. Having severed himself from "you," the boy actor is able to consolidate his political metaphor by the speech's midpoint as he describes women in the third person:

> Such duty as the subject owes the prince,
> Even such a woman oweth to *her* husband;
> And when *she* is froward, peevish, sullen, sour,
> And not obedient to his honest will,
> What is *she* but a foul contending rebel,
> And graceless traitor to *her* loving lord? (159–64)

This speech has now run nearly the same length as the comparable speech in *A Shrew* (24 lines to 27), and it has fully developed its central political metaphor. But it restarts, with its only use of the first person singular: "I am ashamed." This declaration can have a good deal of naturalist resonance for the woman actor in the modern theater. In Gale Edwards' RSC production, Josie Lawrence was able to give the momentary impression that she was embarrassed to have lost the battle for power and her self-esteem to Petruchio's bullying. But the aggression immediately turns outward towards "women":

> *I* am ashamed that women are so simple
> To offer war where *they* should kneel for peace,
> Or seek for rule, supremacy, and sway
> When *they* are bound to serve, love, and obey. (165–68)

Spoken by the boy actor, the I/they structure solidifies a categorical subject/object opposition; "I" can speak about women, and "they" can only listen in silence. The couplet (sway/obey) at least seems to promise that the tirade is over, but the speech restarts yet again, with its broadest and most paradoxical use of the first person plural:

Why are *our* bodies soft, and weak, and smooth
Unapt to toil and trouble in the world,
But that *our* soft conditions and our hearts
Should well agree with *our* external parts?
Come, come, *you* froward and unable worms! (169–73)

The paradoxical "our bodies" highlights the use of the immature male body of the boy actor to stand for an adult woman. The structural similarity of the positions of the boy actor and the mature wife, both subject to the sovereignty of a male master, gives way to their dissimilarity in the transition from "our parts" to "you worms"; the boy will grow out of his dependency, but the woman will never metamorphose into a more mobile being able to "commit *his* body / To painful labour both by sea and land . . . Whilst *thou* liest warm at home" (153–55). Once again, the speech signals closure through a couplet (hearts/parts) before starting up yet again in order to assault the woman spectator with its most offensive address: "you froward and unable worms."

This provocatively divisive figure presages Katherine's most extravagant demand: "place your hands below your husband's foot" (181), a gesture whose cultural resonance has been well documented by Lynda Boose. The actual practice of the bride's prostration during the wedding ceremony was excised from the English Book of Common Prayer in 1549, and Boose records various devices that women used to avoid conforming to a practice that they found distasteful. Boose reads the fictional revival of this spectacle in *Taming* as deeply ambivalent; on the one hand, it redeems a cultural anachronism by evoking "a golden-age lament for a world gone by," but at the same time it "works ever so slightly to unsettle . . . so extremely patriarchal a marriage as a formula inseparable from a perilously divisive politics."[8] Boose's tactful ambivalence about the play's illocutionary logic is inevitably resolved in performance. The most common modern practice is to soften the moment by having Petruchio take Katherine's hand as soon as she begins to gesture towards the floor. This convention was overturned in Edwards' production, where Katherine dropped to the ground in complete abjection, prompting Petruchio to fall to his knees in horror when he realized how deeply he had damaged her. Miller thoroughly fudged the moment; his entire company is seated at dinner, so that Katherine can only place her hand on the table, to be joined by Petruchio's. Miller's production closed with a fully developed "golden age" tableau; within a visual spectacle that Miller said he based on "such Dutch artists as Vermeer . . . who celebrated in an almost religious way, the sanctity of the sober domestic life," his company joined in the singing of a Puritan hymn in which, in Miller's words, "marriage is celebrated not as a social convention but as a manifestation of the ideal relationship between man, woman and God."[9]

There is no documentary evidence of how close the body of the boy actor got to the floor of the stage of Shakespeare's Globe when Katherine pronounced that her "hand is ready" to "do him ease," nor any proof of whether this gesture was so extreme as to disturb the domestic and theological harmonies being brought within Petruchio's reign. But there are substantive grounds for speculating about the disquieting potential of Petruchio's response to this offer—"Why, there's a wench! Come on, and kiss me, Kate" (184)—and to the subversive comedy of his next line: "Come, Kate, we'll to bed" (188). This "kiss me, Kate" marks the third iteration of this demand, and if the first instance can be dismissed as purely comic (2.1.316), this cannot be said of its second appearance. When Petruchio demands a kiss from Katherine as the price of their entry into her father's house, Katherine's initial resistance—"What, in the midst of the street?" (5.1.124)—creates a metatheatrical moment in which the theater itself functions as the public space of the street, and the audience becomes the onlookers who would be scandalized by a public display of affection. The significance of this moment for an orthodox production of *Taming* can be seen in Miller's staging of the scene; once Katherine acquiesces in the kiss, she and Petruchio linger in each other's arms, the camera comes in for a romantic closeup, a lute tinkles in the background, and Petruchio's breathy, intimate whisper of "Is not this well?" (5.1.129) confirms that the primary motivational force of the play's action is in fact "love."

In Petruchio's condensation of the principles of "love, and quiet life; / An aweful rule and right supremacy" (5.2.112–13) and in Katherine's definition of a woman's obligations to "serve, love and obey" (5.2.168), the word "love" is the entire argument that justifies this asymmetrical structure of supremacy and obedience as the ideal relationship between a man, a woman, and a natural order. The two kisses that frame the play's final scene are crucial to the enactment of this argument, but the facility with which the word "love" circulates through the play disguises its ability to compact so many competing definitions. Baptista's warning to Petruchio that he must get Katherine's "love, for that is all in all" (2.1.127) imposes a requirement that does not apply to Bianca's suitors. When Baptista says "love," he simply means personal volition; he sets this requirement not out of concern for Katherine's emotional well-being but because he recognizes that he cannot compel Katherine to do anything she does not want to do. Petruchio's reassurance to Baptista, Gremio, and Hortensio after his courtship scene with Katherine that "she loves me" (2.1.299) is very different from his earlier dismissals of this requirement ("that is nothing" [2.1.128]; "Tell me her father's name and 'tis enough" [1.2.90]). When Petruchio is rebuffed by Katherine, he does not ask Baptista to join with him in imposing their patriarchal prerogatives upon her; instead, in terms that eerily foreshadow the modern defense of domestic abuse as a private, family matter ("being alone . . . If she and I be pleased, what's that to you" [2.1.295–96]), Petruchio tells Baptista that his daughter's domestic life is none of his business. In Petruchio's assertion that "she loves me," "love" means the elevation of the marital pair bond above all other familial or social relations. When Katherine asks Petruchio to stay for the wedding dinner in the name of "love" ("Now, if you love me, stay" [3.3.77]), she appeals to this concept that marital love supersedes all other bonds. Gremio and Tranio have already asked Petruchio to stay in order to meet a social obligation. If Petruchio were to accede to Katherine's request after denying theirs, he would signal that he does indeed hold a sacramental view of both marriage and love. But he does not agree, and the play defers the consecration of their marriage to the spectacle of a semi-coerced man/boy kiss. The reassuring sight on the modern stage of a man and a woman in a consensual display of affection legitimates Petruchio's regime of taming Katherine, but when that heterosexual spectacle is portrayed in the early modern theatre by a same-sex kiss, *Taming* lets the rule of compulsory heterosexuality slip away just when it is most needed.

While an orthodox view of early modern performance practices would minimize the scandalous potential of the kiss between Petruchio and Katherine, it is difficult to judge, at this historical remove, how often the man/boy stage kiss incited the erotic currents that alarmed John Rainolds when he warned against both theatrical cross-dressing and stage kisses because of the erotic power of "beautifull boyes" who "by kissing doe sting and poure secretly in a kinde of poyson, the poyson of incontinencie."[10] Dessen and Thomson estimate in their *Dictionary of Stage Directions in English Drama 1580–1642* that "roughly 360 signals direct figures to *kiss*" in this period, and they note that this constitutes "a small percentage of the actual onstage kisses."[11] The very frequency of the act, some will argue, indicates that it should take some unusually elaborate stage business or textual innuendo in order to activate its erotic or subversive implications. Michael Shapiro's survey of the erotic complications engendered by transvestite plots on the early modern stage offers a few instances in which characters or audiences are scandalized by man/boy stage kisses,[12] but the best indication of the subversive comic potential of this particular moment resides in the echoes of *Taming* that appear in the conclusion to its sequel, Fletcher's *The Woman's Prize, or, The Tamer Tamed*. In *The Woman's Prize*, once Petruchio's new wife Maria has constructed an egalitarian relationship in which "I have tam'd ye, / And now am vowd your servant," she offers Petruchio a consummation of their bond: "Nor feare what I say to you. Dare you kisse me?" (5.4.45, 47).[13] The ensuing dialogue indicates that they kiss three times, that this has an exciting effect on Petruchio, and that the spectators find his arousal comic because the kisses make it impossible to ignore the patent visibility of the boy actor's body in the woman character:

> PETRUCHIO: Once againe?
> MARIA: With all my heart.
> PETRUCHIO: Once again Maria!
>   O Gentlemen, I know not where I am.
> SOPHIE: Get ye to bed then: there you'l quickly know sir.
>   (5.4.48–51)

Sophie's innuendo that Petruchio has a surprise awaiting him in bed comes full circle back to the Induction of *Taming,* where Bartholomew the page is suborned to pose as Sly's wife and the play leaves it an open question whether his impersonation of a woman can survive a trip to the marriage bed. Fletcher's joke echoes the quick transition from the final iteration of "kiss me, Kate" (5.2.184) to Petruchio's triumphant command "Come, Kate, we'll to bed" (188). In the final line of *Taming,* Lucentio expresses some mild doubt ("'Tis a wonder, by your leave, she will be tamed so" [193]) over whether Petruchio really has "won the wager" (190) as fully as he thinks, but it is in the action of the play, in the removal of Petruchio and "Katherine" to the marriage bed, that this question rises to the metatheatrical level of representation.

The latent presence of the boy actor only generates some incidental static to the vision of a naturally gendered hierarchy in Katherine's lecture, but when he becomes fully manifest in a homosexual joke that comes at Petruchio's expense, the audience that has been divided by gender into two distinct factions is reunited in mockery of Petruchio. This unified formation is so readily available because Petruchio has never really solicited the partnership of other men in his assertion of his own male privilege. He not only beats his servants, he bullies his equals, including his prospective father-in-law, demanding that the Paduans believe him ("she loves me") and not their own ears ("I'll see thee hanged on Sunday first" [2.1.291]) as obdurately as he later tells Katherine that the sun is the moon. While Katherine's lecture describes a two-gendered model of social identity grounded on a biological differentiation of bodies, Petruchio operates on a unitary model in which masculinity and femininity are only the opposite poles of an imbalance of power. In asserting his dominant masculinity, Petruchio both claims a place in a social order and satisfies the conventions of a genre. New Comedy asks not only for multiple marriages; the form wants a ranked hierarchy with a clearly identified primary couple. Although Petruchio and Katherine establish their narrative centrality in their first meeting, they do not become the dominant couple in the social world that centers on Baptista's house until Petruchio wins the bet in the play's conclusion. When Baptista tells Petruchio that "I think thou hast the veriest shrew of all" (5.2.65), he sets Petruchio's place in the hierarchy of men; having married the least desired woman, one that is difficult to control, Petruchio is assigned the lowest status. He redeems his dominance as alpha male by showing that he can in fact compel his wife to perform the three basic functions that one teaches to a domesticated being: come, fetch (Bianca and the Widow), and drop (the cap). In the mimetic economy of the play, the character of Katherine is thoroughly dominated by Petruchio, but the bodily materiality of the boy actor reframes the unequal terms of a gender war that operates as a closed system: In the homosexual kiss, "femininity" becomes the place of the mobile trickster and "masculinity" a futile aspiration to mastery of that elusive force. The ironies of Fletcher's revision of *Taming* are reiterated in

Edwards' closing figure of a defeated Petruchio which, while it takes extensive liberties with the text of the play, sustains its problematic vision of the
tension between inequality and love.

In *As You Like It*, a much nicer play, the role of dominant masculinity is quickly conferred on Orlando as he beats up two men, secures the
allegiance of the old family retainer, and compels two women to fall in
love with him in the first two scenes of the play. The instantaneous cou-
pling of Orlando and Rosalind occurs without the friction of verbal fore-
play generated by Petruchio and Katherine. While text-centered criticism
generally attributes their immediate attraction to circumstance, suggesting
that Rosalind and Orlando recognize and sympathize with each other's
dispossession, Celia, who is not dispossessed, also seems to be in love with
both Rosalind and Orlando. The relative lack of initial erotic motivation in
the characters of Rosalind and Orlando and the ease of their affiliation is
counterpointed by the situation of Celia, whose excess of desire is doubly
unrequited. Celia first complains that Rosalind "lovest me not with the full
weight that I love thee" (1.2.6–7), but only minutes after Celia expresses
this unbounded love for Rosalind and asks her to "love no man in good
earnest" (1.2.22–23), both Rosalind and Celia flirt with Orlando. Celia is
actually far more forward than Rosalind in showing her desire for Orlando;
her tribute to Orlando's prowess in the wrestling match, that "If you do
keep your promises in love / But justly, as you have exceeded all promise,
/ Your mistress shall be happy" (1.2.209–11), is pretty suggestive talk for
a princess. Having watched Orlando engage in strenuous physical activity,
she tells him that if his wrestling was any indication of what he could do
"in love," he could make a girl very happy. Celia offers no indication that
she is deferring to Rosalind in aspiring to that happiness. If Celia's mobile
desire is viewed not as a matter of realist characterization but as a position
in the narrative structure of the play, Celia can be seen to express the desire
of the audience. In order for the play to acquire narrative momentum, an
audience has to cathect, and not just identify, Rosalind and Orlando as its
primary erotic objects. The theme of dispossession plays only a minor role
in the creation of this collective desire. As Rosalind and Orlando act out
their roles as subjects and objects of desire, choosing each other rather than
Celia, both their characters and their actors construct and dominate the
play's erotic hierarchy.

The absence of verbal friction in the first encounter between Rosalind
and Orlando is belatedly supplied by the Ganymede/Orlando scenes, but
the problem of motivational absence reappears in a particularly glaring
form in the meeting of Celia and Oliver. Again, attempts at naturalistic
explanations of Celia's behavior—imagining that her indiscriminate desire
simply moves to a third object, or that she recognizes in Oliver the enemy
of her enemy ("Was't you that did so oft contrive to kill him?" [4.3.133])—
are less compelling than a structural motive: Celia and Oliver effortlessly

take up their places in what Rosalind describes as a "market" (3.5.61). They are above a shepherd and a shepherdess, and certainly above a clown and a peasant, but not, "in the lineaments of Nature" (1.2.35–36), in the same class as Rosalind and Orlando. They are made for each other, and somehow they know it.

The ease with which this structural efficiency enables spontaneous behavior by making up for internal motivational deficiencies informs Louis Montrose's classic analysis of *As You Like It* as a play in which marriage functions not as a vehicle of erotic fulfillment but as a mechanism for homosocial bonding.[14] In an even broader way, this imbalance seems to bear out Stephen Greenblatt's argument for the irrelevance of psychoanalytic readings of early modern plays. Greenblatt argues that the psychoanalytic concept of a "continuous selfhood" that is "guaranteed by the fixity, the certainty of our own body" (*LTC* 135, 138) is less central to the early modern concept of identity than "communally secured proprietary rights to a name and a place in an increasingly mobile world" (*LTC* 141). *As You Like It* implies an erotic substrate to the construction of social privilege when it suggests that the dominant positions claimed by Orlando and Rosalind are the effect of Nature overcoming the vagaries of Fortune, but as it casts its characters as the objects rather than the agents of this erotic hierarchy it dissipates the significance of individual psychic histories.

The figure who most obviously does not stay within the lines of this efficient pastoral fantasy is Ganymede, whose unfixed body generates a homoerotic tension that both jeopardizes the restriction of object-cathexis to monogamous heterosexuality and suggests an erotic foundation to the male bonds whose ostensible purpose is the transmission of power, property, and title. Ganymede plays a central role in Valerie Traub's queer-inflected, psychoanalytically oriented argument that "the homoerotics of Shakespearean comedy are most accurately perceived as a cultural intervention in a heterosexually overdetermined field,"[15] but Montrose has little difficulty dispensing with Ganymede; for Montrose, Ganymede is simply a fictional disguise taken on by Rosalind, whose "holiday humor" is granted "a temporary, inversionary rite of misrule" (51) before she is shoved back into the container of marriage. Montrose's description of the Epilogue of *As You Like It* as spoken by "the androgynous Rosalind—boy actor and princess—address[ing] Shakespeare's heterosexual audience" (53) effectively makes Ganymede disappear by reifying the border between the fictional and the nonfictional in the staging of this address. In Montrose's account, reality is equated with heterosexuality ("the heterosexual audience"), Rosalind is divided into her mimetic ("princess") and nonfictional ("boy actor") identities, and the metafictional Ganymede disappears into a concluded temporality. But as the early modern theatre locates the Epilogue speaker and the audience in a unified physical space, it blurs the reified distinctions between the fictional princess Rosalind, her fictional emanation Ganymede, and the nonfictional boy actor. As the Epilogue speaker shifts the mode of representation from mimesis to narrative, he shares our knowledge that *As You Like It* is a fiction, and he can pretend to doubt whether it really is "a good play" (*Epi.* 8). This teasing doubt sets up the coyness of his address to an audience that he explicitly divides by gender. With no imaginary fourth wall separating him from the audience, his categorical division of the playhouse spectators into men and women makes it impossible to ignore the question of who is speaking; calling attention to the materiality of their bodies, he can no longer camouflage his own. His imaginary gender mobility ("If I were a woman" [*Epi.* 14–15]) and his offer to kiss the men in the audience does not subsume androgyny within heterosexuality; instead, embodying the appeal of the Ganymede, the boy actor keeps alive the possibility of a desire that is something other than the market-driven, exclusive, heterosexual object-cathexis that organizes the plot and the subjects of the play.

While Traub turns to psychoanalysis as a discourse that offers access to the multiple identities and erotic options embodied in Rosalind/Ganymede, Greenblatt's dismissal of the relevance of psychoanalytic approaches to early modern drama casts psychoanalysis as an essentialist discourse founded on the "dream of authentic possession" of "a centered, imperial self" (*LTC* 134), and he opposes this essentialism to Hobbes's equation that "'a *Person* is the same that an *Actor* is'" (*LTC* 142). Through this opposition between the discourses of psychoanalysis and performativity, Greenblatt concludes that psychoanalysis falls short of Hobbes's understanding that "Identity is only possible as a mask" (*LTC* 143). Greenblatt's own critical method in "Psychoanalysis and Renaissance Culture" is unusual. Instead of engaging any actual psychoanalytic readings of early modern texts, Greenblatt constructs his own psychoanalytic interpretation of the case of Martin Guerre, and then shows that the courts that adjudicated Guerre's case did not adhere to Freudian principles but simply saw "Martin Guerre" as a role to be filled in a larger network of "relations, objects and judgments" (*LTC* 137). In Traub's critique of Greenblatt's "hierarchical discourse" in this essay, she objects that Greenblatt "privileg[es] external force relations over interiority to the point" that "'normative structures' are themselves a given" (*Desire* 13–14), and she asks, "Norms may *appear* to be 'natural,' but when did 'nature' become 'normal'?" (14). Traub's readings of the comedies in *Desire and Anxiety* exemplify the way in which psychoanalysis has become the standard vocabulary for recovering a mobility of desire that precedes its normative regulation; as Traub describes *As You Like It*, the "Freudian notion of the polymorphously perverse" (21) is reduced by "the heterosexual imperative of matrimony" into the "singularity of monogamy" (127), while the same normative forces position homoeroticism as "unnatural, criminal, and heretical" (129). But the centrality of Ganymede to this analysis raises a question about straight-cast productions of cross-dressed plays. If the homoeroticism of Shakespearean transvestite comedy is originally "a cultural intervention in a heterosexually overdetermined field," can any straight-cast *As You Like It*, or any critical analysis that unproblematically refers to Rosalind as "she," ever deliver a critical perspective on that overdetermination, or will it inevitably ratify the equation of the normative and the natural?

The queerness of *As You Like It* is curiously diffuse; the critical function of the boy actor jokingly taking on the identity of Ganymede is not immediately obvious in a play where the closest relationship is between two women whose bond is "dearer than the natural bond of sisters" (1.2.242–43). One attempt to recover the homoerotic focus of *As You Like It* in performance was an adaptation of the play that appeared at the Southwark Theatre in London in 1996, created and directed by Julie-Anne Robinson, with the title *Wicked Bastard of Venus* ("that same wicked bastard of Venus," *AYLI* 4.1.181). *Wicked Bastard* reduces *As You Like It* to three characters—Rosalind, Orlando, and Celia. The play is straight-cast, and it remedies the dearth of Celia's lines in the latter half of the play by giving her much of Phoebe's part. The homoerotic focus is located not between Orlando and Ganymede, who is only a transparent disguise for Rosalind, but between Rosalind and Celia/Phoebe. The revelatory center of the production is the continuity of character that becomes apparent once Celia begins to speak Phoebe's lines. When the character who asks in the early part of the play if "Rosalind, lack'st thou then the love / Which teacheth thee that thou and I am one"? (1.3.90–91) begins to write poetry to Rosalind in which she laments that "the scorn of your bright eyne / Hath power to raise such love in mine" (4.3.50–51), *Wicked Bastard* becomes more than a modern play that manages to use some Shakespearean language. As the language of *As You Like It* begins to demonstrate the seamless continuity of Celia/Phoebe's character, *Wicked Bastard* shows how *As You Like It* works as a covert queer play; as "Phoebe" becomes an alias for Celia, she serves as the conduit for the primary erotic current in the play, while heterosexuality, as Montrose so lucidly shows, operates as a conventional vehicle of male dominance and social stability. The reason for Celia's rhetorical disguise as "Phoebe" is obvious; if sexual love between women is a topic that is not to be broached on the early modern stage, the only way to suggest that Celia is in love with Rosalind is to express that desire through an alias whose excuse is that she believes that Rosalind is a man.

This excuse is necessary not only at the level of the story, where Phoebe can be forgiven for simply having made a mistake, but at the level of authorial enunciation. An author who splits "Celia" into a figure whose declarations of love for Rosalind stop just short of being explicitly erotic and an alias ("Phoebe") whose erotic admiration ("There was a pretty redness in his lip, / A little riper and more lusty-red / Than that mixed in his cheek" [3.5.121–23]) can be written off as a mistake can still claim deniability when he says that "never two ladies loved as they do" (1.1.97) and that their "loves / Are dearer than the natural bond of sisters" (1.2.242–43). In the modern reception history of *As You Like It*, this deniability is honored even in Traub's "lesbian-affirmative analytic," where Traub finds these lines sexually innocuous; Traub observes that when "Le Beau describes the love of Rosalind and Celia as 'dearer than the natural bond of sisters,' despite the fact that his words imply that their love is *more dear* than is natural, his tone is admiring, and presumably no one would have raised an eyebrow."[16] But an audience listening to *Wicked Bastard* could have no doubt that when "Phoebe" is finally able to declare that "Whiles the eye of man did woo me / That could do no vengeance to me" (4.3.47–48), that Celia is in love with Rosalind, that she cannot say so, but that she has been saying it, below the radar, for four centuries.

The wholesale liberties taken with the text of *As You Like It* in *Wicked Bastard of Venus* might seem to fulfill W. B. Worthen's injunction that modern Shakespearean production should not be "a vehicle of the work" but should "produce the work anew,"[17] but Worthen's privileging of "trans-formative" performative practices over those that are "committed to recovering meanings already inscribed in the text"[18] depends upon a simplified, and not altogether consistent, concept of "text." On the one hand, Worthen casts the "text" as an impediment to the freedom of performance when "text" is associated with an "ideology of print" that grounds the "literary understanding of dramatic performance." Within this textual ideology, Worthen argues, "conference-paper performance is illustrative" of an emphasis on "regularity and reproducibility."[19] But Worthen also uses "text" in a loosely Barthesian sense, as a field of semiotic possibilities waiting to be "transformed" in reception—i.e., in theatrical performance. The progress from semiotic possibility to perlocutionary effect is then carried out solely in performance, as though a "text" is not in itself a performative that acquires its coherence in its illocutionary modes.

The scapegoating of "text" that eventually leads Worthen to declare the "essentially nontextual identity of performance"[20] originates in the substitution of perlocutionary consequences, i.e., reception history, for illocutionary motive, or intentionality. This substitution is based in the subject matter of *Shakespeare and the Authority of Performance*, where Worthen critiques a series of performative and critical practices that engage in a rhetoric of self-legitimation by presenting themselves as vehicles of Shakespearean intentionality. These practices then claim, as Worthen shows, the authority of "Shakespeare." Worthen acknowledges at the outset of *Shakespeare and Authority* that this is a review of a reception history, in which "texts and performances are not really the issue, but how they are construed as vessels of history, of canonical values, of hegemonic consensus" (6), but as the book goes on, Worthen becomes a good deal more categorical about establishing an essential distinction between text and performance, arguing that "Stage meanings are not 'translatable' from the text, because meaning in the theater arises from the application of productive practices *to* the text . . . that stand outside and beyond the text" (51–52). When Worthen asserts that "A performance of *Hamlet* is not a citation of Shakespeare's text, but a transformation of it," he identifies the "text" of *Hamlet* with its locutionary surface (which would be realized in "conference-paper presentation") and its perlocutionary history (of "canonical values" established by "hegemonic consensus"), as though those terms fully define the performative logic of *Hamlet*.[21]

A reviewer of *Wicked Bastard* suggests a more complex relation between textual legacy and modern performance when he compares *Wicked Bastard* to a contemporaneous London production of *As You Like It* in terms of the relation of the two productions to the Shakespearean "subtext." Adrian Turpin asks, "If the BAC *As You Like It* begs the question 'How little attention to the sub-text can you get away with in Shakespeare?' *Wicked Bastard of Venus* demands 'How much?'"[22] Turpin's suggestion that the performative meanings of *Wicked Bastard* do not, as Worthen argues, "stand outside and beyond the text" of *As You Like It* but that they emerge from its "sub-text" describes *Wicked Bastard* performing the cultural function that Joseph Roach calls "surrogation." As Roach describes the process of surrogation, "as actual or perceived vacancies occur in the network of relations that constitutes the social fabric . . . survivors attempt to fit satisfactory alternatives."[23] Where Worthen constructs an oppositional relation between the hegemonic authority of reified texts and the freedom of present performativity, Roach presents a fluid relation between the past and present moments of cultural performativity—or as Derrida would call them, "events."[24] In this case, the two events, *As You Like It* and *Wicked Bastard of Venus*, are joined not at the level of reproducible statement but at the level of purpose, as "intervention[s] in a heterosexually overdetermined field." Historical continuity is always implicitly conservative in Worthen's oppositional relation between the past and the present, but Roach's concept of surrogation embraces the continuity of dissident cultural formations, such as those that emerge around prohibited sexual practices, as marginalized subjects address persistent structures of repression. When *Wicked Bastard* shows that Celia loves Rosalind in the same way that Orlando claims to do, the play gets its theatrical force by becoming a better interpretation of *As You Like It* than a straightforward, "conference-paper presentation" of the play in which the words are clearly enunciated, the story is easy to follow, and the theatrical experience offers little affect and no intellectual challenge. The success of *Wicked Bastard* as a surrogate for *As You Like It* depends upon the way in which it enables the words of *As You Like It* to recover a sense of illocutionary purpose. When Phoebe/Celia's declaration that if Rosalind "my love deny, / And then I'll study how to die" (4.3.62–63) can be weighed in the same scale as Orlando's promise "to live and die her slave" (3.2.141), an audience that returns to the text of *As You Like It* is no longer compelled to make the words "dearer than the natural bond of sisters" mean less than they say.

Wicked Bastard of Venus shows that on a level playing field, the language addressed to Rosalind by Celia/Phoebe is more intimate and more erotically suggestive than that used by Orlando, but it also demonstrates the importance of the gender of the performing body in constructing a "cultural intervention in a heterosexually overdetermined field." Traub's formula is tactfully ambivalent about whether this "intervention" is inscribed in Shakespeare's text (or subtext) or supplied by modern interpreters. The compulsory presence of the boy actor on the early modern stage offered an obvious vehicle for such interventions, but by following critical conventions that elide that body simply by calling Ganymede "she," and that distinguish Celia's words from Orlando's along the axis of the nonsexual and the sexual, we privilege the mimetic illusion of transvestite plays over their material embodiments and clean up the past, making it into something like Turpin's description of an ordinary straight-cast *As You Like It*: "a jolly Arden."

A sense of the limitations of our present resources for recovering the critical edge of the early modern transvestite stage could be gleaned from the all-male *Twelfth Night* that appeared at the Middle Temple and the New Globe in London in 2003. It was a lively and popular production, with little subtext. The only hint of eroticism was a near kiss between Orsino and Viola, a bit of stage business that has become standard practice in performances of *Twelfth Night* ranging from the RSC to regional college productions. The gesture also occurs in Trevor Nunn's film of the play, and if my playgoing experience is any guide, Nunn's film is a reasonable index to the minimal degree of sexual tension that exists in most modern productions of *Twelfth Night*. This may not have been the case in the play's original setting.

Inferring the original illocutionary logic of *Twelfth Night* is particularly challenging because of the indications, which do not rise to the level of absolute proof, that the play was written for a specific audience and a specific occasion: the law students celebrating their accession to the bar at the Candlemas revels of the Middle Temple on 2 February 1602. The evidence of John Manningham's notebook entry about that performance has been supplemented by an extensive treatment of the play within the context of the Inns of Court culture by Anthony Arlidge. Arlidge argues that the Candlemas performance recorded by Manningham was a first, commissioned production, and he provides a wealth of evidence about circumstances of production and allusions in the play to individuals, cases, and issues that would have been familiar to the members of the Inns. If it remains impossible to prove conclusively that the production on 2 February 1602 was the first performance of *Twelfth Night*, Arlidge nevertheless demonstrates, as Peter Parolin judges, that "we need to understand the Inns of Court as an important context for the play."[25]

In Arlidge's focus on the festive potential of *Twelfth Night* as an entertainment, he notes, but pays less attention to, the political and cultural tensions that run through both the play and its elite audience. The two most salient characteristics that would distinguish an Inns audience from a Globe audience are that an Inns audience would be all male and far more learned. They would not, however, be politically homogeneous; the history of the Middle Temple indicates the significant presence of both Catholics and Puritans in its membership in 1602. And while it will inevitably strike a modern reader that the Inns of Court, an all male institution made up largely of the products of a residential, all male educational system, would exemplify Bruce Smith's observation that the "structures of power in early modern England fostered the homosexual potentiality in male bonding,"[26] the records of the Inns offer no indication that homosexuality was either a common activity or a matter of concern within the Inns culture. The recorded criticisms of the licentiousness of the younger residents of the Inns in this period are almost always connected with their patronage of female prostitutes, an emphasis that suggests that homosexual activity in the Inns was either nonexistent or a matter of great discretion, at least when it came to the scrutiny of the outside world. Smith argues that the circulation of Richard Barnfield's *The Affectionate Shepherd* in the 1590s, when Barnfield was a resident of Gray's Inn, shows the appeal of a coded homoerotic text for the "coterie readership" (103) of the Inns. So too, I would suggest, for the performance of *Twelfth Night*.

The demographics of the Inns population suggest an immediate basis for the cross-generational structure of desire that pervades the play. The average age of enrollment in the Inns during the years 1587–1603 was between seventeen and nineteen, seventy percent of the resident population in that period was between seventeen and thirty, and about half had spent some time at Oxford or Cambridge.[27] Alongside this young population there was an older cohort, some of whom kept rooms at the Inns throughout their lives. Some of the older group served as instructors, or Readers, while others paid a fee for reserving the right to keep rooms at the Inns without taking on the duties of instruction.[28] The permanent members who did not take up positions as Readers were known as the "ancients," and a table was set aside for them in the Middle Temple in 1595 called the "ancients table."[29] Orsino's opening lament over Olivia casts him as one of these ancients. As Philip Finkelpearl shows, extravagant love poetry was the norm in the Inns in the 1570s, when George Turberville wryly observed that though his own "minde were free," living among "sundry gallants" who had been struck by "the blinded archer with his bow" meant that he had to feign love poetry himself: "Yet must I seeme love wounded eke to be." But Turberville feigned so well that when he died in 1595 and his florid style had gone out of fashion, he became the object of satire in funeral elegies for his "Drerye Drops of doleful plaintes." When Orsino asks for "an old and antic song" (2.4.3) and Feste sings of being "slain by a fair cruel maid" (53), the song resonates with the 1595 satire of Turberville, "whom cruel death hath slaine, whom cruel death hath slaine."[30]

Orsino is notably older than his model Apolonius in Shakespeare's source, who is called a "verie yong man,"[31] and his attraction to Viola sets in motion the dominant structure of desire in *Twelfth Night* in which the mature characters (Orsino, Olivia, Antonio) pursue the younger, androgynous figures of Viola, Cesario, and Sebastian. This cross-generational structure in which older, masculine subjects pursue younger, effeminized objects, and in which Olivia's wealth grants her the masculine privilege of buying youth, is presented as spontaneous, natural, and axiomatic. Since Orsino advises Cesario that a difference in age is crucial to a successful marriage and that it is the woman who must "take / An elder than herself" (2.4.28–29), it is somewhat paradoxical that Stephen Orgel should find the use of the boy actor in *Twelfth Night* to reflect the principle that "homosexuality is generally, though not exclusively, conceived to be pederastic in this period."[32] Using the term "pederastic" to describe erotic partnerships in *Twelfth Night* at least requires the term to be equally distributed across same- and opposite-sex relationships. The implicit inequality in the category of "pederasty" would be both blurred and resonant for an Inns audience. In order for Viola and Sebastian to be plausibly indistinguishable to the other characters in the play, the actors playing these roles would need to be similar to each other in age and appearance. These theatrical apprentices would also be close in age to the youngest members of the Inns audience. Viola's initial dilemma upon arriving in an unfamiliar city and having to find patronage reflects a common experience of the younger members of the Inns, whose population was largely made up of the sons of the landed gentry and the sons of merchants. The Inns were an arena in which young men of uncertain fortune made the connections (or not) that enabled them to rise in the world. John Manningham, whose residence at Middle Temple was maintained by an older male relative with no heirs (who referred to Manningham as his "son in love"), and who made an advantageous marriage to his roommate's sister, was an example of those who successfully converted homosocial personal connections into public advancement.[33]

Viola is initially vague about her reason for wishing to enter into Olivia's service upon her arrival in Illyria. When she says only that she hopes that she "might not be delivered to the world / Till I had made my own occasion mellow, / What my estate is" (1.2.38–40), she does not specify what she is protecting herself from, but the hazard becomes clearer when she assumes that in order to enjoy comparable safety in Orsino's court she will have to disguise her sex. There are two implicit assumptions in Viola's plans: the first is that unprotected young women will be the targets of sexual predators, and the second is that young people are safe from sexual advances when they are in the company of their own sex. The histories of the Inns offer no indication of how often young men who had been privately educated were disabused of the latter notion upon their entry to the Inns, but it is difficult not to imagine that it was a common occurrence.

There is a big difference between Viola's two assumptions: The first is true, and the second is not. That the manifest falsehood of this second premise, the supposed nonexistence of homosexuality, can nonetheless function as a plot device is central to *Twelfth Night's* critique of the discursive rules of its sociosexual culture. But when this critique is framed in terms of Alan Bray's influential theses—that Tudor society "lacked the idea of a distinct homosexual minority" and that homosexual activity occupied no distinct category in the Renaissance mind but was simply part of "a more general notion: debauchery; and debauchery was a temptation to which all, in principle at least, were subject,"[34] the play loses much of its critical force. Orgel puts Bray's theses into their strongest form and brings them to bear on *Twelfth Night* when he argues that

> The binary division of sexual appetites into the normative heterosexual and the deviant homosexual is a very recent invention; neither homosexuality nor heterosexuality existed as categories for the Renaissance mind. . . . Men in the period who preferred not to marry—like two of Shakespeare's Antonios—were eccentric, certainly, but they did not therefore constitute a special class, nor are they associated with the discourse of sodomy.[35]

Bray and Orgel describe homosexuality as a category whose invisibility is the effect of discursive underdetermination—the activity exists, but it hasn't enough significance to merit a name—but Viola describes something very different in her lament that

> As I am man,
> My state is desperate for my master's love.
> As I am woman, now, alas the day,
> What thriftless sighs shall poor Olivia breathe. (2.2.34–37)

Viola assumes that homosexuality does not exist, not as a category, but because the activity cannot happen. Viola's ingenuous perplexity, when raised to the level of authorial enunciation and audience awareness, becomes disingenuous; the audience is complicit in the knowledge that what is inconceivable to this fictional character is actually quite common in real life. Antonio's condition at the end of the play, free and unpartnered, is unremarkable only from the naive perspective of Viola. If all one man can ask of another is platonic friendship, then Antonio is simply where Orgel places him: a little off the center of the marriage plot, but in no definable category. But this is far too benign a description of Antonio's place in the resolution of *Twelfth Night*, where his single status is a structural necessity and not an expression of his own eccentric preference. Antonio cannot be partnered, with Sebastian or anyone else, because that would require an explicit crossing over into the discourse of sodomy. Judith Butler's formula that "The performative queer operates alongside, as a deformation of, the marriage vow"[36] is as relevant to *Twelfth Night* as it is to modern American wedge politics.

Antonio's exclusion from the erotic bonds formed in the conclusion to *Twelfth Night* enacts the logic of compulsory heterosexuality articulated in Viola's speech; it presents the binary division of desire into hetero- and homosexuality as a distinction not only between the normative and the deviant but between the real and the impossible. But a dizzying array of displacements and substitutions in the play's final scene, which includes but is not limited to Viola/Cesario's gender ambiguity, mocks this coercive logic. At the level of the plot, Orsino's and Antonio's claims that Cesario has spent the previous three months in their respective companies and Orsino's dismay at hearing Cesario described as a "husband" (5.1.138) are simply mistakes that are explained away by the arrival of Sebastian. But at a deeper narrative level, these two mistakes construct and deconstruct the presumptive impossibility of homosexual desire. The impasse between Orsino and Antonio over the recent whereabouts of Cesario is founded on an agreement in principle: Both Orsino and Antonio agree that the figure in dispute cannot be divided and cannot go both ways. The conflicting claims of same- and opposite-sex object cathexes are activated in Orsino's shock at hearing Cesario described as Olivia's "husband," where it is not at all clear whether Orsino is more distraught over losing Olivia or at losing Cesario, whom he has just described as "the lamb that I do love" (5.1.126). While the presence of the woman actor playing Viola in the modern theatre allows audiences to accommodate the ambiguous vector of Orsino's dismay by anticipating Cesario's resumption of the identity of Viola, the surprised identification of a boy actor on an improvised stage in the Middle Temple dining hall in 1602 as a "husband" would have a very different effect. In a culture in which the homosocial graded into the homosexual and the roles of pursuers and pursued were largely determined by age, the loss of an attractive young man to the path of matrimony would have been a regular source of regret at the ancients' table. The figure who actually inhabits this perspective, the man who really is disappointed to discover that his object of desire has become a husband, is not Orsino but Antonio. The screening of Antonio's unrequitable desire for Sebastian behind Orsino's shock that "Cesario" has become a husband hides the real homosexual cathexis in *Twelfth Night* in the same way that Phoebe's desire for Ganymede screens what cannot be spoken in *As You Like It*, Celia's desire for Rosalind. In each case, the screen representation is excused as a mistake; Phoebe mistakes Rosalind for a man, and in Orsino's case the audience knows that he is doubly mistaken: He does not know that he is in love with Cesario and not with Olivia, but it's okay because he will soon discover that Cesario is really a girl.

That the most sustained representations of sexual desire in *As You Like It* and *Twelfth Night*, Celia for Rosalind and Antonio for Sebastian, are so deeply buried in subtext suggests the inadequacy of the Foucault/Bray hypothesis for explicating the rules that make these desires invisible. Foucault/Bray, in its strongest form, attributes the lack of representation of homosexuality in Renaissance England to an absence of conceptual recognition, but keeping Antonio out of the marriage plot of *Twelfth Night* requires both a firm sense of recognition and a coercive regime of self-censorship. When *Twelfth Night* declines to name "the shamefull sin of sodomy, which is not to be named,"[37] it accedes to the rule that, as Bruce Smith puts it, requires that "In order not to say something one has to have a precise sense of what that thing is."[38] An Inns audience would have a very precise sense of how homosexuality remains recognizable but inexplicit throughout the play. When Sebastian confesses to Antonio in their first onshore conversation that "my name is Sebastian, which I called Roderigo" (2.1.13–14), everyone understands that "Roderigo" is the equivalent of a fake phone number, an alias that Sebastian uses under temporary circumstances such as being at sea, and which he relinquishes when he returns to land.

The strength of the Foucault/Bray hypothesis lies in its depiction of the historical mutability of the construction of homosexual identity; an early modern audience would not have found an "interior androgyny"[39] in Antonio, a "notable pirate" (5.1.63) who stops an Illyrian duel as effectively as Othello terminates a Venetian brawl. But when the dissociation between the concept of homosexual identity and the practice of homosexual behavior leads Orgel to assert that *Twelfth Night* shows how "The love of men for boys is all but axiomatic in this period" and, in his larger thesis, that the transvestite theatrical practices of the Renaissance indicate that "despite all the age's heavy rhetoric about the monstrous unnameable crime against nature, the problem of sex between men involves a good deal less anxiety" (71) than does heterosexuality, the reification of "this period" and "the age" leads Orgel to underestimate the complexity with which *Twelfth Night* stages a tension between residual and emergent formations. In the schematic pairbonding that brings the marriage plot of *Twelfth Night* to closure, Orsino gets Viola, Olivia gets Sebastian, and Antonio's desire for the same object that appeals to Orsino and Olivia, the androgynous "master-mistress," disappears into impossibility; Antonio's Roderigo has become Cesario, a chimerical, attractive young man who desires other men, but who is too good to be true. The premise in the early modern discourse of "debauchery" that homosexuality was a universal temptation is an easily recognizable implication of Orsino's and Olivia's attraction to Cesario, but in *Twelfth Night* this residual premise is consistently layered beneath more explicit assertions of the exclusivity of heterosexual object-cathexis. When the appearance of Sebastian consigns Cesario to the fictional realm of Roderigo, compulsory heterosexuality acquires a coercive force that determines the erotic fates of Orsino, Olivia, Viola, and Antonio.

The conventions of the two-hour comedy that takes multiple characters from first encounter to the altar necessarily accommodates the expeditious representation of courtship, but in dealing with its main characters, *Twelfth Night* stretches these conventions to the point of farce. Orsino is a reverse image of the gull in the satirical boy-bride plot, intimated in the Induction to *Taming of the Shrew* and brought to fruition in *Epicoene*, in which an old and unlikable man is punished by the discovery that the object of his desire is actually a boy. Orsino's happy ending depends on his discovery that his object of desire is really a girl, and it takes only that moment of discovery for him to decide to marry her. That neither Orsino nor anyone else notes the history of his desire preserves the conspiracy of silence over homosexuality, but it also empties out Orsino as a desiring subject. Orsino's character, alternately aloof, whiny, condescending, and sadistic, is not designed to engage an audience's desire, an absence that leaves a corresponding void in Viola's motivation. In realist terms, are Viola's prospects with Orsino ("let the woman take an elder to herself") really much better than Katherine's with Petruchio? Olivia is shielded from the discovery that her desire was homoerotic by the fact that this revelation is occasioned by the appearance of a figure who has all the attributes of the original object plus the one thing that would legitimate her original desire, so she marries him. Sebastian is propositioned by someone who is recognizably wealthier than he is, so although she seems to insist on calling him Cesario, he immediately agrees to marry her. Presumably, such a decision would not surprise the Manninghams in the Inns audience.

In the absence of individual motivation in the marriage plots, *Twelfth Night* locates its affective closure in the reunion of Viola and Sebastian, and the representation of their reunion becomes as absurdly excessive as the erotic motivations of the marrying characters are ridiculously deficient. The elaboration of the colloquy between Viola and Sebastian far exceeds the bounds of realism; if the person whose appearance solves the riddle of Olivia's husband were to declare that his father did not have a mole on his brow, would Viola conclude that he was just someone who looked a lot like her brother Sebastian? The sentimental privileging of the presexual sibling bond joins with the irrepressibility of queer humor (Cesario's woman's clothes are in the care of a man who has offered to pretend to be a mute, "nature to her bias drew" Olivia to Viola) to undermine the coercive force of the marriage plot and to establish a critical vantage on the principle that underlies the construction of a rigorous distinction between a healthy heterosexuality and an unspeakable Other—the imposition of an excessive significance on "the fictitious point of sex" (*HS* 156). Orsino asserts this significance when he imagines the force that will compel Olivia to transfer her affections from her deceased brother to a prospective husband; in terms that identify sex as the supreme corridor of both affection and power, Orsino predicts that "liver, brain, and heart / Those sovereign thrones, are all supplied and filled . . . with one self king" (1.1.38–40). When *Twelfth Night* makes object-cathexis funny and locates primary affect in families rather than in sexual partners, it asks, more obliquely but just as effectively as Foucault, why "the fictitious point of sex" has been given the metaphysical burden of telling us "the secret which seems to underlie all that we are" (*HS* 155).

Twelfth Night does not end with the resolution of its marriage plots. It goes on to offer two supplementary developments: the return of the vengeful Puritan, and a mock pastoral song from the Clown. The clash between these two events speaks to the tensions between the dissonant cultural and political factions of Middle Temple; Malvolio speaks for the city Puritans, and Feste for the country Catholics. The retrospective focus of Feste's rustic song, which looks back to "When that I was and a little tiny boy" (5.1.376), counterpoints the prospective threat that has just been issued by his natural enemy, the "kind of puritan" (2.3.125) Malvolio: "I'll be revenged on the whole pack of you" (5.1.365). Malvolio is more than a representation of hostile figures from outside the theatre, the "London disciplinarians, those Puritan aldermen who . . . condemned holiday revelry, bearbaiting, and the theatre."[40] Puritans were an important political faction inside Middle Temple in 1602, and the Malvolios were in the room at the Candlemas performance of *Twelfth Night*. Their presence in Middle Temple had been encouraged by the government in the 1580s, when Cecil arranged for the appointment of Richard Travers, who had strong Puritan leanings, as a lecturer in order to counteract a Catholic faction in Middle Temple, but by 1602 Middle Temple students with Puritan sympathies were protesting against participation in an entertainment for the Queen.[41] It is not clear whether their reluctance was fueled primarily by a disapproval of royal authority or of theatrical performance, but this resistance showed how the Inns were deeply embroiled in a culture war whose ostensible central issue was the relative authority of English common law against that of the ecclesiastical courts.[42] As in any such event, the battle lines were overdetermined, even along geographic lines; the Puritan faction consisted largely of London city merchants, while their opposition was mostly made up of country gentry.[43]

Shakespeare had an intimate link to Middle Temple in 1602, and it ran through Warwickshire. Christopher Whitfield has documented a broad network of connections between Shakespeare and dozens of Middle Templars from the Stratford region, and Shakespeare's most intimate connection was with Thomas Greene, to whom he was related by both blood and marriage.[44] Greene graduated from Middle Temple in 1603 and moved to Stratford, where he lived with the Shakespeare family in New Place. His children, born in 1604 and 1608, were named William and Ann. Considering Shakespeare's familial and professional connections with the country faction in the Inns, his response to the Puritan threat is relatively muted. Feste's final ballad is positioned to serve the summary function of an Epilogue, but it offers only an oblique connection to the action of *Twelfth Night*. The nostalgic aura of the song echoes the tone of the sentimental exchange between Viola and Sebastian, as both their colloquy and the song look back to childhood as a better, simpler time. As Feste's ballad traces a progress from the sheltered world of "a little tiny boy" to the rougher tides of "man's estate," the song sets the rhythms of the country against the friction of the city. As far as we know, Feste's song is a Shakespearean invention, a piece of cultural surrogacy that sounds so perfectly archaic that it allows an audience of young men on the make in London, where their gender privilege was likely to be subverted by economic contingencies that made them into objects, rather than subjects, of desire, to find themselves in two places at once: both in the brisk and giddy-paced present ("When I came to man's estate"), where there is robust, subversive comedy in the fact that the difference between Viola and Cesario is a hidden parcel of women's clothing, and back in an organic order of being ("When that I was and a little tiny boy") where songs are sung by "the spinsters, and the knitters in the sun, / And the free maids that weave their thread with bones" (2.4.43–44), and where boys and girls really were nothing different.

3 Racism and Homophobia in *The Merchant of Venice*

The past generation of historically inflected critical work on *The Merchant of Venice* has generally accepted the premise that Shakespeare wrote an antisemitic play structured, as Stephen Greenblatt puts it, on "the central dramatic conflict of Jew and Gentile, or more precisely, of Jewish fiscalism and Gentile mercantilism."[1] Those who find *Merchant* frankly insulting to modern sensibilities have good reason to be suspicious of the ways in which the virulent expressions of antisemitism in the play have been treated both in critical commentary and in the work's performance history. Faced with a performance tradition that generally attempts to mitigate that virulence by encouraging the lead actor to use all of the resources of naturalist theatre in order to sentimentalize Shylock, and with a critical reception history that regularly describes the Venetian characters as exemplars of a civil generosity that reflects theological values, there is ample reason for Alan Sinfield's dismissal of the argument that *Merchant* might have been intended as a satire on the sanctimonious avarice of the Christians and of their hypocrisy in projecting their own worst traits onto the scapegoated figure of the Jew. Sinfield argues that there is less difference than there seems between those who idealize the play's Christian characters and those who see the play as a critique of the flaws of those characters, and he suggests that "even a 'sympathetic' presentation, with Shylock as victim" ends up saying that "the Christians are as bad as the Jews—who function, therefore, as an index of badness." Both the idealized reading and the darker reading, Sinfield contends, accept "an underlying us-and-them pattern" in the play.[2]

While I share Sinfield's distaste for productions and readings of *Merchant* that try to muffle its expressions of antisemitism, I would nevertheless take issue with his assumption that the play proceeds from a unitary Christian subjectivity ("us") that constructs Jewishness ("them") as an object of inquiry. The stability of the "us-and-them" pattern in *Merchant* depends on the reification of an unstable identity category—not "Jewish," but "Christian." As Greenblatt's reference to Shylock's adversaries as "Gentiles," rather than "Christians," indicates, the adversarial structure of *Merchant* is overdetermined by the overlapping of racial and religious categories that are not entirely congruent. This definitional instability is the subject of recent studies of the play by Janet Adelman and M. Lindsay Kaplan, who note that the intractability of the religious conflict in *Merchant* (Jewish/Christian), which is framed in residual theological terms, seems to prefigure an essentialist concept of race (Jewish/Gentile) that we think of as modern.[3] Nevertheless, neither Adelman nor Kaplan questions the presumption that the play presents an unambiguous opposition between two groups, Gentiles/Christians and Jews, in which Italian Catholics stand unproblematically for Christian values. But in a play set on an early modern London stage where the exemplary Christian figure is a homosexual Italian Catholic merchant, Christianity becomes a problematic subject position from which to initiate an inquiry into the ontological status of the Jewish Other. In a cultural setting where an anti-alien handbill directed at Italians in London in 1593 could complain that "Your Machiavellian merchant spoils the state . . . Like the Jews, you eat us up like bread,"[4] the conflicts between Italians and Jews in *Merchant* displace the theological differences in the play to the level of superstructure, and the play's persistent evocation of the vocabulary of Biblical allusion becomes a vehicle for a critique of English xenophobia.

When Portia says of the Prince of Morocco that "If he have the condition of a saint and the complexion of a devil, I had rather he should shrive me than wive me" (1.2.109–10), two conceptual frames are brought into juxtaposition; the first is theological ("the condition of a saint") and, according to Christian doctrine, it ought to outweigh the second, racial marker, "the complexion of a devil." As Paul explains, the difference between Christians and others is not a matter of the body but of the spirit; when asked if a man who has been circumcised can still become a Christian, Paul responds affirmatively, because "He is a Iewe which is one within, and the circumcision *is* of the heart, in the spirit, not in the letter" (Romans 2:29).[5] Portia's racism is, in a precise and even heavyhanded way, unchristian, and it reflects a structure of hypocrisy that informs *Merchant's* treatment of its central financial issue: the legitimacy of interest. The universal access to Christianity through the willingness of the spirit is at the heart of Aquinas's defense of anti-usury laws; when Aquinas argues that "The Jews were forbidden to take usury from their brethren, i.e. from other Jews. By this we are given to understand that to take usury from any man is evil, simply because we ought to treat every man as our neighbor and brother,"[6] he relies on the distinction between the precept in Deuteronomy that "Unto a stranger thou mayest lend upon usurie, but thou shalt not lend upon usurie unto thy brother" (Deut. 23:20) and Luke's admonition to Christians to "loue ye your enemies, and do good, and lend, looking for nothing againe" (Luke 6:35). While *Merchant* claims to depict this distinction in the difference between the business practices of Antonio and Shylock, this distinction has no such relevance in 1590s London. When England legalized interest in 1571, the state recognized a longstanding business practice associated largely with Italian immigrants. Not only were there no Jewish moneylenders in London in 1594, but the hated foreign usurers in London in the 1590s were mostly Italians, and there was a long history of English resentment of Italian merchants. From the time of the expulsion of the Jews from England in 1290, Italians served as the primary source of foreign capital, and from the fourteenth through the sixteenth centuries Italian moneylenders were subject to a series of parliamentary petitions calling for their expulsion and to xenophobic riots by the London working class. The "good Parliament" of 1376 appealed to Edward III for the expulsion of all Italian merchants, and a parliamentary petition for restraint of "Marchaunds Straungers Italyans" was set aside by Henry VI in 1455, after which London apprentices and servants launched anti-Italian riots in 1456 and 1457.[7] The "evil May-Day" riot of 1517 in London was precipitated by the abandonment of an English merchant by his wife, who set up housekeeping with an Italian trader.[8] A royal edict of 1559 that tightened the currency regulations on "merchant strangers" warned that "The Italians above all other to be taken heed of, for they . . . lick the fat even from our beards."[9] When *Merchant* opens with three Venetians discussing their concerns over their "merchandise" (1.1.40), it presents a familiar tableau of acquisitive Italian merchants. It was not axiomatic to an Elizabethan theater audience that Italian merchants were more economically virtuous than Jews; Robert Wilson had a good deal of success in the 1580s and 1590s with *The Three Ladies of London* (revived in 1588 and reprinted in 1592), a play that pitted a morally upright Jewish merchant against an unscrupulous Venetian.

Historicist readings of *Merchant* have generally gathered their persuasive force by framing the play within broad historical currents,[10] but a close reading of *Merchant* within the micropolitics of its immediate historical moment suggests that its focus is more local than global; English anti-Italian prejudice is a significant element in its composition, and the treatment of Shylock is largely an antiracist response to the hanging of Elizabeth's Jewish doctor Rodrigo Lopez in London in 1594. This public execution, according to Camden's *Historie*, was accompanied by a virulent display of antisemitism. As Camden depicts the scene, Lopez, a convert, protested his innocence on the scaffold and claimed that he "loved the Queene as hee loved Jesus Christ, which from a man of the Jewish profession was heard not without laughter."[11] Gratiano's reference to Shylock as a "wolf . . . hanged for human slaughter" references this execution, and his further suggestion that "from the gallows did his fell soul fleet" (4.1.133-34) offers Shylock as Lopez's actual reincarnation. As the trial scene develops, this slur fits neatly into a triumphalist Christian narrative in which the Christians once again overcome the demonic Jew. But even as the play's insistent repetition of the words "Christian" and "Jew" seems to suggest a tribal identification by the London mob with the Venetian Catholics, the stability of this formation is unsettled by the repeated juxtaposition in the play of inconsistencies, contradictions, and hypocrisies in the Tudor stereotyping of Jews and Italians. The very frequency with which the Venetians are called "Christians" indicates the stress borne by the word as it tries to persuade a Tudor audience to see Italian Catholics standing for the same values as English Protestants. The words "Christian" and "Christians" appear twenty-seven times in *Merchant*, which is over three times the count for any other individual play, and constitutes over a third of all of the appearances of those words in Shakespeare's works. This insistent repetition functions like the double cross-dressing adopted by all three of the major female characters in the play; the slippage of the signifier exposes the unstable relation between the sign and the referent. Just as double cross-dressing forces a recognition of the artificiality of representing women with boy actors, the repeated references to Italian Catholics as "Christians" call attention to the ambiguity of this designation for a Tudor audience.

In order to view *Merchant* as a play that deliberately constructs a critical distance on the cultural phenomenon of antisemitism, it is necessary to depart from a central presumption of naturalist, or aristotelian, theater, the premise that a play should solicit some sort of identification from the audience. *Merchant* consistently frustrates any possibility of identification with its characters as it cites, rather than iterates, the stereotypical Jewish/ Christian opposition. In the play's original performance setting, its audience would find none of "us" on stage; at a time when Protestant writers routinely referred to Catholics as "infidels," asking an English audience to accept Italian Catholics as representative Christians puts the word "Christian" into quotation marks and gives the term a critical force that makes it possible, in Brecht's terms, to "alienate the familiar" and make an audience "distrust what they are used to" (*BOT* 192).

The Tudor audience was certainly used to antisemitism, and that prejudice is initially invoked both by Shylock's self-caricaturing statement that he will avoid the smell of pork and by his first aside to the audience ("I hate him for he is a Christian" [1.3.37]), but the proximity of Italians and Jews in the Tudor imaginary is shown in the 1593 handbill that complained, "Your Machiavellian merchant spoils the state, / Your usury doth leave us all for dead / . . . And like the Jews you eat us up like bread." The metaphoric equivalence of the "Machiavellian merchant" and "the Jews" might suggest that Elizabethan xenophobia did not make much of a distinction between Italians and Jews were it not for the fact that this handbill appeared in the year before the Lopez trial, when there was no "Jewish question" in London. The simile that joins the "Machiavellian merchant" and "the Jews" describes a structural relation in the Tudor imaginary between the Italians widely present in London and the archetypal figure of the Jew, a structure that is reflected in the first confrontation between Shylock and Antonio. When Shylock easily gets the better of Antonio at every turn in their battle of wits, he gives the crowd an opportunity to see the alien usurers in their midst being beaten at what was supposed to be their own game by a figure who is perceived as their prototype. The scene solicits a series of contradictory responses as it plays one prejudice against another; anti-Italian xenophobia is partly disabled by the identification of Antonio as a "Christian," but the certainty of the moral superiority of the Christian/Catholic over the Jew is eroded in the course of the scene by Shylock's scathing account of his customary treatment by Antonio, an account which suggests that Shylock's hatred does not originate in his nature as a Jew but is the result of having been continually harassed while conducting a business that is legal by the laws of both Venice and London.

Antonio's status as an exemplary Christian is further clouded by his offer to Bassanio that "my person . . . lie[s] all unlocked to your occasions" (1.1.138–39). The suggestiveness of Antonio's metaphor is reinforced by English stereotypes of the sexual behavior of Italians. As Coke asserted, "Bugeria is an Italian word," and according to his parliamentary history (published in 1628), the fourteenth century appeal for the expulsion of "Lombard merchants" charged not only usurious business practices but also accused the Lombards of having "brought into the realm the shamefull sin of sodomy, that is not to be named."[12] This accusation appears in a similar context and in a similarly euphemistic form in Thomas Wilson's *Discourse Upon Usury* in 1572, where Wilson charges Italians with a propensity "to sin horribly in suche sorte as is not to be named."[13] This stereotype allows the Tudor audience to complete the innuendo of Solanio's teasing challenge to Antonio "Why then, you are in love" (1.1.46) when they see Antonio's response to the arrival of Bassanio, and it enables them to understand what is not quite named when Solanio says of Antonio's tears at Bassanio's departure, "I think he only loves the world for him" (2.8.50). Bruce Smith's formula that "In order not to say something one has to have a precise sense of what that thing is"[14] accommodates thoroughly contradictory purposes; something can remain unspoken either because it is too horrible to be named or too inconsequential to be mentioned.

As the work of James Shapiro and Alan Bray has shown, both the presence of Jews and the practice of sodomy were open secrets in Tudor England.[15] What was forbidden by law was routinely overlooked in everyday affairs, unless a Jew or a "sodomite" ran afoul of the law, in which case his sexuality or his Jewishness quickly became a marker of his probable guilt. Another way of describing this phenomenon would be to say that both homophobia and antisemitism were ordinarily latent presences; it took some special circumstances to make them active forces. The hanging of Lopez in 1594 was one of these circumstances, which involved the exposure of one open secret and the maintenance of another. Even as the Elizabethan mob easily articulated the common understanding of Lopez's true religious allegiance, they overlooked a second open secret maintained by his prosecutors. Lopez's chief antagonists consisted of the homosocial network of Essex's men, and the task of chronicling the Lopez trial for the Essex faction was undertaken by Francis Bacon, whose openly secret homosexuality was well protected by the Essex clique. At the time of the Lopez trial, Essex was attempting to secure Bacon's appointment as Attorney General at the same time that he was pursuing a vendetta against Lopez over the resistance of Cecil and of Elizabeth herself. But Bacon's homosexuality, and particularly his association with Antonio Perez, was probably among the reasons for Elizabeth's resistance to his appointment.[16]

Perez, a Spanish émigré who had been investigated by the Inquisition for sodomy in 1592 and who was particularly disliked by Elizabeth, was one of two "Antonios" in the Essex circle at the time of the Lopez prosecution, and Francis Bacon was intimately involved in the circulation of political, financial, and personal favors with both of them.[17] The other "Antonio" was Anthony Bacon, Francis' brother, who had been charged with sodomy in France in 1586 and who was by 1594 deeply in debt for money he had borrowed and passed on to Francis.[18] When Francis Bacon was passed over for the Attorney General's position (which went to Coke), a number of Essex's political rivals offered their support for Bacon's appointment to the Solicitorship as a compensatory gesture to Essex. Coke, however, who was to become a forceful polemicist against "the shamefull sin of sodomy, that is not to be named," continued to argue strongly (and successfully) to Elizabeth against Bacon's advancement. Bacon's description of Lopez in his *True Report of the Detestable Treason Intended by Doctor Lopez*, that he was "of nation a Portugese, and suspected to be in sect secretly a Jew, (though here he conformed himself to the rites of the Christian religion)"[19] shadows Bacon's own maintenance of his openly secret sex life.

The outcomes allotted to Shylock and Antonio at the conclusion of *Merchant* reflect the fates of Lopez and Bacon in 1594: The Jew's life is destroyed, and the semi-covert homosexual is excluded from the center of the social structure. The downfalls of both characters are produced by the figure of Christian feminine authority, Portia, whose success, as Jonathan Goldberg has argued, "unleashes energies that are racist and homophobic."[20] Both Antonio and Shylock function as scapegoats to the play's comic resolution, and the asymmetrical parallel between them takes its form from the Book of Leviticus, where two goats are chosen, one to be sacrificed, the other to be sent to wander in the wilderness (16:8–22). Portia's question, "Which is the merchant here, and which the Jew?" (4.1.169), recreates the moment in Leviticus when the two goats are poised to discover which is to get the worse news. Through this double scapegoat structure, *Merchant* outlines the structural similarity of the positions occupied by homosexuals and Jews in Tudor England.

The importance of Antonio's sexual orientation in securing the Christian/Jewish opposition in the play becomes clear in critical commentary on the nature of the Antonio/Bassanio relationship. Joseph Pequigney, who sees the Antonio/Sebastian relationship in *Twelfth Night* as a consummated homosexual partnership, in this case offers a version of Bassanio's logic ("I didn't give it to a woman, I gave it to a lawyer") when he argues that the "Christian ethic that saturates *The Merchant of Venice*" and is defined by "right conduct" makes it impossible for this Antonio to be a homosexual.[21]

According to Pequigney, Antonio isn't a homosexual, he's a Christian. Pequigney's error is to take this contradiction too literally; when Solanio declines to spell out his understanding of Antonio's "love" for Bassanio, he implies essentially the same thing about Antonio that Pequigney does, but Solanio's reticence is a matter of conscious discretion. The either/or distinction (homosexual or Christian) that Pequigney applies to Antonio shows how firmly the moral clarity of the Christian/Jewish opposition in the play depends upon Antonio's uncorrupted sexuality, but it also shows that nothing guarantees that innocence except the premise that a "Christian ethic" is able to "saturate" the play. In a more productive account of Antonio's contradictions, Seymour Kleinberg describes the conflict between Antonio the Christian and Antonio the homosexual as internal to the character and as the cause of Antonio's vicious antisemitism. Kleinberg calls Antonio "the earliest portrait of the homophobic homosexual," and he suggests that Antonio projects his self-loathing onto the stigmatized figure of the Jew "in a classic pattern of psychological scapegoating."[22]

The strength of Kleinberg's interpretation of Antonio's character is that it both makes the extremity of Antonio's bigotry explicable (there is no mention of any other Venetians routinely assaulting Shylock on the Rialto) and it shows the play giving a coherent form to a pressing social issue. As Bray argues in "Homosexuality and the Signs of Male Friendship in Elizabethan England," by the 1590s there was a good deal of anxiety over the difficulty of distinguishing the "orderly 'civil' relations" of friendship from the "subversive behavior" of sodomy. According to Bray, one sign of a proper friendship was that the bond between the friends was "personal not mercenary"; otherwise, it became impossible to distinguish "the bribes of the one from the flow of gifts and the ready use of influence of the other."[23] Antonio's showering of gifts, or bribes, on Bassanio creates precisely this ambiguity.

Bray's larger thesis, that Tudor society "lacked the idea of a distinct homosexual minority" (2), would seem to rule out the possibility of identifying Antonio as a homosexual, but Bray's orthodox Foucauldian paradigm is, to borrow its own metaphor, too superficial to account for the overdetermined evasions that keep homosexuality visible in Shakespeare's comedies without making it explicit. This structure of overdetermination informs the moment in the unraveling of the ring plot when Gratiano defends himself against Nerissa's charges of infidelity by protesting of his missing engagement ring that "I gave it to a youth, / A kind of boy, a little scrubbed boy" (5.1.160–61). The ease with which the performative function of an excuse is conveyed through the constative declaration that the ring was given to a boy indicates that although Nerissa claims to disbelieve her husband's excuse, she has no trouble understanding that this statement is an excuse. Both the fiancées onstage (played by boys) and Shakespeare's audience (watching fiancées played by boys) immediately grasp the inference that Gratiano could not be guilty of sexual infidelity if he gave the ring to a boy because, everyone spontaneously agrees to assume, his relationship with another male could not possibly be sexual. The mimetic fiction of Gratiano's consistency as a betrothed character clashes with the dramatic device of cross-dressed actors, and the audience is offered simultaneous access to two contradictory models of same-sex desire, one that presumes its impossibility and another that suggests its pervasive presence. Gratiano's impending marriage to Nerissa seems like the inevitable fate of a young, unmarried male character in a comedy, yet at the same time Antonio's devotion to Bassanio suggests the potential intensity of same-sex male bonds, and performance embodies and eroticizes that potential in the cross-dressed (sometimes doubly cross-dressed) boy actors.

The contradiction between the premise that Gratiano, an imminent husband, is therefore immune to the possibility of same-sex desire and the transvestite evocation of an ambiguous border between boys and women as objects of male desire prises open the question of the relation between sexuality and interiority in the early modern period, a question that is foreclosed by the Foucault/Bray hypothesis of a clear epistemic shift that separates early modern from modern conceptions of homosexuality. The premise that turns Gratiano's statement into an excuse, the assumption of his immutable heterosexuality, suggests a deeply fixed connection between sexual desire and personal identity, but Antonio's hopes for Bassanio suggest that sexuality might become the contingent effect of cultural determinants and individual choice. When the Foucault/Bray hypothesis is posed in its strongest form, it leads to the conclusion that it would be impossible for Shakespeare's audience to combine the innuendo of the play with their stereotypes of Italians in order to perceive Antonio as different from Gratiano, but *Merchant* is both expansive and ironic in its deployment of ethnic and religious stereotypes. When Antonio offers Bassanio free access to his "person," the audience is led to believe that they have spotted one of "them," an Italian sodomite, but when the same sodomite is identified as the "Christian" antithesis to Shylock, the audience is forced to weigh the subtle caricature of Antonio against the blatant stereotyping of Shylock. The stereotypical moral distinction between Christian and Jew is unraveled by the introduction of a middle term, the sexually and economically ambiguous "Machiavellian merchant." In the sexual economy of the play, the cross-dressed boy takes up the liminal position that is occupied in its financial sphere by the "Machiavellian merchant." Just as the "Machiavellian merchant," neither "Christian" nor "Jewish," erodes the moral distinction between those terms, the cross-dressed boy undoes the difference between the desires that inform the heterosexual marriages in the play and Antonio's desire for Bassanio.

While Foucault's history of sexuality provides the critical tools for the dismantling of a particular modern stereotype, that of "the homosexual," *Merchant* offers a critique of the essentializing operation that produces stereotypes and scapegoats when it shadows the representation of Shylock's

Jewishness with the paradoxical treatment of Antonio's ethnic, sexual, and religious identity. The oft-noted symmetry between Antonio and Shylock reflects a repetitive historical process: The cultural formation that Foucault describes, the production of the irredeemably perverse homosexual who is defined not by his actions but by his "interior androgyny" (*HS* 43), was anticipated by the imposition of the concept of blood purity on early modern Jewish converts to Christianity. Just as homosexuality has come to be perceived in the modern era as an interior essence that is more than the sum of the actions of a subject, Christian converts from Judaism in the early modern period were stereotyped as possessing an essential Jewishness, an interior perversion that transcended their actual behavior. In early modern Europe, neither the personal participation in Christian rituals such as baptism nor the Christian practices of several generations of ancestors could protect Jewish converts or their descendants from the perception that they remained "really" Jewish.

As members of a proselytizing religion, Christians should have acknowledged that there was no doctrinal basis for distinguishing old Christians from the newly converted, but as Rodrigo Lopez and his Iberian ancestors discovered, experience often proved otherwise. The "conversos" of Spain and Portugal were subject to the regime of "blood purity" as the Spanish "old Christians" deplored the contamination of pure Spanish blood by racially inferior Jews.[24] In *Merchant*, blood becomes a contested sign of moral and biological differences. Morocco believes either that his "blood is reddest" (2.1.7) or that there is no distinction between European and African blood, yet both his belief and Shylock's apodictic claim of his sameness with Christians ("If you prick us do we not bleed?" [3.1.54]) are belied by Salerio, who insists that there is no common essence shared by Christians and Jews, or by Europeans and Africans. Salerio asserts that Shylock's blood is precisely what sets him apart from the Christians, and even from his "New Christian" daughter: "There is more difference between thy flesh and hers," he claims, "than between jet and ivory; more between your bloods than there is between red wine and Rhenish" (3.1.33–35). The most volatile reference in the play to the centrality of blood imagery in Christian antisemitic mythology is slightly more indirect; when Shylock first proposes that Antonio pledge "a pound of flesh" to guarantee their bond, he evokes the Christian blood libels that told of Jews desiring Christian flesh (particularly that of children) in order to reenact the crucifixion on Jewish holy days.

The trial scene of *Merchant* brings together the sacrificial narrative and the blood imagery that served as bases of early modern Christian antisemitism. As the play raises the specter of the judicial execution of an exemplary Christian by a Jew, it both invokes the Christian symbolism of the crucifixion and brings that symbolism back to its Judaic roots. Antonio depicts himself as the Christlike sacrificial "lamb" (4.1.73), and Portia's role in the ritual is drawn from the medieval morality play *Processus Belial*, from which she takes the Marian part of advocating a more generous standard of judgment than the strict standard of justice called for by the devil/Jew.[25] Shylock's rejection of her pleas for mercy and his declaration "my deeds upon my head" (4.1.201) put him in the archetypal role of the Jews in Matthew's gospel who say of Christ, "His bloud be on us, and on our children" (Matthew 27:25). The triangulation of Portia, Antonio, and Shylock iterates a symbolic structure that first appears in Western literature with the launching of the First Crusade in the late eleventh century, when the rise of European antisemitism was accompanied by the emergence of a cult of the virgin mother of Christ and the corresponding infantilization of the figure of Christ. The most familiar occurrence of this tripartite structure in English literature is Chaucer's "Prioress's Tale," where the Jewish attack on the Christian child is prompted by the child's song to the Virgin Mary. This combination of images—the protective Madonna, the vulnerable Christ-child, and the predatory Jew—reflected the medieval Christian mythology of Jewish murders of Christian children and the ritual use of their bodies and blood.[26]

When Antonio identifies himself first as a "lamb" and then as "the tainted wether of the flock, / Meetest for death" (4.1.113–14), he invokes a symbolism that is both Christian and Jewish. Antonio is both Christ and the Levitican scapegoat who is, in patristic exegesis, a figure for Christ; as Tyndale puts it, Christ "is the oxe, the shepe, the gote, the kyd and lambe; he is the oxe that is burnt without the host and the scapegote that caryed all the synne of the people away into the wildernesse."[27] In Tyndale's explication, the Jewish ritual of the scapegoat foreshadows Christ's sacrifice on the cross, where Christ fulfills the roles of both goats, both the scapegoat and the sacrificial goat (or lamb); according to Tyndale, "just as their worldly synnes coude no otherwyse be purged then by bloude of sacrifice / even so can oure synnes be no otherwyse forgeven then thorow the bloude of christ." Antonio's self-identification as the "tainted wether" invokes both the roots of the sacrificial Christ-figure in the Jewish Bible and the Christian mythology of predatory Jewishness. A wether is a castrated ram, and the nexus of castration and circumcision suggests that Shylock's desire to cut off a piece of Antonio's body is characteristic of a perverted Jewish lust for Christian flesh.[28] But as a "*tainted* wether," Antonio becomes not the lamb "without blemish" called for in Leviticus which would serve as the pure sin offering, but the scapegoat who has "all the iniquities of the children of Israel, and all their transgressions in all their sins" (Tyndale) put upon his head so that they can be carried off.

In Portia's legal challenge to Shylock, "This bond doth give thee here no jot of blood" (4.1.301), *Merchant* both crystallizes and collapses the doctrinal and metaphoric distinctions between Jew and Christian. Shylock's downfall is brought about not only by the letter of the law but by a provision that he should have anticipated. This fictional statute in Venetian law is based on the prohibition in Leviticus against ingesting blood ("Ye shal eat the blood of no flesh" [17:14]), a principle that is maintained in the custom of koshering meat.[29] Blood has a deeply paradoxical status in Leviticus; it is at once sacred ("the life of all flesh is his blood" [17:14]) and unclean; Leviticus is pervaded with instructions for the careful disposition of sacrificial blood, and if the blood of a sin offering falls on a piece of clothing, the garment must be taken off and washed "in the holy place" (6:27). *Merchant* never quite comes to the point of testing the Christians' claim of their essential difference from Jews by performing the ritual of blood sacrifice called for in both Levitican ritual and in Christian doctrine (recalling Tyndale's principle that "oure synnes [can] be no otherwyse forgeven then thorow the bloude of Christ"). If Shylock were to cut a pound from Antonio's heart, would the blood he spilled be distinguishable, as Salerio claims, from Shylock's own blood that would be taken in retribution?

The two Biblical stories that the trial scene invokes, the Levitican story of the scapegoat and the crucifixion of Christ, allow for two interpretations of the trial scene in *Merchant*. In Christian world-historical narrative, the peripetia through which Shylock is defeated shows the Jews (in the person of Shylock) receiving their deserved fate: "His bloud be on us." When the grounds upon which Shylock's life is spared—some property confiscation and a forced conversion—are summarized as an example of "the difference of our spirit" (4.1.363), the Duke invokes the proverbial difference, articulated by Paul, between the people who abide by the spirit of the law and those who remain committed to the letter: "He is a Iewe which is one within, & the circumcision *is* of the heart, in the spirit, not in the letter" (Romans 2:29). This "difference" secures the Christian mythos of the relative wrongs of Jews and Christians. As the Christian narrative goes, they may harass the Jews a bit, confiscate their property from time to time (as a punishment for their greed), and sometimes force them to convert, but they don't (usually) just kill them, whereas the Jews killed Jesus Christ. Jewishness functions as *the* "index of badness" (Sinfield 6) in Christian world-history, so that whatever lapses Christians exhibit from doctrinal ideals, the scapegoating of Jews allows them to believe that at least they are not as bad as the people who murdered the son of god.

From a Jewish perspective, the singling out of a Jewish individual for an arbitrarily shifting punishment—a death threat, a confiscation of a shifting amount of property, and a forced conversion—confronts Christian historical myth with an accurate summary of the experience of Jews in early modern Europe, and particularly with that of the Iberian and English Jewish communities from which Rodrigo Lopez emerged. The increasingly severe tallages levied on the Jewish community in England before their final expulsion in 1290 culminated in a late attempt at conversion of English Jews by Edward I in 1280, when Jews were allowed to retain half of their property upon conversion.[30] After the expulsion from England, many English Jews moved to the Iberian peninsula, where their descendants had the option of living as Jews until 1492, when they were compelled by the

Inquisition either to convert or emigrate. Antonio's demand that Shylock "become a Christian" does not reflect the contemporary practice of Venice, which preferred that Jews remain Jewish and live in the Jewish ghetto, but that of the Spanish Inquisition. In either case, the fate of converted Jews in Spain or in Venice does not bode well for Shylock. In Spain, Conversos were routinely found guilty of heresy by the Inquisition, which was self-funded through the confiscation of the property of those it found guilty, and so had a double imperative to doubt the religious sincerity of the "New Christians." Not only was the Inquisition run by the "Old Christians" who resented competition from the conversos, its bureaucracy was directly funded by every guilty verdict.[31] In Venice, Jews who lived as Jews were not subject to the Venetian Inquisition, but those who claimed to have converted to Catholicism in order to move out of the ghetto were liable to face charges of heresy if the sincerity of their conversions became suspect. Venice was a city in which Catholic icons were ubiquitous, and failure to show due respect to icons could easily attract suspicion of a secret attachment to Judaism. Shylock's new status as a nominal Christian also disables his livelihood; Christians (even "New Christians") were not allowed to loan money at interest, and converts were unable to collect interest on any loans they had outstanding and were required to restore all money that had been earned as interest.[32]

Shylock's disappearance from *Merchant* at the end of the trial scene reflects the expulsion of the Levitican scapegoat, but the scene ends with the play's affective entanglements unresolved and the Levitican ritual incomplete. Although one scapegoat has effectively been exiled, there has been no blood sacrifice, and Antonio's self-confessed "taint" seems to have had no consequence. The entire structure of the Levitican scapegoat ritual is brought to completion in the play's conclusion through the development of the symbolic roles acquired by the characters of Shylock, Antonio, and Portia in the trial scene. The material for the play's last act is generated when Antonio speaks what he believes will be his last words to Bassanio, and issues a challenge to the supposedly absent Portia:

> Commend me to your honourable wife.
> Tell her the process of Antonio's end.
> Say how I loved you. Speak me fair in death,
> And when the tale is told, bid her be judge
> Whether Bassanio had not once a love. (4.1.268–72)

If the greatest proof of love (in both Christian and romantic terms) is to die for it, Antonio has set an impossibly high sacrificial standard for his rival for Bassanio's love. Bassanio's immediate offer that he would "sacrifice" everything, including "my wife," if it would save Antonio (4.1.279), and Portia's aside "Your wife would give you little thanks for that / If she were by to hear you make the offer" (4.1.283–84) seem momentarily to divert the trial scene from a theological melodrama into a domestic farce, and when Gratiano and Nerissa reenact the roles of a husband verging on errancy in front of his disguised wife, the play veers even further into the conventions of domestic comedy. The resolution of these domestic conflicts in the play's final scene is darkened by the symbolic overtones of the theological melodrama. While Shylock is not physically present in the play's conclusion, his death is prefigured in the play's final lines in Nerissa's bestowal upon Jessica and Lorenzo "From the rich Jew a special deed of gift, / After his death, of all he dies possessed of" (5.1.291–92). Lorenzo's description of this prospect as "manna" for "starved people" (293–94) makes Shylock's death and his transformation into a sacrificial host the vehicle of financial salvation for Lorenzo and his New Christian wife. The story in Exodus of the manna found by the Jews in exile (16:12–15) becomes, in Christian exegesis of the Jewish Bible, a foreshadowing of the communion host, but as the communion also signified the reenactment of the blood sacrifice of the crucifixion, it acquired a disturbing symbolism. When the doctrine that the "bloude of Christ" is the necessary condition for the standard of "mercy" that enables Christian salvation was joined to the infantilization of the figure of Christ in the early modern Church, the communion ritual inspired anxiety over oral-aggressive fantasies of killing and eating the Christ-child. A thirteenth century preacher explained that Christ did not visibly appear in the communion because it would be too disturbing to the congregation; assuming the infantilization of Christ's bodily form, he asked "Who would like a little child to have his little head, or his little hands, or his little feet bitten off?"[33] By the end of the sixteenth century, Protestants were able to restrict this suggestion of cannibalism to the Catholic belief in transubstantiation; the Catholics, Reginald Scot charged, "in the end of their sacrifice (as they say) they eat him up raw, and swallow down into their guts every member and parcel of him."[34]

The substitution of Shylock for Christ as the sacrificial offering who is devoured by the spiritually purified community reverses the imaginary construction in the 1593 handbill of "Jews, [who] eat us up like bread," a reversal that is more than a figure for the permeability of religious traditions. The insertion of Shylock into the role of the sacrificial offering outlines both the rules of the game and the place of the Jews in the compromises between Christianity and commerce that accompanied the transformation of European states into capitalist enterprises. Antonio, Shylock, and Portia all affirm the impossibility of altering the terms of a written contract, even in a life-threatening situation, suggesting that everyone understands that the Venetians are prepared to allow Antonio to die—and they will watch the gruesome execution take place in a public courtroom—in order to preserve the "trade and profit of the city" (3.3.30). This calculation reflects the decision made by the English government in response to the anti-Italian "evil May-day" riots of 1517, when Henry VIII publicly hanged (with "extreme cruelty," suggesting drawing and quartering) fourteen Englishmen as an assurance to the resident Italian merchants that the full force of the English state would be brought to bear on anyone who interfered with the ability of foreign merchants to do business in London. As Henry well understood, the brutality of this practice cannot represent the official state ideology. Several days after the fourteen had been hanged, Henry brought the other four hundred men and eleven women arrested in the riot to the gallows, where, according to Hall's Chronicle, "the prisoners together cried, 'Mercy, gracious lord, mercy.' Then the lords altogether besought his Grace of mercy, at whose request the King pardoned them all." Two other chronicles offer a more dramatic story; in Stow's Annals and in Godwin's history, the pardon ensues from the intercession of three kneeling Queens—Katharine of Aragon and Henry's sisters, the Queens of Scotland and France.[35] Portia's "quality of mercy" speech, delivered in a feminine persona, is the official statement of values of a system that, when forced to choose, will allow the spilling even of native blood if it is necessary to maintain the "trade and profit of the city."

The figure of the Jew thus serves as a double scapegoat figure for the Christian-capitalist condominium. The final epithet applied to Shylock, "the rich Jew" (5.1.291), indicates his specific function in carrying off the taint of greed. Shylock is, at this point, possessed of less wealth than Antonio, both by the margin of an unspecified fine and by the "life and living" (285) Antonio has just received from Portia, and Shylock is barred from his former livelihood; he remains, nevertheless, the archetypal "rich Jew." When mercenary excess is assigned to Jewishness, the Christians can revel all they like in their wealth, since the stigma of greed has been carried off by the designated scapegoat. The broader scapegoat function of the Jews derives from their assignment to the role of the Christ-killers. The guilt that accrues to the beneficiaries of a culture based on blood sacrifice, the killing, dismembering, and eating of the Christ-child, without which "oure synnes [could] no otherwise be forgeven," is displaced onto a group of "aliens," and whenever the system needs venting—whenever blame has to be fixed somewhere for a failure or shortcoming—the guilt of these figures makes them the obvious choice to be offered up as the sacrifice. Just as "Gentile mercantilism" devises elaborate ways to destroy Shylock and still claim that he brings about his own demise, the fall of Rodrigo Lopez instances the difficulty of playing the Christian game as an alien. The Lopezes went through the entire gamut of choices presented by Christian sovereignties to the Jews within their borders in the early modern period. Rodrigo Lopez came to London about 1559, and he was among the second generation of Lopezes in England. This means that both Rodrigo Lopez and some of his ancestors became Catholics in Spain and then reconverted to Protestantism when they emigrated to England, and yet, in the case of Rodrigo Lopez, he still ended up on the scaffold being denounced for Jewishness. While the judicial evidence that led to Lopez's conviction remains open to dispute, the historical record indicates that his partisans—including Elizabeth herself,

the alleged victim of his plot—could not save him because of his identification as a Jew.[36]

Shylock eventually takes the place that seemed to have been prepared
for Antonio as the sacrificial sin offering for the worship of money by the
Italians, and Antonio, though he is finally less unlucky than Shylock, slides
into the role of the exiled scapegoat in his exclusion from the marriage plot.
His fate, like Shylock's, is laid out by the all-powerful Portia, who articulates the rules of the sexual economy of Belmont as deftly as she explicates
the judicial principles of Venice. In her chastisement of Bassanio for having
lost "the ring," Portia assumes the most severe aspect of the Blessed Virgin
in ballad tradition. As Hyam Maccoby puts it, Mary is "a fearsome figure
when her will is crossed,"[37] and she takes on the role of a phallic mother
disciplining an infantilized Bassanio in her harangue,

> If you had known the virtue of the ring,
> Or half her worthiness that gave the ring,
> Or your own honour to contain the ring,
> You would not then have parted with the ring. (5.1.198–201)

Portia teases Bassanio in terms that do not make literal sense, but which
clearly establish the rules of the game from which the "tainted" Antonio is
excluded. She tells Bassanio, first, that she is sure that "some woman had the
ring" (5.1.207); next, that she will be "as liberal as you" (225); and, finally,
that she now has the ring, showing that "the doctor lay with me" (258).
Gratiano's incredulity, "What, are we cuckolds ere we have deserved it?"
(264), does not capture the inconsistency in Portia's logic. Portia's supposed
infidelity with the (presumably male) doctor is presented as a reciprocation
("as liberal as you") for Bassanio's tryst with "some woman," but if the ring
was in the hands of a male doctor when Portia next saw it, this would seem
to confirm Bassanio's excuse, not to refute it; he says he gave it to a man,
and Portia says she received it from a man. But this constative inconsistency
is overridden by an illocutionary logic that allows Portia to maintain both
of her claims: first, that the ring could not have been lost unless Bassanio
had slept with "some woman," and second, that in recovering the ring by
lying with the doctor, Portia has simply been "as liberal as you." Just as it
is inconceivable for Gratiano to have been unfaithful with "some scrubbed
boy," Portia contends that her ring could not have passed directly from Bassanio to a man. Portia's story needs two intermediary fictional characters;
the first is "some woman" to whom Bassanio gave the ring (in return for
her sexual favors), and the second "a doctor" (i.e., a man) who received it
from that woman (for his favors), and then gave it to Portia. Portia's parable
has a succinct moral; as the ring comes to stand for genitalia, Portia warns
Bassanio that if yours goes into circulation, so will mine.

Both Portia's insistence on the reality of this fictional "some woman"
and the audience's immediate understanding of her accusation of Bassanio's

heterosexual infidelity depend upon the presumption that sexual desire is exclusively heterosexual. Thus Portia, and the audience, deny the possibility of what they have just witnessed: that the marital bond could be threatened by a same-sex, rather than an opposite-sex, bond. Where Antonio embodies the possibility of same-sex desire and Gratiano its impossibility, Bassanio is saved for compulsory heterosexuality by the grace of Portia, as the "sin which is not to be named" is silently censored into invisibility. Antonio is protected from anti-sodomy laws, and from Shylock's fate, through a conspiracy of discretion that does not name his difference from the other Christian characters, but that difference is nonetheless registered in his lack of a partner in the play's conclusion. The taint associated with Antonio's separation from the married couples serves a specific function in assuaging the anxiety about marital fidelity manifested in the nervous, obscene jokes that permeate the play's final scene and that culminate in Gratiano's final pun on the precarious sanctity of "Nerissa's ring."[38] Leviticus, which provides the story of the scapegoat, is also the source of the Biblical injunction that to "lie with the male as one lieth with a woman" is an "abomination" (18:22), a passage that is elevated to a dominant position in modern Christianity in establishing "a difference betweene the uncleane and cleane" (11:47) in matters of sexuality. The Marian cult of virginity is the extreme version of this obsession with sexual purity that informs Portia's lesson to Bassanio, and the threat to the sexual purity of Christian marriage has to be assigned elsewhere, to an alien scapegoat, just as the taint of greed is carried away from the financial behavior of Christians by its stereotypical assignment to Jews. The play does not indicate that Antonio's assignment to his "homosexual role" is directly derived from his actual sexual practices. There is no suggestion that Antonio has an active sex life; it is only his declaration that he will dispose of the wealth he gained from Shylock to Jessica and Lorenzo, and not to any possible heirs of his own, that secures his separation from the structures of alliance that are formed through marital bonds of blood and property. Antonio's lack of heirs also reflects the fate of the usurer in Wilson's *Discourse,* where the merchant finally accedes to the preacher's arguments and acknowledges that "my goods [are] not mine to bestow after my death, if I should die a usurer."[39]

   What happens to Antonio is structurally similar to what happened to Jews, like Rodrigo Lopez, who tried to become Christians by changing their behavior and participating in Christian rituals. Since Jews fulfilled the necessary scapegoat roles of embodying both the specific guilt associated with money and the more general guilt produced by a religion that taught that the salvation of its members depended upon a blood sacrifice, their conversions were never really trusted; they were always suspected of being "really" Jewish. So with Antonio; his relationships with Bassanio and with other men may not be overtly or actively sexual, but the cultural obsession with sexual purity means that a suspicion of his essential difference causes him to be stigmatized and compelled to live the role of an internal exile.

I have tried to suggest how *Merchant* fit into a particular cultural moment in London in 1594–96. The production history of the play has given us a work with a volatile and uneven life on the stage, even down to the present day. The restored Globe Theatre in London presented a *Merchant* in 1998 that was unabashedly partial to the Christians, and in the participatory space of the Globe this led to a disturbing response from the audience. As Michael Billington reported in *The Guardian*, "Last Friday afternoon I heard a Jew being hissed in south London. Not . . . at a National Front rally but at a performance of *The Merchant of Venice* at Shakespeare's Globe."[40] The production received mixed reviews, but few reviewers other than Billington mentioned the unembarrassed antisemitism that it courted from the audience. In 1999, possibly in response to the Globe production, Trevor Nunn staged a *Merchant* at the Royal National Theatre that was entirely sympathetic to Shylock and Jessica. The production was a popular and a critical success, and both Nunn and Henry Goodman, whose Shylock oscillated between public urbanity and private rage, won Olivier awards. For all of their differences, both productions took place on the axis described by Sinfield: one was sympathetic to the Christians, while the other showed them to be equal to Shylock in ruthlessness. Goodman's Shylock was, in fact, far more ferocious in the trial scene than was Norbert Kenthrup in the Globe production, and his Olivier award reflected his successful realization of the values of realist theater.

The original performative impact of *Merchant* cannot be recreated today. English anti-Italian xenophobia is not the force it once was, and the cross-dressing of the play's female characters is not a common stage practice. But the divided response to one of the most famous of all Shylocks, that of Charles Macklin, may help to indicate how a Brechtian political effect can be created in an audience by forgoing "empathy" and instead appealing to "righteous anger" and "a sense of justice" (*BOT* 227). Macklin's was, famously, an elementally powerful performance. Whether his Shylock was meant to be sympathetic is harder to determine, even from contemporary accounts. While Francis Gentleman thought that Macklin's Shylock was "a most disgraceful picture of human nature . . . subtle, selfish, fawning, irascible and tyrannic," James Boaden felt that Macklin "in the trial scene, 'stood like a TOWER' . . . He was 'not bound to *please*' anybody by his pleading; he claimed a right grounded upon LAW, and thought himself as firm as the Rialto."[41] Macklin spent a good deal of time researching his role with the Jews of London; he read extensively in Josephus's *History of the Jews*, and he commented on his reading in his commonplace book: "Jewes Their history an instance of human incertainty—from the Creation to the Flood—in Egypt leaving it . . . go thro the history of it—act the great characters."[42] He wore a red hat in his production when he learned that Venice required Jews to wear red hats when they traveled in the Christian part of the city. It is easy to find a basis for Macklin's interest in Shylock's Jewish background. "Macklin" was born Charles McLaughlin or

Melaghlin in County Donegal and first appeared on a Drury Lane playbill as "Mechlin." He chose a less ethnic name for himself when he arrived in London, apparently feeling that it would be helpful to his theatrical career if he were less obviously Irish.[43]

Macklin's experience of passing in London undoubtedly informed his characterization of Shylock, and the response he provoked suggests that an unsentimental Shylock can be more disturbing than a sympathetic one. Macklin was best remembered for the trial scene; his power was realized not in the appeal "Hath not a Jew eyes" (3.1.50) but in his indecorous challenge to the justice of Venetian law: "You have among you many a purchas'd slave" (4.1.89). Slavery was an institution that produced categorical distinctions between Christians and others; in early modern Europe, the Catholic church insisted that only non-Christians could be enslaved, and that European Jews could not own slaves. The Church objected to the symbolism of a Jew exercising dominion over anyone, even an African, but it did not object to slavery as long as it were practiced by Christians over non-Christians.[44] As Shylock points not at an individual moral failure but at how inequities are enshrined in law, he makes "difference" not a matter of personal "spirit" but the effect of systematic inequalities based on accidents of birth—Christians over Jews, Jews over slaves. Shylock thus articulates the principle of Brechtian realism: "*Realist* means laying bare society's causal network / showing up the dominant viewpoint as the viewpoint of the dominators" (*BOT* 109).

The motive for the derogation of Macklin's Shylock into something subhuman is supplied by George Lichtenberg's contemporary account of Macklin's performance: "The sight of this Jew," he writes, "suffices to awaken at once in the best regulated mind, all the prejudices of childhood against this race."[45] In some parts of his audience, Macklin's Shylock revived the fear of the Jewish bogeyman that was used to scare children, while others, like Boaden, seemed to understand the uncompromising brutality of his character as a matter of aesthetic necessity. This polarity of responses indicates that in producing an unapologetic Shylock, Macklin desentimentalized the question of whether Shylock was to be sympathetic or unsympathetic and instead demanded from his audience a recognition of the human face of a sociological effect. The divided response to Macklin's performance shows that the aesthetic force of the play came to depend, in a manner that Brecht would appreciate, almost entirely on one's political beliefs. We have a modern genre that is able to produce a similar polarization in our cultural moment: Gangsta rap, whose vocabulary is centered upon both the insistent repetition of the "n-word" and the framing of that word within quotation marks, does not ask for empathy for the downtrodden; instead, its embrace of violence demands a recognition that members of a social underclass are capable of "better[ing] the instruction" (3.1.61) they have received about the devaluation of their own lives. If "Jew" was the n-word of 1596 London, *Merchant* displays the word so often and so ostentatiously that it does for "Jew" what gangsta rap does for our own n-word; when Shylock declares "I am a Jew," he reappropriates and destigmatizes a word whose persistent repetition in the play functions as a nagging reminder of the pervasive social violence of bigotry. The original performance effect of *Merchant* involved Burbage not only asking a Globe audience "Hath not a Jew eyes?"; one year after the lynching of a Jew, he also looked out into the Globe pit and said "I hate him for he is a Christian" (1.3.37). It was up to the Globe audience to decide whether this was the revelation of the nature of a subhuman species, or if there was a significant back story to this hatred. Is the story of a "wolf [i. e., Lopez/*lobos*] . . . hanged for human slaughter" (4.1.133) really an occasion for theological triumphalism, or is it only a category confusion?

The sort of stereotyping that produces Shylock's "difference" as "an inhuman wretch" (4.1.3) is familiar in American political rhetoric. When young people who live in urban ghettos are apprehended for violent crimes and show little remorse, the media is apt to echo Shakespeare's Duke in telling us that they seem to lack "human" feeling. By the point that Shylock pursues what even he recognizes is "a losing suit" (4.1.61) against Antonio, he has gone beyond trying to improve his own life; he can only imagine dragging his antagonists down to the level to which he has been reduced. Young people who live in ghettos often ascribe their indifference to the deaths of their victims to the fact that they have seen friends their own age die. They don't see why you should be exempt from what happened to their friends. Neither does Shylock.

4 Love and Object-Cathexis in *Troilus and Cressida*
Just One of Those Things

Although the story of the removal of Cressida from Troy to the Greek camp does not appear in Homer's *Iliad*, her transfer so closely iterates the legend of the kidnapping of Helen that Shakespeare is able to use the triangular character structures precipitated by Cressida's story—the first consisting of Troilus, Cressida, and Pandarus, and the second made up of Troilus, Cressida, and Diomedes—to join his text to a series of Homeric figures that reflect upon the central themes of the *Iliad*. The challenges faced by Troilus, where he must first deal with a substitute father-figure, Cressida's uncle Pandarus, and then with Diomedes, a coeval rival, reflect the multiple pressures faced by Agamemnon in the opening episode of the *Iliad*, where the demand for the forfeiture of Agamemnon's war bride Chryseis by her father, the priest Chryses, leads to Agamemnon's conflict with Achilles over Achilles' war bride Briseis. Homer never hints that these triangular structures are metonyms for the war over Helen, but seeing them as such places a subtle frame over the entire *Iliad*. Just as the final image of Hector's funeral pyre foreshadows the fire that will consume Troy at the war's conclusion, the rivalries that inform the opening scene of the *Iliad* present a condensed figure for the cause of the war: a recurrent structural formation in which two men cannot resolve a dispute over the possession of one woman.[1]

As Cressida's transfer reverses the path of Helen's abduction, the conflict created between Troilus and Diomedes also reflects the war's central coeval rivalry of Menelaus and Paris, while the fact that Cressida's removal is carried out at the behest of her priestly father Calchas echoes Homer's account of the repatriation of Chryseis, whose forfeiture is ultimately demanded by the entire Greek army, led by Achilles, who have been convinced by Calchas that the reason the Greeks are enduring a plague is that Apollo has been offended by Agamemnon's refusal to return Chryseis to her father Chryses. Homer is typically reticent about the implications of this episode. He never hints that the image of a disease pervading the Greek camp is meant to suggest that the behavior of the Greek warriors as they traffic in women is pathological; we do not hear from Briseis or Chryseis bewailing their fate, Achilles and Agamemnon have more to say about their honors than they do about their affections for Chryseis or Briseis (although

Agamemnon compares Chryseis favorably to Clytemnestra), and Calchas locates the cause of the plague in Agamemnon's insulting response to Chryses rather than in his treatment of Chryseis. In the medieval revisions of the legends of Troy, the image of disease returns with a clear metaphoric purpose in a story about Cressida's forcible removal, Henryson's fifteenth century supplement to Chaucer's *Troilus and Criseyde*. In Henryson's account, Cressida suffers from leprosy. Her affliction is a figure of poetic justice; as a euphemism for venereal disease, it is Henryson's way of punishing Cressida for betraying Troilus.[2]

In Shakespeare's revision of the story of the Trojan war, Thersites wields the threat of sexual disease with a similar sense of moral retribution but with a different target when he suggests that all of the warriors engaged in the war over Helen deserve a venereal disease; "the Neapolitan bone-ache," Thersites contends, is "the curse dependent on those that war for a placket" (2.3.16–17). In the Epilogue to *Troilus and Cressida*, where Pandarus metamorphoses into a diseased Southwark pimp, Shakespeare spells out the presentist moral implications of this curse. Shakespeare's Pandarus is derived from Chaucer and Boccaccio, who transform the traditional blocking agent, the *senex iratus*, into a facilitator, a transformation that illustrates both the multiplicity of the functions performed by patriarchal authority and its ultimate amorality. In the *Iliad*, Calchas serves as Chryseis' advocate against Agamemnon, but when Shakespeare extends the transformation of the father-figure from a priest into a pimp, his most pointed revision is neither of Homer nor of Chaucer but of Henryson. As Shakespeare transfers the image of sexual disease from a commodified woman to a paternal commodifier, he identifies sexual pathology not with a promiscuous woman but with a paternal metaphor.

The modern reception history of Troilus *and* Cressida suggests that we are confident in our ability to diagnose the sexual pathology that envelops Troilus, Cressida, and Pandarus. In our postfreudian wisdom, we know that desire is not really about object-cathexis, and that what looks like rivalry is actually a form of homosocial collaboration. As Rene Girard argues,

> The conquest of a beautiful woman makes an inexperienced young man like Troilus feel on top of the world. To be fully enjoyed, this great triumph needs witnesses. . . . It always takes other men to make an erotic or a military conquest truly valuable in the eyes of the conqueror himself.[3]

Girard's theory of mimetic desire provides the central motive for a series of psychoanalytic readings of *Troilus and Cressida* in which the primary culprit is not Pandarus but Troilus. Linda Charnes' contention that "Helen and Cressida are the conduits through which these men form crucial political and psychological connections with each other," Carol Cook's claim that "the heterosexuality founded on a traffic in women is a mediated homosexuality," and Valerie Traub's argument that the play "defies any effort to imagine a sexuality that is not defensive or diseased" are all based on Girard's principle of mimetic desire in which "identity is constructed in the envious gaze of the other."[4] The presumptive inescapability of this formation is registered in Charnes' contention that the choice of such notorious protagonists confers an aura of futility over the play from the outset, so that Shakespeare's dramatic strategy is to show his characters' "inability to be new, even to themselves" (418). As Lacan so eloquently puts it, "What is love other than banging one's head against a wall, since there is no sexual relation?"[5] But Lacan's gloomy conclusion on the final page of *Feminine Sexuality* follows several attempts, in short chapters taken from his seminars, to discover a non-phallic sexuality that could be free from determination by the symbolic order. In these essays, "God and the Jouissance of the Woman" and "The Love Letter," Lacan looks for a feminine *jouissance* that would not be identified with the body but that would depend upon conscious alienation from the symbolic order. Lacan offers his usual objection to materialists like Freud who base desire on the drive, arguing that this is "an attempt to reduce the mystical to questions of fucking" (147), but he does not, like Girard, simply dismiss object-cathexis as an uninteresting side effect of more sophisticated motivational structures. Lacan is at his most polemical when he insists that he uses the word "love" as a deliberate affront to the "subject who knows" in arguing that "Speaking of love is in itself a jouissance" (154).

Despite Lacan's dismissal of courtly love as simply an excuse for the absence of the sexual relation ("For the man . . . the only way of coming off elegantly from th[is] absence" [141]), his use of terms like "love" and even *la mystique* to describe dimensions of sexuality that are neither simply alibis for the drive nor pure iterations of the symbolic function draws him into the orbit of the classic analysis of courtly love offered by Denis de Rougemont, who argues that the precepts of courtly love were actually derived from the religious practices of Catharist mystics. De Rougemont, like Girard, has little use for object-cathexis; in de Rougemont's history of desire, romanticized sexuality is only a corruption of a spiritual principle.[6] But Shakespeare's Troilus and Cressida are the legatees of a complex tradition, one that identified sexual passion with a quasi-religious sense of personal identity, but which was at the same time highly aware of the ironies that arose from attaching spiritual qualities to a bodily practice. The paradoxes of this tradition were deep, but they were not opaque to its adherents. Andreas Capellanus warns that love and marriage are incompatible because marriage imposes an obligation that deprives desire of its spontaneity—"if the parties marry," writes Capellanus, "love is violently put to flight." But this does not prevent Capellanus from also instructing his readers that "It is not proper to love any woman whom one would be ashamed to seek to marry."[7] This contradiction illustrates how the task facing Shakespeare's

Troilus and Cressida, that of making their love perpetually spontaneous, is both familiar and inescapable.

Girardian readings of *Troilus and Cressida* illuminate the common structures that inform the treatments of the Trojan War by Shakespeare, Homer, and the medieval romance tradition, but in their presumption of the deterministic force of homosocial bonding and in their disinterest in the particularities of object-cathexis, these readings underestimate the scope of the play's sometimes spectacularly vulgar critique of the imaginary constructions that are created around sexual behavior. The Greek council scene offers a graphic map of the motivational forces that drive both armies to the war. The rhetorical field of the scene is rich in metaphor and synecdoche, and it is anchored by two particularly vivid figures, both of which are offered by Nestor. In the first, he compares a soldier to a ship, imagining how "the strong-ribbed barque through liquid mountains cut, / Bounding between the two moist elements / Like Perseus horse" (1.3.39–41); in the second, in "small pricks . . . there is seen / The baby figure of the giant mass / Of things to come at large" (337–40). In the first case, the ship stands for a soldier, the stormy sea represents adverse circumstance, and the point of the metaphor is that it is only in adversity that character, figured by Agamemnon as "nobler bulk" (36), reveals itself. The equation of size and virility informs Nestor's subsequent images of a "small prick" or "baby figure"; these figures are metaphoric vehicles of a synecdoche, where the tenor of the metaphor is the single combat that is being arranged in response to Hector's challenge. Following the imagistic logic of the *Iliad*, this individual contest is a synecdoche for the entire war, and so Nestor proposes that, according to this synecdochic logic, Achilles should stand for the Greek side because "the success, / Although particular, shall give a scantling / Of good or bad unto the general" (334–36). So the small prick (ostensibly a scratch, not a penis, though the pun is obvious) and the baby figure are metaphoric vehicles for single combat, single, "particular" combat is a synecdoche for the "general" war, and Achilles is the "small prick" who, according to Nestor, should stand for the entire Greek army. But by what standard is Achilles only a small prick? According to Nestor's first figure, a soldier is like a ship, and a ship is like a horse. By analogy then, a soldier is also like a horse. This analogy is reiterated when Ulysses and Nestor contest Achilles' claim to supremacy in the Greek camp; they complain that if brute strength is the only criteria of value, then "the ram that batters down the wall" (206) is of more worth than any soldier, and, therefore, "Achilles' horse / Makes many Thetis' sons" (211–12). As the equine and phallic imagery that pervades the scene measures Achilles' prick against that of his horse, this relentless phallicism leaves little doubt that the two moist elements between which Perseus' horse bounds, rising and falling, are not only the sea and the sky but the genital complement to the phallic horse. Thersites' critique that this is a war over a placket is borne out in the hum of sexual imagery that glides through the play barely below the threshold of awareness of its users. The figures that are knit together in this scene will be dispersed throughout the play; the "particular" and the "baby figure" will return as Hector's "toucheth my particular" and Troilus' "private part" and "infancy of truth," Thersites will proclaim the mismeasure between Ajax's' "inches" and those of a horse, and there will be no lack of euphemisms for battering rams and moist elements.

As the vulgarity of *Troilus and Cressida* undermines the heroic ethos of the epic tradition, a rampant cynicism pervades a play whose theatrical fortunes have often benefited from the worst of circumstances. The Vietnam era revivals of *Troilus* showed the play's relevance for an audience that had become suspicious of the viability of its own symbolic order in the midst of an interminable war of dubious origin. The juxtaposition of the two young lovers against a backdrop of massive militarism extends the persecutory structure of *Romeo and Juliet*, where the repressive forces are specifically concentrated on the romantic protagonists, into a more encompassing representation of a society that will crush the development of sexual love through crude indifference. No one particularly objects to the joining of Troilus and Cressida; their separation is simply an afterthought to those who determine it. In the Girardian reading, though, the failure of the romantic couple in *Troilus and Cressida* comes from within. It is Troilus's fault, whose "highly artificial lyricism" in the morning after speech to Cressida, Girard believes, "cannot be sincere":

> O Cressida! But that the busy day,
> Waked by the lark, hath roused the ribald crows,
> And dreaming night will hide our joys no longer,
> I would not from thee. (4.2.10–13)

The imagery here iterates the nightingale vs. lark debate between Juliet and Romeo, but Girard hears only Troilus's "indifference"[8] to Cressida. This perception is echoed in Mihoko Suzuki's contention that Troilus "acquiesces quite readily" in Cressida's transfer to the Greek camp, and in Charnes' claim that "he immediately accepts the verdict that she must go to the Greeks; he offers no resistance."[9] But placing the blame for this erotic failure on Troilus's insufficient emotional investment in Cressida strikes a very different balance than Shakespeare does. Shakespeare's Troilus follows through on the promise that Chaucer's Troilus makes but never redeems. Shakespeare's character actually takes the risk of surreptitiously entering the Greek camp in order to meet Cressida, where Chaucer's Troilus decides that it's just too dangerous:

> And ofte tyme he was in purpos grete
> Hymselven lik a pilgrym to desgise
> To seen hire; but he may nat contrefete
> To ben unknowen of folk that weren wise,

Ne fynde excuse aright that may suffise,
If he among the Grekis knowen were;
For which he wep ful ofte and many a tere.[10]

When Shakespeare's Troilus finds his way to Diomedes' tent, his response to his discovery of Cressida's perceived infidelity is dramatic; he is transformed from a hyperbolic idealist to a nihilistic cynic. Troilus's problem does not reside in a lack of attachment to Cressida, but in the contradiction adumbrated by Capellanus between private and public eroticism. In Lacan's terms, Troilus does not recognize the conflict between the imaginary and the symbolic, between the particularity of the *a* and the universality of the O. Where Charnes charges that Troilus and Pandarus jointly "'produce' Cressida's desirability by comparing her relentlessly to Helen,"[11] it is really only Pandarus who engages in a methodical production of resemblances. Troilus's single inadvertent use of the same figure, a pearl, to valorize Cressida and Helen (1.1.96 and 2.2.80) suggests his inability to dissociate the imaginary (the dyadic) from the symbolic (the triangular), but it does not indicate an indifference to the libidinal force of the imaginary.

Shakespeare's Troilus and Cressida both enter into their romantic roles demonstrating a good deal of book knowledge that has not been tested by personal experience. When Cressida's knowing caution that "That she beloved knows naught that knows not this: / Men price the thing ungained more than it is" (1.2.266–67) and Troilus's metaleptic observation that Helen's reputation for beauty is not the cause of the war but the effect of the amount of blood shed over her ("Helen must needs be fair / When with your blood you daily paint her thus" [1.1. 86–87]) puncture the cliches that always threaten to deflate romantic idealizations, their characters appeal to a knowing audience that wants to see a "truth tired with iteration" (3.2.163) renewed by eloquent variation. Troilus's literary training is on early display in a speech whose originality lies at least as much in its graphic subtext as in its surface eloquence. Responding to Pandarus's advice that Cressida is worth pursuing because her beauty compares with Helen's while her intelligence rivals Cassandra's, Troilus protests, in Petrarchan rhetoric, that it has become painful to contemplate the catalog of her virtues:

O Pandarus! I tell thee, Pandarus,
When I do tell thee 'There my hopes lie drowned',
Reply not in how many fathoms deep
They lie endrenched. I tell thee I am mad
In Cressid's love; thou answer'st 'She is fair',
Pourest in the open ulcer of my heart
Her eyes, her hair, her cheek, her gait, her voice;
Handlest in thy discourse, O, that her hand,
In whose comparisons all whites are ink
Writing their own reproach, to whose soft seizure

The cygnet's down is harsh, and spirit of sense
Hard as the palm of ploughman. (1.1.45–56)

The initial figure, which measures Troilus' emotions by the depth of the
ocean, is neatly structured but familiar. The syntactic elision of the subject at line 50 ("[Thou] Pour'st") initiates a loosening of structure, and the
ensuing blazon runs through a series of potential metaphoric sites before
settling on one: "her hand." The figuration that follows is deft in its com-
pactness and deeply embedded in literary tradition; Cressida's hand is so
much whiter than any other whiteness that it transforms the standard of
comparison, a piece of paper ("whiter than the paper it writ on / Is the
fair hand that writ" (*Merchant* 2.3.13–14) into the blackness of the ink
that writes on that paper. But the final, elaborated figure of the softness
of Cressida's hand reaches a different level of complexity as it folds back
on itself. This figure makes two comparisons: The first is that Cressida's
hand is softer than the feathers of a swan, and the second is that Cressida's
hand is softer than the "spirit of sense," which is, in comparison, as hard
as a workingman's hand, just as all other whites are black as ink in comparison to the whiteness of her hand. But now there are two hands in this
metaphoric field; one is the material tenor (Cressida's hand) and the other
("the palm of ploughman") might be called a negative vehicle, or a vehicle
once removed. This coarsened hand is not directly compared to Cressida's
hand—its place in the metaphoric field is that it is as rough as ink is black—
but it is easy to establish the grounds of difference between the two hands:
The ploughman's hand is rough because it has seen a good deal of use.

   If the ploughman's hand is, as Diomedes later says of Helen, insuscep-
tible of sensation due to excessive activity ("a flat tamed piece" [4.1.64]),
Troilus's speech implicitly adds one more virtue to Cressida's catalog; she
not only has the beauty of Helen and the brains of Cassandra, she is also
unused. In Troilus's imaginary, the value of Cressida's virginity is not as a
guarantee of legitimate heirs, and its worth will not be apparent to anyone
beyond its first possessor. The difference between the subject tenor (Cressida's hand) and the negative vehicle (the ploughman's palm) can only be
realized through the intermediate vehicle, the "spirit of sense," the ineffable
medium that transmits and transforms sensory impressions into interior
states of mind and soul. As this vehicle is resituated to the level of the material tenor, where it serves as the substance that picks up sensation transmitted through the surface of the hand, the displacement from the imaginary
("cygnet's down") to the material realm ("spirit of sense") reinflects the first
stage of the figure. The comparison of the "soft seizure" of Cressida's hand
to a cygnet's feathers describes the sensation that would be felt by someone
who was grasped by that hand; at this point, Cressida is the active agent
and the someone seized is the recipient witness of her softness. But in the
reversal of tenor and vehicle, as the quality of the sensation transmitted
along the spirit of sense is imaginarily conditioned by its point of origin, the

comparison between Cressida's hand and that of the ploughman makes her the recipient of sensation. Her value, which resides in a heightened sensory ability, is dependent on her difference from Helen, who, having had two husbands, is beyond being impressed by yet another display of virility. In contrast, Troilus imagines that an untouched Cressida cannot help but be overwhelmed by her first sexual encounter.

The gap between the sexual fantasies of Troilus and Diomedes and the easy recognition by a modern reader that their perceptions of Cressida and Helen are projections born of their own sexual anxieties establishes a critical distance that is reflected in Shakespeare's revision of Henryson's leprous Cressida into the venereally diseased Pandarus. The relocation of Pandarus to Winchester in the play's Epilogue is a reflexive and presentist gesture, one which suggests that in modern London just as in ancient Troy, the source of sexual pathology resides not in women's excessive sexuality but in the governing term of a patriarchal social order—as Lacan calls it, the law of the father. As Shakespeare returns to the archetypal plot of romantic tragedy, displaying the transience of desire through the depiction of a great one night stand, the paternal blocking agent becomes a facilitator, and the threat to sexual happiness is realized not in a power that forbids sexuality (Capulet) but in a power that instructs and manages it (Pandarus). Shakespeare's diagnosis of this pathology is less monolithic than that offered by Girard or Foucault. His characters are the descendants of a medieval lineage that punningly opposed a Church of Love—"Amor"—against the institutionalized power of "Roma."[12] In this heretic ideology, only a love that existed outside the recognition granted through legal marriage truly deserved the name of love. Lacan is at least willing to take the question of "love" as seriously as it was taken in the medieval romance tradition, and Lacan's account of the fragmented structure of desire offers a compelling critical vantage on the vagaries of desire in *Troilus and Cressida*. But at the final level of agental motivation and in the scope of its vulgarity, the play sometimes exceeds even Lacan's account of the causative powers of representation and more closely tracks the elemental logic that Julia Kristeva calls the semiotic order.

With Troilus, Cressida, and Pandarus occupying the three positions in Lacan's formulation of the triangle that shapes desire—the perpetually immature male subject, the objectified woman, and the morally indifferent paternal metaphor—the debased quality of the governing symbolic order in *Troilus and Cressida* is shown by the way in which for the second position, the terms "whore," "woman," and "slave" have become interchangeable. In this play, the word "whore" never describes women paid for sexual services; instead, it refers to those who have been forcibly transferred from one man to another, Helen (4.1.68) and Cressida (5.2.114). It also covers the case of Patroclus, a man who, for lack of "stomach to the war" (3.3.213) has been made a sort of woman, a "masculine whore" (5.1.19.1), and "Mistress Thersites" (2.1.34). The sexuality of the Greek army is so fully dependent on the positioning rather than the biological essentialism of subjects that in the absence of biological women, Patroclus and Thersites have become "women." The Hegelian master-slave dialectic that underlies Lacan's account of the negation of the woman in patriarchal heterosexuality accurately describes the sexual practices of the Greek heroes; through their valor on the battlefield, Achilles and Ajax have become masters and the natural proprietors of slaves, while those who will not fight to the death to protect their sexual honor become "women" or "whores." When Thersites accuses Achilles and Ajax of allowing themselves to be treated by Agamemnon and the ruling clique like "barbarian slaves" and claims that he himself "serves here voluntary," Achilles corrects him, insisting on the difference between a "man" and a "slave": "no man is beaten voluntary. Ajax was here the voluntary, and you as under an impress" (2.1.46, 91–94). In this sexual economy, the greatest prestige accrues to the "men" who can keep possession of the most women/whores/slaves. The complete irrelevance of the actual woman being fought for is shown in the declension of the role of the *femme fatale* from Helen to Cressida to Thersites. Ajax's fury when Achilles has "inveigled his fool from him" (2.3.84)—i.e., when Thersites leaves Ajax for Achilles—is the *reductio ad absurdum* of the triangular relation that launches and sustains the war.

The reduction of women to the status of slaves, however, introduces an unstable Hegelian dialectic of power into the values of the sexual economy. The dependence of the Hegelian master on recognition by his slave is illustrated in Thersites' deconstruction of Ajax's manhood. When Ajax claims the privilege of the master to beat his slave, Thersites threatens to "tell what thou art by inches, thou thing of no bowels" (2.1.47–48). Since Ajax beats him anyway, Thersites offers a deflationary measure of Ajax's "inches"; punning "bowels" to "balls," Thersites tells Achilles that Ajax "wears his wit in his belly," but "has not so much wit . . . As will stop the eye of Helen's needle" (2.1.70, 75, 77). If Ajax were unable to satisfy Helen, Thersites suggests, the fault would reside with Ajax, not Helen. Thersites thus demolishes the legend of Ajax, of whom George Peele's "The Tale of Troy" claims "the stomacke of the man was great."[13] As Thersites delivers this truth from the woman's position, his analogue on the Trojan side is Cassandra. Thersites' curse on those who "war for a placket" is echoed by Cassandra's prophecy that "Our firebrand brother, Paris, burns us all" (2.2.109). Although the first reference to Cassandra in the play casts her as the exemplar of "wit" (1.1.44) as Helen is the pattern of beauty, once Cassandra questions the rationale for war her prediction is ignored as madness; Troilus dismisses her from the debate simply by saying "'tis our mad sister" and "Cassandra's mad" (2.2.97, 121). Cassandra's archetypal fate, to be the voice of a potentially liberating truth that seems like madness to properly interpellated subjects, calls out from the position of the Lacanian Other.

The phallic subjects in *Troilus and Cressida* are constructed cross-culturally and from within a unified metaphoric field, one in which gender construction plays the dominant role. Ajax's shortcomings of "bowels" and "belly" foreshadow both Patroclus' effeminization due to his "little stomach to the war" (3.3.213) and Hector's challenge to "some knight . . . / That hath a stomach" (2.1.119–20). Hector uses the gastric metaphor self-referentially when he compares himself to a "lady of more softer bowels" in his plea to "let Helen go" (2.2.10, 16), but his sensible computation of the cost of the war loses out to Troilus's production of the tautology that results from the contract between aspirational masculinity and the law of the father: "manhood and honour" (2.2.46) are at stake. As Hector and Troilus debate the message sent to Priam, the Trojans recreate the divided condition of the Greeks. Both societies are in the transitional state described by Freud in *Totem and Taboo*, where the father figure has lost his place and the brother cohort negotiates the possession of women,[14] but the Trojans have evolved far enough to mystify this condition. Troilus insists that his motivation is not in fact sexual, that it is "glory that we more affected / Than the performance of our heaving spleens" (2.2.194–95), but the *double-entendres* that run through the scene belie his idealistic claim. Hector introduces the excessively suggestive imagery of the scene with his declaration that

> Though no man lesser fears the Greeks than I,
> As far as toucheth my particular . . .
> There is no lady of more softer bowels,
> More spongy to suck in the sense of fear . . .
> Than Hector is. (2.2.8–13).

Troilus takes up the figure of the male "particular" with his protest that "For my private part, / I am no more touched than all Priam's sons" (124–25), and his rhetorical query "Will you . . . buckle in a waist most fathomless?" (29) adds an infinite depth to Hector's figure of soft, spongy bowels. The bowels that are primarily at issue here are those of Helen, and the question of their fate is raised by Priam in his charge that Paris has the "honey" and everyone else "the gall" (143) of Helen's possession. Paris's response momentarily seems to suggest that he sees the justice of sharing this "honey" with his brothers: "I propose not merely to myself / The pleasures such a beauty brings with it" (145–46). In the slightly less civilized Greek camp, such "sharing" nearly happens to Cressida in the stylized gang rape that takes place on her arrival. All that Paris actually proposes to share, though, is the fame of keeping Helen, and this is the argument that carries the day. Troilus proclaims her "a theme of honour and renown" (198) and he imagines that, in defending and keeping her, "fame in time to come [will] canonize us" (201). Ironically enough, although Helen is the legal wife of Menelaus and the Greeks win the war, she does go down in legend as Helen of Troy. The complementarity of the fame of female possessions and of their male possessors is conveyed in elegantly graphic terms when Troilus says that "the world's large spaces cannot parallel" (161) Helen. He means to say that the entire world cannot offer her equal, but what he actually produces is a "parallel" between Helen and "large spaces." The convergence of Helen and Trojan honor allows the imagery of "large spaces" to join the vehicles of a "waist most fathomless" and soft, spongy bowels as figures for the immeasurability of Helen. In the imaginary world of phallic subjects, Helen has not the tiny-eyed needle suggested by Thersites but a vast, spongy, fathomless depth, and Trojan honor will be recorded as the manhood commensurate with its challenges.

The spurious autonomy of the penis as the phallus and the dependence of male identity on the woman it negates are the primary themes of Lacan's sexualizing of the Hegelian dialectic of the master and the slave. Although Hegel calls the relation between master and slave dialectical, and Lacan posits the mirror stage as the originary consolidation of the subject through its reflection of the imago of the human form,[15] neither Hegel nor Lacan imagine a dyadic identity as more genuine than one imposed by a cultural order. Hegel's teleology of the state and Lacan's omnipresent symbolic order relegate the Aristophanic myth of perfect complementariness to the realm of escapist fantasy. In Lacan's formulation of the primal triangle, a father figure sets the primary pattern of identification for an ego formed as a mimetic entity, and the triad of ego/objects/others trains the ego to imitate the desires of others and to compete with them for the objects of their desires.[16] Lacan thus grounds Hegelian competition in a phase of psychic development in which the male subject learns to place a higher value on the possessions of others than on material satisfaction. The result is the emergence of the gap between need and demand—the gap in which desire first appears.

Kristeva has come closest, among analysts influenced by Lacan, to imagining the Aristophanic myth of the romantic couple as a viable basis of an identity which could satisfy both need and desire, finding "the object of love a metaphor for the subject, a constitutive metaphor, its 'unary feature.'"[17] Kristeva stresses the liminality of this formation, calling it an "idealization on the edge of primal repression" (282), hovering between fragmentation and the symbolic code. *Troilus and Cressida* uses the mirror imagery that informs both the Renaissance sonnet tradition and the Lacanian theory of subject formation as the entry point into more graphic sexual imagery that grounds male identity not in specular recognition but in the act of sexual intercourse. The conjunction of specular and sexual imagery is developed in a conversation between Ulysses and Achilles that is initially pervaded by reflective images. Ulysses tells Agamemnon that his plot will show Achilles that "Pride hath no other glass / To show itself but pride" (3.3.47–48), and Achilles quickly discovers that "What the declined is / He shall . . . soon read in the eyes of others' (70–71). Ulysses explicates the point to Achilles through the teaching of an unnamed "strange fellow"[18] who writes that "man, how dearly ever parted . . . feels not what he owes, but by reflection"

(91–94). Except for the suggestive phallicism of "dearly . . . parted," Ulysses remains within a familiar field of specular reflection, but he defamiliarizes this imagery when he goes on to add "As when his virtues, shining upon others, / Heat them, and they retort that heat again / To the first giver" (95–97).[19] At first, Achilles recognizes only what is conventional in Ulysses' argument; he objects that "this is not strange" and, in a figure that suggests that these ancient Greeks are familiar not only with Aristotle but with the Renaissance sonnet tradition, he reminds Ulysses that it is universally understood that "The beauty that is borne here in the face" is incapable of self-recognition until it "commends itself / To others' eyes," where, "eye to eye opposed," it is "mirrored there / Where it may see itself" (98–106). But Ulysses corrects Achilles, warning him that he has missed the salient point; reiterating the significance of "parts," he argues that it is not visual reflection that confirms romantic identity:

> no man is the lord of anything . . .
> Till he communicate his parts to others.
> Nor doth he of himself know them for aught
> Till he behold them formed in th'applause
> Where they're extended—who, like an arch, reverb'rate
> The voice again; or, like a gate of steel
> Fronting the sun, receives and renders back
> His figure and his heat. (110–18)

The imagery of sexual intercourse is vivid, with extended parts entering a gate that replies to its own penetration. There is no longer a mismatch of paltry inches and immense, spongy spaces but a perfect fit of moving parts, like Perseus' horse bounding between moist elements. In this metaphoric field, it is not the possession of the trophy woman, nor the homosocial admiration of that achievement, but the woman's response to male sexual performance that confirms the identity of the master.

Lacan's interest in taking the psychoanalysis of sexuality away from the drive follows the Hegelian path of distinguishing the specifically human desire for prestige from the merely biological satisfaction of material need, but these terms can be difficult to disentangle in *Troilus and Cressida*. When Pandarus warns Troilus that he "must be witty" (3.2.29) at Cressida's arrival, his surface meaning is that Troilus must retain the presence of mind necessary to speak in a proper courtly fashion, but the sexual innuendo that Thersites attaches to the word "wit" in his quarrel with Ajax gives Pandarus' warning a subtext of performance anxiety. This sexual subtext is developed in Cressida's concern that lovers might "have the voice of lions and the act of hares" (81–82) and in Troilus' recognition of the principle that "desire is boundless and the act a slave to limit" (77). It would be reductive, as Lacan suggests, to reduce all of this figuration to questions of sexual performance; desire is "boundless" because there is more at stake in sexuality than the satisfaction of need. The desire to find a self in the reflective surface of the other fuels Troilus' doubt that "constancy" "could be in a woman" (148, 145), a confession which, far from being a sign of his personal misogyny, marks the moment at which he confronts and rejects the misogynist tradition of texts like Henryson's *Testament of Cresseid*. Cressida's corollary fear that "They say all lovers swear more performance than they are able, and yet reserve an ability that they never perform" (78–79) similarly cites the authority of tradition only to reject it. Troilus and Cressida thus expose themselves to the risk of entering into the romantic pair bond as a "utopic wager,"[20] short-circuiting the competitive triangles of self/objects/others identified by Hegel and Lacan as the means of achieving fully self-conscious identity. As Kristeva asks,

> If desire is fickle, thirsting for novelty, unstable by definition, what is it that leads love to dream of an eternal couple? Why faithfulness, the wish for a durable harmony, why in short a marriage of love—not as a necessity in a given society but as desire, as libidinal necessity. (225)

Unlike Romeo and Juliet, Troilus and Cressida say nothing of marriage, but in this they are simply true to their medieval roots. As Capellanus shows, the precepts of courtly love call for a union which has all of the qualities of the marriage bond but which is never granted the legal and social recognition that makes that bond into an obligation rather than a perpetually spontaneous renewal of desire. The absence of a public contract suggests a couple that has passed Lacan's course, of which he says that "My entire teaching is to dissociate the *a* and the O."[21] Kristeva's answer to the question "why the couple?" is that, even after technological advances

> render the eternal couple socially and scientifically useless, and do the same for marriage as a social necessity that insured the optimal conditions for the reproduction of the species . . . the faithful couple that the law used to wish for, remains for many a therapeutic erotic necessity caused by the open multiplicity of pleasures and *jouissances*. . . . the couple is a durable mirror . . . binding in self-esteem [*amour-haine*] partners who are tied to such and such a partial object furnished by the other.[22]

For Hegel, the desire for recognition by the Other is the mainspring of the specifically human quality of desire, and the triangular relation of competition for the desired objects of others creates that recognition as the winners prove their ability to force others to recognize their claims. But if, as Alexandre Kojeve realizes in unpacking Hegel, "to desire a Desire is to want to substitute oneself for the value desired by this Desire,"[23] why could that recognition not be achieved directly through dyadic mirroring? The war over Helen is driven by a desire for recognition by an imaginary third term called "fame" by Troilus, but every time that term is invoked in the play it marks an alienation of desire. Paris appeals to this imaginary tribunal when he asks Diomedes, "Who in your thoughts merits fair Helen most, / Myself or Menelaus?" (4.1.55–56), a query that suggests a classic Girardian structure in which Helen's value to Paris resides not in herself but in Diomedes' opinion of her possessor. Achilles extends protection to Thersites even though he fills no real need that could not be filled by Patroclus, because keeping Thersites as dessert ("my cheese, my digestion" [2.3.36]) establishes Achilles' ability to defend multiple possessions and thus enhances his prestige. The narrative of young, first love seems to suggest that the central question asked by *Troilus and Cressida* will be whether the sexual relation between Troilus and Cressida can be distinguished from the bonds between Paris and Helen and those between Achilles and Thersites, but as the story evolves, even that question will be shadowed by the interaction between Cressida and Diomedes.

Shakespeare's account of the sexual relation between Troilus and Cressida incorporates a wide range of themes from within the courtly love tradition. When Troilus responds to Cressida's fear that "all lovers swear more performance than they are able, and yet reserve an ability"—i.e., fidelity— "that they never perform" (3.2.78–79), he adopts a metaphor that casts her as his sovereign: "Praise us as we are tasted; allow us as we prove. Our head shall go bare till merit crown it" (83–85). The motive for the male lover to subordinate himself to the woman's judgment is, as Kristeva describes it, a "therapeutic erotic necessity" because of the inadequacy of the satisfactions available to the position of the master; as Hegel explains, once the master has won the struggle for prestige by making the other his slave, he discovers that when "he is recognized by someone whom he does not recognize," this "is a recognition without value for him. For he can be satisfied only by recognition from one whom he recognizes as worthy of recognizing him."[24] This paradox informs Lacan's story of the primal triangle and the alienation of desire. In Lacan's account, the male child initially sees the mother as having the phallus, since she is the source of satisfaction of his needs. When he learns that she is not all, he gives up the body of the mother in order to find a place in the world of the fathers, the symbolic order. Lacan's insistence that there is nothing coherent outside the symbolic order leads him to overlook the deduction that Kristeva and Shakespeare's "strange fellow" make about the couple: that in order to recover the pleasure that is deferred when the male infant relinquishes the body of the mother, he will have to return the phallus to the woman if he is to reconcile need and desire. In order to obtain the pleasure of being the desired of the Other, he has to grant her the power of recognition of the phallus.

Even this account of the libidinal value of the couple for the male position puts the woman in an ambiguous role in the case of an idealizing, courtly lover like Troilus. Can he really love her, or is the woman only the *petit a* who is obliterated as she serves as the vehicle of his consummation with the grand O? Lacan derides the premises of courtly love, declaring that chivalry "is always the discourse of the master" where the "lady was entirely, in the most servile sense of the term, his female subject."[25] But the literary record is not so unequivocal. Capellanus's *Art of Courtly Love*, which shares with its predecessor Ovid's *Art of Love* a tolerance, under certain circumstances, for rape,[26] also acknowledges that the most intractable disputes between lovers can only be resolved through the woman's choice. Capellanus records a number of complex cases in which knights assert claims in a court of love based on promises made by a woman. The classic situation involves a woman whose first lover unexpectedly returns from a lengthy incommunicado period during the Crusades only to find that she has taken up with a new partner. In such situations, according to Capellanus, the court can only conclude that "The resolution of the immediate question depends more on the will or desire [*arbitrio vel voluntate*] of the woman than on an understanding of precept of law" (206–07). In such cases, it is left to the woman to decide how she is moved by the "impulse to love [*spiritus movetur amandi*]."[27]

The reliability of Capellanus's text as a historical document is problematic. It has been widely argued that the courts of love never existed, and that women's adultery could not have been widely practiced in the tightly regulated sexual climate of the medieval aristocracy. De Rougemont cites Rene Nelli's thesis that, in a society where marriages were contracted not out of love but from "material and social conditions . . . imposed on the parties regardless of their feelings," the literature of courtly love, as it idealized adultery, offered to women "a spiritual antipode to marriage, the state into which they had been forced."[28] But even the hypothesis that these texts served as escapist fantasy for a readership of women suggests the persistence of the Lacanian principle that, in a culture whose sexuality is structured around the pleasures of one sex, the other will find its *jouissance* "elsewhere," in a supplementary (not a complementary) *jouissance* that exists "beyond the phallus" and outside the law.[29]

Cressida's first soliloquy shows that she fully understands both the power and the jeopardy of her cultural position. She alludes to the danger of being reduced to a "thing," and she counsels that the only way to avoid such debasement is to "hold . . . off" (1.2.265, 264). A woman who convinces men that her desire is difficult to attain thereby enhances its value, while a woman who shows her desire too openly does more than lower her own worth; she positively inspires male paranoia. In one of the most misogynist passages in *The Art of Courtly Love*, Capellanus warns against women who "grant favours readily," and he shows why Cressida is so justifiably wary of sexuality and why she is ultimately defamed anyway:

> A woman of this type cannot unite herself to anyone with bonds of love because of her excessive sexual appetite; she seeks satiety through the lust of many. So in vain do you seek her love, unless you regard

yourself as so virile in sexual matters that you can satiate her lust. But this would be more difficult than draining the seas completely of their waters. . . . Though you can obtain your will and win her embraces to the full, the consolations she offers will be the occasion of intolerable pain and the source of abundant griefs to you when . . . you come to realise that she is lending herself to another's lust.[30]

If a woman's desire is independent of male inspiration, there is no telling where it might go or what it might say. As Thersites' description of Ajax to Achilles shows, a woman's potential sexual mobility can threaten the material basis of male identity. The reaction to this threat is the representation of the woman as infinitely promiscuous, as a "whore."

Shakespeare's Troilus enters into the field of courtly love bearing a deep familiarity with both the idealistic rhetoric and the paradoxical logic of that tradition, but his penchant for baroque figuration disappears when he tries to engage the contradictions between the idealization of desire and the debasement of women:

> O that I thought it could be in a woman—
> As, if it can, I will presume in you—
> To feed for aye her lamp and flames of love,
> To keep her constancy in plight and youth,
> Outliving beauty's outward, with a mind
> That doth renew swifter than blood decays. (3.2.145–50)

This speech confronts Henryson's misogyny with Capellanus' principle that "Character, alone, is worthy of the crown of love."[31] The desire for "a mind / That doth renew swifter than blood decays" takes Cressida entirely out of Helen's shadow, and Troilus's imagined response to such "constancy" brings in just the slightest hint of the sexuality that informs the romantic pair bond; before such an ideal woman, he thinks, he would be "uplifted" (3.2.155). Cressida's half-line response, "In that I'll war with you" (158) is the dramatic hinge of the scene. Nothing is agreed until Cressida inverts the play's equation of love and war and Troilus accepts the inversion by saying "O virtuous fight, / When right with right wars who shall be most right" (159–60). Overturning the Hegelian struggle for mastery, Troilus and Cressida both pledge to offer faithful service. This seeming mutuality is not symmetrical, though, as the terms of their succeeding vows show. Just as Troilus believed that fame would canonize his manhood if he stood by his honor and fought for Helen, now he imagines that fame, through the agency of "True swains in love . . . in the world to come" (160) will celebrate his fidelity to Cressida. Cressida imagines the opposite; her negative vows ("If I be false, or swerve a hair from truth" [171]) show that she understands that the best she can expect from fame is anonymity. Cressida sees that her only place in a symbolic order is not a happy one; when a simple mutuality of desire is alienated to the judgment of a totalizing authority, women become the "things" men use to find their place in that order. As Cressida understands, the contradictions between Lacan's *petit a* and grand O really are intractable.

The symbolic order that has brought about this war is a metaphoric structure of substitution in which Cressida stands for Helen and Helen for an abstraction, while the romantic narrative that Cressida seeks to inhabit is a purely metonymic structure in which she is simply herself. The genius of the absolute distinction made in the courtly love tradition between love and marriage, and the insistence on the complete secrecy of the true love bond, depend upon a recognition of the fundamental incompatibility of the binary (Lacanian imaginary) and triangular (Lacanian symbolic) structures of desire. Peter Dronke offers a spiritualized description of the covert romantic bond, explaining that "The secrecy of *amour courtois* springs from the universal notion of love as a mystery not to be profaned by the outside world, not to be shared by any but lover and beloved,"[32] but Capellanus' grasp of this principle has a more practical cast. When he counsels that "He who is eager to preserve his love undamaged ought to take the greatest precautions to ensure that his love is not divulged to anyone beyond its limits, but preserved secret from all,"[33] he locates the threat to the romantic couple in the active hostility of their closest friends and relatives. Capellanus warns that lovers who come upon each other in a public place should behave like strangers, "lest some person spying on their love should have opportunity to spread malicious gossip" (152). The immediate reappearance of Pandarus after the lovers' exchange of unscripted vows casts the shadow of the public order over their spontaneous performance. The symbolic order may legislate monogamy as a means of its own reproduction, but it does so only by channeling desire into an idealization that turns the other, the *objet petit a*, into a marker of prestige. When this function is at its peak, all male desire will be channeled not into individual partnerships but into a fight to the death over Helen of Troy, the most beautiful woman in the world. The character of Pandarus spans the paternal metaphor that governs this economy. In its most benign manifestation, his jokes about Cressida's sexual experience—"hast not slept tonight? Would he not—a naughty man—let it sleep?" (4.2.33–34) are the Nurse's jokes in *Romeo and Juliet:* "For the next night, I warrant / The County Paris hath set up his rest / That you shall rest but little" (*RJ* 4.4.32–34). But when the war requires that Cressida be sent to the Greeks, Pandarus becomes old Capulet disowning Juliet. Pandarus' concern for how this separation will affect Troilus ("The young prince will go mad" [4.3.2]) and his curse on Cressida, "Would thou hadst ne'er been born. I knew thou wouldst be his death" (4.3.10–11), illustrate the disinterest of the patriarchy in the fate of its daughters.

Troilus' response to Cressida's exile bears out his self-description as "plain and true" (4.5.108); he really is a "baby figure" (1.3.339), "simpler than the infancy of truth" (3.2.157) in comparison to the cynical veteran Diomedes. Troilus speaks the language of chivalric challenge to Diomedes as if it is simply a game:

> If e'er thou stand at mercy of my sword,
> Name Cressid, and thy life shall be as safe
> As Priam is in Ilium. (4.5.114–16)

Diomedes, who understands this rhetoric as only a temporary deferral of the brutal reality of the battlefield, simply ignores Troilus' offer of mercy and speaks directly to Cressida; praising "the lustre in your eye, heaven in your cheek" and informing her that "to Diomed / You shall be mistress" (4.5.118–20), he effectively dismisses Troilus' claim to knightly heroism. The difference between Troilus' and Diomedes' characters is delineated in Ulysses' later account of Troilus and Thersites' description of Diomedes. Ulysses confirms Troilus' reputation for being "matchless-firm of word, / Speaking in deeds and deedless in his tongue" (4.6.100–01), while Thersites describes Diomedes as the epitome of the "all lovers" feared by Cressida; Diomedes will "promise like Brabbler the hound, but when he performs astronomers foretell it: that is prodigious" (5.1.83–84). Cressida's sensitivity to this difference leads her to conclude, even as her affections are shifting from Troilus to Diomedes, that Troilus is the "one that loved me better than you [Diomedes] will" (5.2.90). But Troilus plays his part in producing her alienation through his challenge to Diomedes. When he effectively tells Diomedes that he is Cressida's lover, he casts her as an object of desire and of competition. Troilus' revelation of his love for Cressida violates the courtly code of secrecy, and it begs the question of whether Troilus, like Paris when he asks Diomedes who "merits fair Helen most" (4.1.55), is looking for the prestige that would be conferred by Diomedes' recognition.

Cressida's character arc is broader than that of Troilus, and the difference corresponds to their different positions in relation to the symbolic order. His pledge of love to her takes place in an extemporaneous near-sonnet of twelve lines (3.2.158–70) in which he makes the traditional turn, at the ninth line, from listing archetypal standards of fidelity to holding himself out as the truest standard of all. Cressida's near-sonnet response (also twelve lines) is phrased as a negation; she takes up the topos of Shakespeare's grandest sonnet, Sonnet 55 ("Not marble nor the gilded monuments / Of princes"), which compares the enduring properties of edifices and documents, and she allows for the ultimate extinction of both. The "stones of Troy" (173), she mistakenly imagines, will erode over time, and the city itself will be forgotten, "characterless" (175) in the historical record. Her fate, she prophesies, if ever she "swerve[s] a hair from truth" (171), will be to face an infamy that will last longer than either Troy or the record of its existence. Knowing that she will receive nothing from the symbolic order, Cressida makes no attempt, as Troilus does, to identify herself with its values. When she receives word of her exile, she does not appeal to an imaginary higher order of justice; she threatens self-mutilation, and to Pandarus's admonition to "be moderate" she offers an eloquent and immoderate refusal:

> Why tell you me of moderation?
> The grief is fine, full, perfect that I taste,
> And violenteth in a sense as strong
> As that which causeth it. How can I moderate it?
> If I could temporize with my affection
> Or brew it to a weak and colder palate,
> The like allayment could I give my grief.
> My love admits no qualifying dross;
> No more my grief, in such a precious loss. (4.5.2–10)

Cressida's narcissistic masochism puts her in the conventionally male position of the unrequited lover in the romance tradition, echoing Petrarch's insistence that "I so feed on the tears and the suffering, deriving from them some kind of dark pleasure, that I must be torn from my misery against my will."[34] The modern theorist of this subject is Kristeva, who writes of the "pangs and delights of masochism" as the lot of the "abject," the subject who has discovered that "all its objects are based merely on the inaugural loss that laid the foundation of its own being."[35] Shakespeare finds in the literary tradition an orphaned young woman who falls in love and tries to establish an identity and a social place through an erotic attachment to a single object of desire, one *objet petit a*. The predictable result is that she finds herself in the position of the abject; even her "own body and ego [become] the most precious non-objects; they are no longer seen in their own right but forfeited" (5), taken by an inexplicable law that demands everything and offers nothing in return.

Cressida's greatest terror in the scene of her parting from Troilus is that she could be unrecognized from within the couple. His repeated exhortations to her to "be true" (4.5.65, 73) draw the seeming *non sequitur* "You love me not" (4.5.83) because his doubts suggest to her that the mirror effect was a mirage. She knows that her "love / Is as the very centre of the earth" (4.3.28–29), and if he does not know this core of her being, then what is he in love with? Lacan argues that the mirror effect in love is always a mirage, that "When, in love, I solicit a look, what is profoundly unsatisfying and always missing is that—*You never look at me from the place from which I see you.*"[36] The self that is projected into the romantic relation is an ideal I, a metaphor of the self, whose function is to persuade the other that I am worthy of love. This fictional being is then idealized into the cause of desire. Cressida looks to Troilus for a recognition that he cannot bestow, a recognition of her essential "centre," but the Cressida he perceives is a fiction, an idealization that has been created through the symbolic order and articulated by Pandarus.

Shakespeare's treatment of the transfer of Cressida's affections to Diomedes is unique. He was corrected by Dryden, who found it puzzling that Shakespeare's "Cressida is false, and is not punished."[37] Dryden, like Chaucer, remedies the fault by making Cressida less false; Henryson's solution is to impose a humiliating punishment. Shakespeare enhances the enigma of Cressida's character by framing her final choice with omissions; her conversation with Diomedes in 5.2 begins with a reference to a conversation the audience has not heard ("Will you remember?" [12]), and the last thing we nearly hear from Cressida is her letter to Troilus, which he tears and throws away (5.3.110–14). The first clue to her feelings towards Diomedes is in her greeting to him, "my sweet guardian" (5.2.7), which suggests a justifiable duplicity. Having barely escaped a group assault upon her arrival in the Greek camp, Cressida now addresses as "guardian" the only man present in that scene who did not try to force himself on her. Her recourse to Diomedes is similar to Thersites' decision to avoid Ajax's beatings by moving in with Achilles. Calling Diomedes "sweet" offers him just enough incentive to provide the protection she needs, but it is not enough to forestall the negotiating process that Chaucer's Criseyde faces from Diomede. In retelling the story of the transfer of Cressida's desire from Troilus to Diomedes, Shakespeare reduces the multiple visits of Chaucer's Diomede to a single dramatic encounter and he alters, in subtle fashion, some of the key terms of Chaucer's account. Chaucer's reluctant narrator recounts the equivocal promises Criseyde makes to Diomede; she tells him that she will only allow him to see her again if he promises to forego any talk of courtship: "To-morweek wol I speken with you fayn, / So that ye touchen nought of this matere" (5.995–96). Chaucer then offers two euphemistic descriptions of what sound like Criseyde's sexual surrender. In the first case, "The morwe com," Diomede returns to Criseyde and pleads his case:

> So wel he for hymselven spak and seyde,
> That alle her sikes soore adown he leyde;
> And finaly, the sothe for to seyne,
> He refte hire of the grete of al hire peyne. (5.1033–36)

The passage suggests, largely through the conclusive "finaly," that the story of seduction has reached its climax and that this euphemistic phrasing of the "sothe" is all that convention will allow and the narrator can bear to "seyne." But only two stanzas later, when Diomede has been wounded in battle, the "sothe" seems to arrive again for the first time when "for to hele him of his sorwes smerte / Men seyn—I n'ot—that she yaf him her herte" (5.1049–50). It is only after this giving of her "herte" that Criseyde begins upbraiding herself for having "falsed Troilus" (5.1053).

When Shakespeare's Diomedes demands of Cressida "Will you remember?" he suggests that she has made some sort of promise to him. Diomedes is more forceful than his Chaucerian predecessor in his attempt to redeem that promise, but his dialogic thrust and parry with Cressida is even more euphemistic than the language of *Troilus and Criseyde*. Where Chaucer's "herte" functions as an easily recognizable anatomical euphemism, Shakespeare's characters enigmatically bandy pronouns ("what" and "that") as they talk around the point before coming to an implicit understanding:

> *CRESSIDA:* What would you have me do?
> . . .
> *DIOMEDES:* What did you swear you would bestow on me?
> *CRESSIDA:* I prithee, do not hold me to mine oath.
>   Bid me do anything but that, sweet Greek
> *DIOMEDES:* Good night. (5.2.23–27)

Cressida's response to Diomedes' question "What did you swear you would bestow on me?" offers only "that" ("anything but that") as a description of "what" he is asking for. When Diomedes names what he has gotten so far—"words" ("let your mind be coupled with your words" [5.2.15])—and "what" he expects to follow, Chaucer's euphemistic "herte" is replaced by the even more discreet "mind." But the displacement from Chaucer's "herte" to Shakespeare's "mind" signals the real stakes of this exchange. These two potential lovers are playing a difficult game. In order for Cressida to satisfy Diomedes' desire, and not just a material need, she has to convince him that she is looking to him for something more than protection. In order for Diomedes' desire to matter to Cressida, he has to convince her that she is the object of his free choice and not just the only biological woman in the Greek camp. While Thersites accuses Cressida of deliberately playing coy to arouse Diomedes, it is actually Diomedes who behaves just as Cressida did in her courtship scene with Troilus; he repeatedly threatens to walk away, as if he has plenty of other options. He makes this threat at least four times in this scene: "Nay, then" (20), "Good night" (27), "And so good night" (42), and "Why then, farewell" (99).

Chaucer's euphemistic "herte" is reechoed when an ostentatious signifier—Troilus's sleeve, his parting gift to Cressida—is put into circulation. The movement of the sleeve is marked by implicit stage directions that attach to the italicized lines below; it is first grudgingly handed over by Cressida to Diomedes, then forcibly recovered by Cressida, and then even more forcefully retaken by Diomedes:

> *CRESSIDA: Here Diomed, keep this sleeve.*
> . . .
> *CRESSIDA:* You look upon that sleeve. Behold it well.

He loved me—O false wench!—give't me again.
DIOMEDES: Whose was't?
CRESSIDA: It is no matter, *now I ha't again.*
I will not meet with you tomorrow night.
I prithee, Diomed, visit me no more.

. . .

DIOMEDES: I shall have it.
CRESSIDA: What, this?
DIOMEDES: Ay, that.
CRESSIDA: . . . *Nay, do not snatch it from me.*
He that takes that doth take my heart withal.
DIOMEDES: I had your heart before; this follows it.

. . .

CRESSIDA: You shall not have it, Diomed. Faith, you shall not.
I'll give you something else.
DIOMEDES: *I will have this.* Whose was it?
CRESSIDA: It is no matter.
DIOMEDES: Come, tell me whose it was?
CRESSIDA: 'Twas one's that loved me better than you will,
But *now you have it,* take it. (5.2.65–91)[38]

When Jan Kott asks why Cressida gives Diomedes, of all things, Troilus's sleeve, he concludes that "She had to kill everything in herself. Cressida goes to bed with Diomedes, as Lady Anne went to bed with Richard who had killed her husband and father."[39] Like Chaucer and Dryden, Kott mitigates Cressida's guilt by diminishing her agency. But something else happens in the physical action of this exchange; Cressida fights Diomedes for the sleeve, and although she loses that contest she comes out of the struggle with greater, not less, autonomy. Diomedes, too, is changed. At every previous sign of resistance on Cressida's part he responds by threatening to walk away, reminding her of his power to throw her to the Greek camp. But in the end he reacts to her most vigorous gesture of resistance, her forcible retaking of the sleeve ("Now I ha't again") by physically fighting back. His repeated question "Whose was't?" is disingenuous. Troilus' behavior at Cressida's parting left no doubt about whose sleeve she carries, but Diomedes wants to hear Cressida put Troilus in the past with her own words. Diomedes' identification of Cressida's "heart" as the prologue to something else, represented by the sleeve, that "follows it" marks the sleeve as the signifier of sexual possession, but what Diomedes wants is something more than Cressida's body. In his demand that Cressida renounce Troilus, and in his inability simply to walk away when she fights for possession of the sleeve, Diomedes shows that he has been pulled into the circuit of desire. He will not be satisfied by resigned sexual submission; he wants Cressida's "mind," her uncoerced desire.

Cressida's ability to knock Diomedes off his diffident game has a rebound effect on her. As Thersites notes, Cressida initially "holds off" with perfect skill. By taking the sleeve back from Diomedes she creates a triangular rivalry and, as Capellanus knows, "jealousy always increases the feeling of love."[40] As Cressida plays this game spontaneously, she makes it new. Cressida and Diomedes are drawn together by something that is not apparent on the page; only the results are there of a skirmish in which, as two bodies wrestle over an empty signifier, everything else disappears. Troilus, Calchas, the war, and all of the circumstances that make this encounter impossibly artificial are momentarily obliterated as Cressida and Diomedes generate a dyadic *jouissance*. Cressida's complicity in this union overrides her better judgment; she understands that Troilus has probably "loved me better than you will," but this does not alter the fact that Troilus is now in the past, and this is by Cressida's choice: "One eye yet looks on thee, / But with my heart the other eye doth see" (107–08). Chaucer's Criseyde passively accepts her fate, lamenting that since "too late is now for me to rewe, / To Diomede algate I wol be trewe" (5.1070–71), but Shakespeare's Cressida puts her heart and her willing self, her eye/I, behind the choice to follow her *spiritus movetur amandi*. What happens between Cressida and Diomedes is the phenomenon that gives desire both spontaneity and exclusive focus, and that Capellanus carefully distinguishes from both lust and marriage; it is love. Where the *Iliad* seems to suggest that there is no means of resolving a conflict between two men over a desired woman other than a world war, the revisionary romance tradition contends that the dependence of romantic love on the spontaneity of desire means that conflicts like this one will be common and unavoidable, and that the principle of uncoerced desire requires that the Cressidas of the world should be allowed the freedom to settle such disputes. Capellanus is quite clear in his exemplary case:

"Q: The lover of a noble woman set out on an expedition with the king. False stories were circulated amongst all that he had died. When she heard this and made careful enquiry, she performed the customary and reasonable mourning-period which she believed obligatory for dead lovers. Then she joined herself to another love. After a short lapse of time the first lover returned, and sought to be given the customary embraces, but the second lover forbade him these, saying that the second love had been consummated and was equally reciprocated. . . .

A: The resolution of the immediate question depends more on the will or desire of the woman than on an understanding of precept of law or special command of love. I indeed believe that the lady . . . acts rightly by giving herself wholly back to her former lover, provided she is stirred by some bond of affection toward him. But even if she is not stirred by the slightest impulse to love, I still maintain that she ought forcibly to compel her will to seek what she originally . . . approved with her heart's desire. . . . But if the lady finds that her will experiences no warmth of attraction, and she realises she cannot revive her dead feelings towards her first lover, she can keep the second. . . . To say she ought to return to the first lover . . . without the persuasion of love's prompting, would be a base claim and a cheating of Love's commands. (205–07)

Cressida makes the required effort to wrest her will back to Troilus when she reflects that Troilus was a more reliable lover than Diomedes and that "one eye yet looks on" him, but her choice to follow the prompting of her "heart" reinvests Chaucerian euphemism with the heat of sexual desire.

If Cressida's desire is more mobile than that of Troilus, this is not the revelation of essentially gendered character but the result of the different promises made to men and to women in a patriarchal culture. The idealization of the Other, which is the support of monogamy, depends upon the psychoanalytic function of condensation, or in linguistic terms, metaphor, so that the *objet petit a* stands for a place in the grand Other where value is confirmed. In a subject with no expectations of gratification from the symbolic order, desire is liable to take its naturally metonymic, promiscuous course. Shakespeare's Cressida, who self-consciously occupies the position of the woman and who tries to escape notice by the symbolic order, ironically gets her wish when her last words become a vivid metaphor of fragmentation; contradicting the most basic dramatic rule of what happens when a character is handed a letter onstage, Troilus does not read Cressida's letter aloud to the audience. He simply shreds the paper and casts the pieces to the wind: "Go, wind, to wind: there turn and change together" (5.3.112). Troilus' incredulity at the seemingly incoherent figure he sees flirting with Diomedes—"If beauty have a soul, this is not she" (5.2.138)—reflects his expectation that he would be rewarded with eternal fame for maintaining his honor both in war and in love. His belief that this unity is registered at the level of the "soul" is a pre-Christian image of immortality that embodies Lacan's principle that "for the soul to come into being, she, the woman, is differentiated from it. . . . Called woman [*dit-femme*] and defamed [*diffâme*]."[41] Troilus finds his world inexplicable because he sees no contradiction between two incompatible Others, one which is a stable, ordered hierarchy that could terminate in the permanence of an immortal soul, and another whose essence is mobility and transience. Cressida is relegated to this second order, and as Diomedes' demand for her "mind" indicates, her defamation depends not upon the fate of her body but on the independence of her judgment; as Thersites imagines her inner monologue, "My mind is now turned whore" (5.2.114). It is ironic that Thersites, who gets his revenge on Ajax from the position of the sexual slave, should be the one to recognize that Cressida's culpability depends on her ability to find her own *jouissance*, but as Lacan puts it, "perverts" have "a knowledge of the nature of things, which leads directly from sexual conduct to its truth, namely, its amorality."[42] Having been denied a place in the symbolic order, neither Thersites nor Cressida need to reconcile their desires with its principles.

Cressida does not want to see herself in Thersites' terms. She retains an image of an ideal-I, and in relation to that ideal the metonymic promiscuity of her behavior seems to her to warrant the name of "turpitude" (5.2.112). But the only means of escaping this infamy for women, including Thersites and Patroclus, is to take Juliet's course, suicide, which generations of Cressida-bashers, from Henryson to the late twentieth century critics, have demanded of her. As recently as 1985, a reviewer could complain about Juliet Stevenson's sympathetic portrayal of Cressida that "It may be hard cheese on the RSC feminist puritans, but Shakespeare is writing about falsity and sexual wantonness, not rape."[43] This judgment of Cressida reflects Diomedes' description of Helen as a "whore" (4.1.68) for having chosen, unlike Juliet, to submit to the "fair rape" (2.2.147) of a second husband named Paris. If Cressida were to choose death instead of betraying Troilus, she would make the Hegelian statement of preferring an idealized value to mere survival and would confirm that Troilus' value exists on a higher plane than biological existence. Troilus believes that he should make this choice, and he follows through on his risky decision to seek out Cressida in the Greek camp. But for women to meet this Hegelian standard is not to take a risk but to commit suicide. Shakespeare's Cressida reenacts the position of the woman as it is depicted in the legends of Troy; she does what she has to, she enjoys what she can, and she is called a whore.

As *Troilus and Cressida* winds down to its anticlimax, a triangular logic links the disappearance of Cressida from the story and the ensuing death of Hector. As Kristeva explains the signifying process of the decline into abjection, "when the condensation function that constitutes the sign collapses"—when Cressida's beauty is no longer a sign of a higher order of meaning—"in that case one always discovers a collapse of the oedipal triangulation that supports it."[44] Troilus's exhortation to Hector to kill all "captive Grecian[s]" (5.3.40) is his way of serving notice to the effective agent of the paternal metaphor that he is no longer bound by any rules of "manhood and honor." Hector himself then becomes a victim of Achilles' decision to do exactly what Troilus advocates, and for exactly the same reason: Achilles has lost his lover to the war.

As de Rougemont summarizes the literature of romantic passion and finds that it is always a literature of suffering and death, he asks "Why does Western Man wish to suffer this passion which lacerates him and which all his common sense rejects?" De Rougemont offers the Hegelian answer that "he reaches self-awareness and tests himself only by risking his life," and he sees this as "the most tenacious root of the war instinct."[45] But what Hegel sees as a field of human glory, Kristeva describes as an "infernal *jouissance*" which, in *Troilus and Cressida*, declines into a disgusted parody of the heroic ethos. Kristeva's name for this syndrome is abjection, the "nocturnal reverse of the magnificent legend of courtliness,"[46] whose logic Troilus revealed early in the play when he described Helen's beauty as painted in blood and as capable of turning crowned princes into merchants, but whose lure he followed nonetheless. With his paternal metaphor dissolved by the death of Hector, Troilus can find no other pattern to emulate other than to "haunt" Achilles "like a wicked conscience" (5.11.28), imitating an Other with no object in view, risking his life with no possibility of reward. The outcome, according to the legends of Troy (including Chaucer's version), is that Troilus will be killed by Achilles. The nadir of the breakdown of the symbolic order arrives in the play's final image, which turns the patriarchal body of Pandarus into a fount of oozing fluids.

With the play's final figure of a patriarchal metaphor who functions as the source of sexual pathology, Shakespeare redeems Cressida from Henryson's curse, and he offers an anticlimactic conclusion that is without the glorious catharsis of grand romantic sacrifice available in *Romeo and Juliet* or *Antony and Cleopatra*. Instead, *Troilus and Cressida* provides pointed revisions of the literary histories of its main characters. The identification of Pandarus with the diocese of Winchester and with its patriarchal authority, the bishop, transforms the priestly father-figures of Chryses, Briseus, and Calchas from protectors of virginity into its peddlers. The members of the romantic couple generated by this corrupted authority become vehicles not of empathy but of trauma, which is inflicted in the gendered forms dictated by a patriarchal sexual economy: humiliation for Troilus, objectification for Cressida. Troilus gets to see his paranoid fear of the swelling parts of the Greek warriors confirmed as he watches Cressida fall for Diomedes, while Cressida is taken to the very brink of becoming the most abject of things when she arrives at the Greek camp without a protector. If her subsequent attraction to Diomedes represents both a preference and an escape, perhaps it would be possible to find a feminist poetic justice in the fact that Shakespeare's Cressida is not punished for changing her mind. This would be a realistic and not a "puritanical" feminism, one in which love neither lives happily ever after nor dies beautifully, but it has its moments.

5 The Exotic/Erotic and the Group
Othello

With a relentless plot that hurtles to a catastrophic climax, *Othello* lends itself to deterministic explanations. In one rich vein of the play's reception history, orthodox psychoanalytic criticism presents an oedipal story of the idealization and disillusionment of the "male sexual imagination"[1] in which Othello's race becomes little more than a contingent aggravating circumstance. In a critical counter narrative, the new historicism has generated an abundance of descriptions of early modern English stereotypes of Moors and Africans in which race functions as the definitive marker of character and hence as the principal agent of a predictable failure of erotic possibility. While new historicist studies tend to grant the play less of a sense of reflexive critique than did G. K. Hunter in his 1978 essay "*Othello* and Colour Prejudice,"[2] these studies have not always agreed on the salient points of Tudor/Stuart racial mythology that bear on *Othello*. Ania Loomba points to two essays that appeared in *Representations* within a year of each other that "suggest absolutely divergent valencies for Islam in early modern England"; where Eric Griffin finds that Islam is the "ally of Protestant England, Hispanic Roman Catholicism was the Other," Julia Lupton contends that "Islam and the Turks are the real adversary" of Christian Europe.[3] Although Griffin and Lupton come to different conclusions about the precise form of English xenophobia for which *Othello* serves as a symptom, they share the new historicist premise that our modern critical task is to discover and to define the differences between the incipient racism of early modern Europe and the later conventions of scientific racism.

The psychoanalytic reception history of *Othello* has, over the past generation, become more divided over the central problematic of the play. While classic Freudian readings have sought to explain the causes and the symptoms of Othello's sexual pathology, Edward Snow's contention that the problem in *Othello* is not Othello but Iago, "not . . . the dark, impulsive id but the punitive, sex-hating superego" neatly summarizes the argument that informs an array of recent psychoanalytically informed readings of the play.[4] As these readings depart from an orthodox Freudian focus on Othello's psyche, they recover a profound ethical question that sits at the heart of *Othello*: Is Othello a morally aberrant figure, guilty of spousal abuse and premeditated murder, or is he the victim of an irrational cultural pathology?[5] This question in *Othello* foreshadows a profound contradiction in Freud's work between the normative oedipal theory and Freud's iconoclastic critique of group psychology. In Freud's most familiar story, told most fully in *Three Essays on Sexuality*, sex is a primitive instinct, "the weak spot" in "human cultural development," and the advance of "civilization" depends upon its repression.[6] This oedipal narrative dovetails neatly with the racist storyline of *Othello*, where Othello's race marks his aberrance as the "weak spot" who violates the civilized norms of the group and murders an innocent woman out of a foolish delusion. But a very different set of values informs Freud's essay on "Group Psychology," where the term that Freud uses for the group is not his usual "*Kultur*" but "*die Massen*": the mass.[7] "Die Massen," as Freud describes it, is a primitive formation; whereas *Kultur* accumulates its subjects through the ethical demands of the superego, die Massen is formed out of "*der Herdentrieb*": the herd instinct.[8] Within this tribal narrative, Othello is situated not as an aberrant criminal but as the victim of an irrational bigotry. Freud's analysis of the group formation shows how an exotic outsider inevitably activates, but cannot control, the erotic currents that provide the sublimated binding force of social structures. As Othello's outsider status incites the "Herdentrieb" of the Globe audience, Freud's analysis of group psychology locates both the source of Othello's power and the inevitability of his downfall in his exotic alterity.

While the relations between the racial and sexual narratives of *Othello* have been the focus of much recent commentary on the play, Shakespeare himself offers one of the canniest readings of their interrelation in the story told in Cinthio's *Gli Hecatommithi* of the "handsome" Moor, the Italian "virtuous lady, of marvelous beauty," and the lost handkerchief.[9] In Shakespeare's revision of Cinthio's novella into dramatic form, as two visual signifiers, skin color and the handkerchief, are transformed from verbal references into visible presences, they acquire a critical significance; as these empty visual signifiers are elevated from their casual connection in the novella into a composite figure for the hollowness of pure signifiers, they join the central themes of the play, sexual jealousy and racism, and illustrate their functional similarity. Othello's obsession within the plot, his irrational fixation on a meaningless object as an "ocular proof" of infidelity, is mirrored by the audience's fascination with another empty signifier, Othello's blackness, as if it provides the key to the narrative action. Both the audience's racism and Othello's sexual jealousy depend upon predispositions that are immune to contradictory evidence, since each seems to its believers to be irrefutably grounded in visible proof.

While the storyline of *Othello* follows a recognizable European racial stereotype, a friction between the play's visual and verbal signifying structures generates a tension between mimetic and reflexive readings of that stereotype. A hypothetical spectator who only saw but did not hear *Othello*

(e. g., the viewer of a silent film *Othello)* would see a character who is visually distinguishable from all of the other onstage characters strangle someone who is smaller than he is and who does not seem to pose a physical threat. An even more hypothetical spectator who had no knowledge of European cultural stereotypes would have very little evidence for the motivation of the strangler except his distinctive skin color, while a viewer armed with a critical understanding of racist stereotypes would see a racist pantomime. Historicist readings of *Othello* typically construct an original audience for the play that is somewhere between these two poles, one that is capable of recognizing racist stereotypes but that is unable to understand those formations as cultural fictions.

The verbal imagery of *Othello* regularly refers to, but often complicates, the visual racial narrative, particularly in the various iterations of the word "black." The power of Iago's and Roderigo's initial slurs against the "thick lips," the "black ram," and the "sooty bosom" (1.1.66, 88; 1.2.71) is dissipated when the Duke describes Othello as "more fair than black" (1.3.289) and the audience is asked to join Brabantio in reevaluating whether skin color is a reliable signifier of character. The overdetermined opposition between "fair" and "black" recurs in Iago's mocking jests at wives, where Iago's use of the term "black" tests the concisive skills of editors. When Iago is asked to compare a "fair and wise" woman to one who is "black and witty," he responds that "If she be black and thereto have a wit, / She'll find a white that shall her blackness fit" (2.1.132–36). If "black" here means, as some editors put it, both "dark-haired" and "dark-complexioned," then Iago's mockery raises two uncertainties.[10] The first, directly expressed, returns to the question of whether there is any correlation between appearance and character—Is fair/black in color a signifier of fair/foul in behavior?—while the second ambiguity undermines the racial category of "black" as it dissolves the distinction between "dark-complexioned" Moors and "dark-haired" Italians. A similar ambiguity informs one of Othello's hypotheses for why Desdemona has betrayed him: "Haply for I am black." Othello offers this as the first of three possible reasons for her betrayal, in a passage that ends with an ambiguous pronoun reference: "Haply for I am black, / And have not those soft parts of conversation / That chamberers have; or for I am declined / Into the vale of years—yet that's not much" (3.3.267–70). The final "that" seems to refer to its immediate antecedent, Othello's age, but this does not clarify whether "not much" means that Othello is not that old, or that a difference in age should not be enough to cause Desdemona to betray him. The unsteady referentiality of "that" opens the possibility of reassessing the relative probabilities of the three possible causes of Desdemona's infidelity: race, age, and cultural difference. This uncertainty is posed against one straightforward proposition that is supported by the visual narrative: Desdemona is unfaithful because Othello is black, since skin color matters, axiomatically, more than cultural difference or age. But the answer is fallacious because it resolves a question that is based on a false premise; there is no actual infidelity to explain. Nevertheless, Othello's life is collapsing for some reason, and when he—played by a white actor with some amount of darkening makeup—speaks directly to the audience and asks if this unfolding disaster is based on this single, inexorable cause, "Haply for I am black [?]", the statement of fact ("I am black") that is contained by the rhetorical form of the question comes up against the fluidity of early modern racial categories and their interrelation with religious allegiances. Shakespeare's audience would have had a good deal of contradictory material to sort through as they contemplated the essentialist premise that the figure personated by Richard Burbage is "black."

The play's racist imagery is reinvoked by Emilia in the final scene ("blacker devil," "filthy bargain" [5.2.140, 164]), when she insists that Othello is not the victim but the agent of blackness, but Emilia's role in bringing about Desdemona's death, her seemingly inexplicable failure to tell Desdemona what happened to the handkerchief, suggests that her accusations are largely deflections of her own guilt. As Emilia's racism, which is very different from the attitudes expressed towards Othello by Cassio, Montano, Lodovico, and the Duke, is joined to that of Iago, Roderigo, and Brabantio, each expression of racism against Othello is clearly located in an underlying grievance; jealousy and guilt find their outlets in the cultural virulence of racism.[11] One subtle but central image in the visual register of the play contributes to the undermining of the premise that blackness is the fundamental cause of all that goes wrong in *Othello*. My imaginary spectator who is limited to visual signs would see one more clue, besides skin color and body language, to the motivation of the play's climactic action. She would see a handkerchief fall to the floor twice, once accidentally (dropped by Desdemona) and then more emphatically (thrown by Bianca), and she would be compelled to wonder what role that piece of cloth plays in bringing about the violent outcome.

In the midst of Othello's confusion over the trustworthiness of Desdemona, Cassio, and Iago, the handkerchief functions like the words "I am black"; it offers a deceptively graphic answer to a mistaken question. In both cases, the persuasiveness of the signifier depends entirely on its visible presence. Othello's demand for "ocular proof" (3.3.365) joins two terms that are in an inherently oxymoronic relation. The visible has no meaning in itself, and can only confirm meanings that are imposed upon it. Nevertheless, as *Othello* shows, the psychic valences attached to the imaginary realm of the visible have an extraordinary motivational force. The verbally induced, visually powerful sexual scenarios that disgust Brabantio and Othello, the black ram tupping the white ewe and "her topped" "with Cassio" (3.3.401, 201) conflate marital and adulterous sex as equally contaminated. The ease with which these repugnant fantasies displace actual or normative events, and the absence of any distinction in kind between Othello's and Brabantio's imaginings and Iago's more prolific and clinically paranoid fantasies of Othello copulating with Emilia, Desdemona with

Cassio, and Cassio with Emilia cause sex to operate, in the verbal register of the play, as a force that is equivalent to race in its ability to generate graphic fictions.

While historicist readings of *Othello* typically produce critical allegories in which the action of the play inexorably reenacts racist stereotypes, orthodox psychoanalytic readings have correlated the seeming inevitability of the plot with the most deterministic of Freudian theories. Arthur Kirsch bases Othello's downfall on the principle that "the Oedipal drama which forms the basis of all human sexual development is fundamentally tragic," while Janet Adelman explains the oedipal roots of Othello's marital problems: "As Othello's love for Desdemona is infused with the language of infantile need, his loss of her is infused with the language of maternal abandonment."[12] The oedipal reading of the play moves fluidly from Othello's hyperbolic fiction about his mother's gift of the consecrated handkerchief to his perception of Desdemona as either angel or whore, but the reverse interpretive path, which makes universal claims for this tragic narrative, is more problematic. It is entirely possible that some Freudian constructions, such as the one he calls the "simple positive Oedipus complex,"[13] are more common within certain social structures, such as those characterized by the sexual division of labor ("She loved me for the dangers I had passed, / And I loved her that she did pity them" [1.3.166–67]) than they are universal. As Freud himself said, "The simple Oedipus complex is by no means its commonest form" (33). Nevertheless, in the orthodox psychoanalytic reading of *Othello,* the play becomes a predictable domestic drama in which race plays an ancillary, even dispensable role. Othello simply enacts the rage of the "male sexual imagination" that is frustrated by its inability to possess the mother, and race is only a secondary means through which Iago can exacerbate Othello's sexual anxieties.

The oedipal reading of the play, Edward Pechter argues in a book length study, continues the work of the Leavisites, the Iago-critics whose corrosively reductive view of human nature diminishes the scale of *Othello,* obliterating any possibility of heroism in Othello's character and hence "drastically reduc[ing] the play's capacity to evoke direct sentiment of any kind."[14] Why, Pechter laments, if Iago is so recognizably a "paranoid psychopath" (62), do modern critics find him so persuasive? Pechter's response to this interpretive history is ambivalent; he first calls for the construction of a "position that responds equally to Othello's and to Iago's voice" (110), but he then explains why it might be impossible, or even undesirable, to recuperate Othello's "heroism." When Pechter muses that "For better or worse or both, we've lost the noble Moor" (112), he betrays an uneasy sense that his sympathy for Othello's heroism might be indefensibly masculinist. As Pechter goes on to offer recuperative readings of the sanity and strength of the play's women characters, his critical narrative tracks and expands upon the final turn in Stephen Greenblatt's reading of *Othello,* which closes by identifying Desdemona's "purposeless pleasure" as a potential vehicle of redemptive value (*RSF* 254). This turn to the women characters as an alternative to the Iago/Othello impasse mirrors the narrative development of the play. The colloquy carried on in women's (or boys') light voices in the Willow Scene interrupts the play's dramatic momentum and suspends the overwrought rhetoric of Othello and Iago with a calm interlude. The intimate, feminine space created by Desdemona and Emilia is a reverse image of the grand public spectacle of the Venetian Senate scene in Act One. In the male Senate, Desdemona, even more than Othello, is the alien presence, while in the Willow scene, the tapping noise that prompts Emilia to say "It's the wind" (4.3.52) intimates the threatening presence of masculinity just outside this oasis. And as Pechter notes, Iago, who has more lines than Othello in the entire play, has only a small percentage of the spoken lines in the final scene, while Emilia achieves such an obtrusive presence that her part has often been cut in order to maintain dramatic focus on Othello.[15]

In the development of Emilia's voice, femininity becomes not the site of essential victimage but the source of a critical perspective on the cultural norms that are shared by the male characters in the play and that are so weighted with excessive significance. The most fluid categories of Freudian analysis, the structuring of the unconscious by displacement and condensation, and the convertibility of object-cathexis and identification, can usefully articulate this perspective if these terms are released from Freud's own imposition of deterministic norms upon their operations in the oedipal narrative. The fault in the oedipal reading of *Othello* lies in its assumption of the ineluctable force of a single, particularly problematic Freudian narrative, the one that results in the "simple positive Oedipus complex." The oedipal narrative grounds Freud's theory of a biologically deterministic process of individual sexual development, but it is based on three of the most arbitrary assumptions in Freud's work. The first is the premise of the infantile determinism of adult sexuality, with the parents presumed to be the first objects of a child's libidinal cathexes; the second is that, for the sake of hermeneutic efficiency, subjects can be assumed to be male, and women can be presumed to be mirror-images of the male norm; the third is that object-cathexis, the desire for sexual possession of the other, precedes identification, so that identification becomes a compensatory process that results from the relinquishment of an object-cathexis. This third premise receives its most categorical formulation in "The Ego and the Id," where the causal relations, first between object-cathexis and identification, and then between identification and the creation of the ego, seem so inescapable that Freud's prose begins to reflect the passivity of the subject caught in the grip of an inexorable process:

> When it happens that a person has to give up a sexual object, there quite often ensues a modification in his ego which can only be described as a setting up of the object inside the ego, as it occurs in melancholia. . . . It may be that this identification is the sole condition under which the

id can give up its objects. . . . [I]t makes it possible to suppose that the character of the ego is a precipitate of abandoned object-cathexes and that it contains the history of those object-choices.[16]

Freud's passive constructions ("which can only be described," "It may be," "It makes it possible to suppose") reflect the deductive inexorability of the oedipal narrative, which allows the (male) subject to become a mature, social being only through the sublimation of the object-cathexis for the mother and an identification with the father. This deterministic narrative leads Freud into some interpretive difficulties; the presumption that every identification is the result of an abandoned object-cathexis does not satisfy Freud as an explanation of the bond between the father and the son, and so he declares this case to be an exception to the rule: "This is apparently not in the first instance the consequence or outcome of an object-cathexis; it is a direct and immediate identification and takes place earlier than any object-cathexis."[17] The "simple positive Oedipus complex," which asserts the unambiguous heterosexuality of object-cathexis and the unambiguous masculinism of identification, thus depends upon two beliefs that exert an insidious force on Othello: The first is the assertion of object-cathexis as the originary and irreducible basis of personal identity, and the second is the necessity for the mutilation of this drive for the sake of the construction of male bonds. The problem with Othello is not that he has an unconscious fixation on his mother; his problem is that he believes in the fundamental principles of the oedipal theory. The more closely Othello looks at Desdemona and Cassio, the more he becomes convinced that object-cathexis is the fundamental truth of their being, and his response is to demand its obliteration.

A series of vacillations in Freud's work indicate his difficulties with the question of the priority of object-cathexis and identification. In *Group Psychology,* published in 1921, Freud asserts that "Identification is known to psycho-analysis as the earliest expression of an emotional tie with another person" (*GP* 46), only to reverse that position in 1923 ("Ego and Id"), a change which required the creation of a single exception (the case of the son and the father) to his new rule. Nevertheless, the temporal priority of object-cathexis to identification has come to be identified with orthodox Freudianism, even though there is no real reason, except for a sense of biological determinism, to grant object-cathexis an automatic temporal precedence over identification. Lacan's most fundamental swerve from Freud, his description of the mirror phase as the first leg of the oedipal triangle, substitutes a structure of identification for a Freudian object-cathexis, and another neo-Freudian theorist, Daryl Bem, has developed a multiphasic theory of sexual attraction he calls EBE ("exotic becomes erotic") from the initial premise, based on studies of sexual orientation, that identification with coevals, and not object-cathexis towards parents or other adults, is the earliest and most significant factor in determining the path of mature object-cathexis. Bem argues that these studies indicate that sexual orientation is neither the effect of family environment, the expression of a lifestyle choice, nor the direct result of a biological determinant, i.e., a "gay gene," but is generally produced in a dialectical relation to identification with coevals. Bem cites Freud's observation that both homosexuality and heterosexuality are equally theoretically problematic and in need of explanation; as Freud puts it, "The exclusive sexual interest felt by men for women is also a problem that needs elucidation and is not a self-evident fact based upon an attraction that is ultimately of a chemical nature."[18] If the statistical prevalence of exclusive heterosexuality needs a cultural explanation, Bem locates its cause in a "gender-polarizing culture."[19] Finding that a high percentage of gay men and lesbian women report having "felt different from same-sex children during the grade-school years" (323), Bem posits the initial existence of biological variables that do not directly produce sexual orientation, but that do generate dispositions to aggression and activity levels. Bem theorizes that children gravitate to and identify with those with similar temperaments, and then feel different from those with dissimilar tendencies. With the onset of sexual maturity, our response to those with whom we have not identified, and whom we find strangely different from ourselves, is a "nonspecific autonomic arousal" (321) that can be culturally coded and experienced either as fear or as romantic or erotic attraction.

Bem accepts Freud's premise of a dialectical relation between object-cathexis and identification, but as he dispenses with Freud's value judgments, he liberates Freud's most incisive analytic tools from the deadening effects of his normative judgments. When Freud clings to the oedipal narrative, he generates rigid accounts of normative development; Freud's argument that the achievement of mature sexuality requires an original object-cathexis to be displaced by an identification produces an individualized version of the larger social narrative in which the advance of *Kultur* depends upon the sublimation of the "weak spot" of sexuality. But in his more expansive moments, Freud offers scandalously sharp insights into the pathologies of the cultural norms that are based on the oedipal supersession of object-cathexis by identification. In his analysis of "Group Psychology," Freud comes to the conclusion that "In the great artificial groups, the church and the army, there is no room for woman as a sexual object" (*GP* 94). Othello's investment in these "great artificial groups" does not bode well for Desdemona.

Freud's suspicion about the destabilizing force of sexuality within the exclusively male "artificial group" is reflected by the ways in which the Venetian men who are most deeply invested in Desdemona's sexuality (Brabantio, Othello, Roderigo, and Cassio) all deny her any direct expression of object-cathexis. Her father is, predictably, the most emphatic in this regard, insisting that Othello could only have won his daughter through abduction and witchcraft, because for her to "fall in love with what she feared to look on" would be "against all rules of nature" (1.3.98, 101). Where

Brabantio presumes that Desdemona could only experience fear in looking at Othello, Bem could instruct Brabantio that he is exactly wrong about the "rules of nature." The rules that govern sexual orientation, where difference enhances desire, also apply to the perception of racial difference; any "nonspecific autonomic arousal" needs to be interpreted, and it can be coded either as fear or as erotic response. In Desdemona's erotic attraction to Othello, racial difference supplements the ordinary path of heterosexual love; most women in gender-polarizing cultures are erotically attracted to those whom they see as different from themselves, men. The First Senator immediately attempts to reinscribe the bond between Othello and Desdemona in terms that deny both eroticism and difference when he asks Othello to reassure the Senate that the two are joined by that which "soul to soul affordeth" (114), but when Desdemona protests that even a temporary separation from Othello would mean that "The rites for why I love him are bereft me" (256) she tells a different story. "Rites" is aurally indistinguishable from "rights," and the pun suggests the legal function of marriage as the legitimation of sexual intercourse. Othello tries to defuse the tension between Desdemona's overt expressions of object-cathexis and the stability of the social order by reassuring his superiors that this marriage will not compromise his allegiance to duty, but as Desdemona's protests refocus attention on the unanswered question "Are you fast married?" (1.2.11), she advances the narrative in which the problematic center of *Othello* becomes the tension between heterosexual desire, which is based on difference, and the masculinist bonds that are grounded in *Herdentrieb*.

Desdemona's declarations of erotic desire jeopardize more than an idealized image of womanhood; the overt expression of object-cathexis is an explosive force in a social structure whose binding forces work through sublimation. Desdemona's love for Othello is, in one sense, entirely unexceptional; nearly everyone in Venice loves Othello. When Othello begins his account of his courtship of Desdemona with the assertion that "Her father loved me" (1.3.127), this is not simply a mistake. The bonds of love between the men of Venice are real, and they are recreated, as this speech proceeds, among both the onstage interlocutors and the audience. Othello's narrative charisma has the same effect on the Senators that he had on Brabantio and Desdemona, an effect that is registered in the Duke's immediate response to his speech: "I think this tale would win my daughter, too" (1.3.170). As the Duke substitutes his daughter for himself, he presents an imaginary sexual attraction in the place of an unimaginable one, and he nearly makes explicit the erotic bond that holds together the Venetian patriarchy, the "desexualized, sublimated homosexual love for other men" that, Freud argues, characterizes a male group formation (*GP* 44). While Freud is careful to distinguish object-cathexis from identification in his description of normative oedipal development, these lines become blurrier in his critique of group psychology, where Freud can only be certain that the binding force in this formation is the libidinal investment in the leader: "the mutual tie between members of the group," he asserts, is ultimately based upon "the tie with the leader" (*GP* 50). Othello's assumption of the role of the leader creates a fiction of his indispensability, and the play illustrates the fantasy nature of this construction. There is a universal presumption in Venice that the outcome of the war against the Turks depends upon Othello's immediate presence in Cyprus even though "we have there a substitute of most allowed sufficiency" (1.3.222–23). When the Venetians learn that the Turkish fleet has been drowned before Othello's arrival, they nonetheless remain at the seaside to "throw out our eyes out for brave Othello," for "the man commands / Like a full soldier" (2.1.39, 36–37). The superfluity of Othello's "News" upon his arrival, his belated announcement that "our wars are done, the Turks are drowned" (2.1.199), is anticlimactic to everyone but him. Othello's presence turns out not to have been necessary at all; his perceived indispensability is not a practical calculation but a fantastic effect of the libidinal economy of the Venetian patriarchy.

Brabantio's separation from this sublimated erotic consensus is brought about by his proximity to a direct expression of object-cathexis. As Freud contends, "Directly sexual impulsions are unfavourable to the formation of groups" (*GP* 93), and Brabantio's loss of love for Othello and Desdemona illustrates the tension outlined by Freud between "those sexual impulsions that are inhibited in their aims [and] which achieve such lasting ties" precisely because "they are not capable of complete satisfaction" and those "sexual impulsions that are uninhibited in their aims [and] suffer an extraordinary reduction . . . every time the sexual aim is attained" (*GP* 59–60). The Duke can calmly imagine his daughter's reaction to Othello's allure because it remains in the realm of the imaginary, and he can articulate his own response to Othello through that imaginary substitution. When the affair between Othello and Desdemona moves from Brabantio's dream world into reality, Brabantio can only imagine this affair to be the effect of an alien force imposed upon Desdemona, "spells and medicines bought of mountebanks" or "witchcraft" (1.3.61, 64). Freud would suggest that Brabantio is closer to the truth than the Senators think. When Freud seeks to illustrate the similarity between romantic love and group formations, he suggests a third phenomenon—hypnosis—that illustrates their common symptoms: a reduction in the rationality of the subject and a forfeiture of will to an idealized other who has "stepped into the place of the ego-ideal." "From being in love to hypnosis," Freud concludes, "is only a short step" (*GP* 58), while the relation between hypnosis and the group formation is even tighter:

> Hypnosis is not a good object for comparison with a group formation, because it is truer to say that it is identical with it. Out of the complicated fabric of the group it isolates one element for us—the behaviour of the individual to the leader. (*GP* 59)

The credulity of Othello's followers, who hang on his stories of "men whose heads / Do grow beneath their shoulders" (1.3.143–44) is, from Iago's perspective, a kind of mass hypnosis. All that Iago hears from Othello is "bombast circumstance" (1.1.13) and "fantastical lies" (2.1.219). The general acceptance of Othello's implausibilities depends upon his ability, as the exotic stranger, to initiate a new libidinal constitution in the ruling group. Iago and Brabantio are unsuccessful in their attempts to reactivate the traditional, fully sublimated social order. When Iago seeks a promotion, he solicits "three great ones" to visit Othello and "Off-cap" (1.1.8, 10) to him. Brabantio cannot imagine that his "brothers of the state" (1.2.97) will deny his claims against "this Moor" (1.3.71), and he believes that he can compel Desdemona to recognize where she owes obedience. But when Desdemona sees Othello's "visage in his mind" (1.3.251) and the Duke sees him as "more fair than black" (1.3.289), Othello's personal charisma reorganizes the Venetian social order and gives it a new center.

Othello fully understands the effects that his physical presence and his narrative gifts have on others; his disclaimer that "Rude am I in my speech" (1.3.81) is an attempt to lower the bar of credibility before he begins to deliver stories of men whose heads grow beneath their shoulders, and his account of a handkerchief woven by a two hundred year old sibyl is equally a conscious fiction, but in each case there is a serious motive behind the fabrication. When Othello reminds the Venetian Senate, on the brink of war, of his own martial history, he molds them into a "great artificial group": an army. When he tells Desdemona of the sacred origins of the handkerchief, he does it to impress a point upon her, that marital fidelity is a matter of supreme importance. In each case, Othello knows that at the level of material fact he is lying, but he believes that people will be morally better if they believe his lies. As Freud says in comparing group formations and romantic couples, "love," a word that Freud argues belongs equally to each formation, is the condition for altruism. In the great artificial group of the army, it overcomes the instinct to self-preservation and causes the individual to risk his life in order to defend the group. In the romantic couple, it overcomes the randomness of the sexual instinct and confines its expression to a single other. But a group formation is not always a vehicle of moral improvement, and the opening scenes of *Othello* illustrate both poles of what Freud describes as the extended moral range of groups:

> When individuals come together in a group all their individual inhibitions fall away and all the cruel, brutal and destructive instincts . . . are stirred up to find free gratification. But under the influence of suggestion groups are also capable of high achievements in the shape of abnegation, unselfishness, and devotion to an ideal. (*GP* 15)

Iago is the hypnotist in *Othello* who is able to unleash "all the cruel, brutal and destructive instincts." In the play's opening street scene, he orchestrates the grafting of racist imagery onto bestial representations of sexuality in a form that would be particularly potent, when the play was performed in the Globe, in appealing to the spectators in the pit. Iago's scorn for "his Moorship" draws upon the racial and economic elements of the Expulsion Order of 1601, in which Elizabeth complained that "blackamoors" were depriving "her own liege people that want the relief which those people consume."[20] When Iago advises servants to defy their masters and look to their own interests, his counsel would have the consolidating appeal of race to solidify the English working class against the alien other. There is a perceptible rise in the moral tone of the play when the scene shifts from the street to the Senate and Iago's vulgar, racist imagery is replaced by uplifting stories of the strenuous rise from slavery to greatness, of the love that binds soul to soul, and by the overt rejection of racism by the Duke and Desdemona. But there is also an underlying utilitarian basis for the Venetian Senators' embrace of Othello; they need him for the war against the Turks. Both the greater racial tolerance and the practical self-interest of the propertied class are reflected in the 1601 Expulsion Order, which, Emily Bartels has argued, was targeted at English masters who had defied Elizabeth's earlier order of 1596 and had attempted to keep their African servants because they were cheaper than English labor.[21]

While the figures involved in this mutually beneficial charade, Othello and his "very noble and approved good masters" (1.3.77), engage in some blend of belief and pretended belief in men whose heads grow beneath their shoulders, Iago and the Iago-critics have been determined to demystify Othello's fabrications in the name of plain, commonsensical truth, but the character of Iago is far from an example of clear-sighted realism. In Shakespeare's transformation of Cinthio's ensign into Iago, he makes the narrative of *Othello* notoriously inefficient; instead of the ensign's clear and direct motivation of desire for Desdemona, Shakespeare makes Iago into an enigma whose opacity requires spinning off another character, Roderigo, who takes up the ensign's original motivation. Iago's own identity formation is easily explicable in Freudian terms as anal-sadistic; money is feces ("put money in thy purse"), drowning kittens and blind puppies is fun, and, according to Freud, the anal personality does not actually hate its object but is indifferent to it. The sense that Iago doesn't really hate Desdemona, but that her death is simply a side effect that barely registers on his consciousness, is consistent with Freud's account of the anal-sadistic personality that has not reached the mature stage of genital sexuality. It is only in the genital stage, that Othello uneasily inhabits, where others can become a source of pleasure and the antithesis to love becomes not indifference but hatred.[22]

An orthodox Freudian diagnosis, however, hardly does justice to the force of Iago's character in propelling the psychological narrative of *Othello* away from the direct expression of object-cathexis and into the realm of the imaginary. In Iago's first soliloquy, he does not complain that Emilia has been unfaithful with Othello; he only suggests that it is "thought abroad"

(1.3.369) that this is true. This indirect claim has a particularly creepy intimacy when offered in the direct address of soliloquy; if Iago speaks directly to the audience, it is as though he is accusing us of secretly mocking him. The speech offers no clue as to where Iago got this idea, but in a later scene Emilia refers to "Some such squire he was / That turned your wit the seamy side without, / And made you to suspect me with the Moor" (4.2.149–51). Emilia's complaint suggests a back story in which Iago confronts Emilia with his suspicion and claims that someone has told him of her infidelity, but he does not provide her with the name of the informant, and he offers no evidence that there really was any such person. In his second soliloquy, Iago now believes that the adultery has actually occurred, that "the lusty Moor / Hath leapt into my seat," and he is determined to be "evened with him, wife for wife" (2.1.282–83, 286). A truly commensurate revenge would require Iago to seduce Desdemona, but Iago is never that simple. He immediately imagines himself "failing so" (287), and so moves on to the next best form of retaliation: not that he would persuade someone else to seduce Desdemona (although he has just said "That Cassio loves her, I do well believe it. / That she loves him, 'tis apt and of great credit" [2.1.273–74]), but that Othello should at least think that this has happened. In other words, he wants to put Othello into the same imaginary state that afflicted him in his first soliloquy: Othello should believe that his wife has been unfaithful, even if it is not true. When Othello demands that Iago elaborate his suspicions about Desdemona, Iago reflects upon the possibility that this entire psychodrama may be his own creation:

> I perchance am vicious in my guess—
> As I confess it is my nature's plague
> To spy into abuses, and oft my jealousy
> Shapes faults that are not. (3.3.150–53)

While Iago's seeming reluctance to accuse Desdemona is part of a strategy to enhance his credibility, this admission goes too far. Acknowledging his suspicions as possible fictions undermines Iago's claim to "know our country disposition well" (3.3.205). The admission suggests less a calculated attempt to manipulate Othello than a momentary revelation of interiority in which Iago recognizes that he really may be a paranoid psychopath.

Iago's obsession with controlling others reflects a classic Freudian reaction-formation; living at the mercy of inner compulsions over which he has no control, Iago reasserts mastery by manipulating those around him. His motivelessness could be taken as a symptom of infantile determinism, so that by the time the play begins Iago is automatically repeating a childhood syndrome. But as *Othello* locates Iago within a specific cultural formation that unifies its subjects through racism and misogyny, the play offers a broader explanation of his behavior. Iago is the spokesperson for ideas that exist at the fringe of the social formation; in the virulence of his xenophobia, he takes ideas that are socially recognizable and casts them in their most extreme form. In order to locate Iago in this cultural space, Freud's oedipal analysis of the sadistic personality benefits greatly from a modification introduced by Bem's EBE theory of sexual attraction. Freud's sadistic personality is simply sexually immature; Freud posits the anal-sadistic stage as the second stage of infantile sexual development, between the oral and the genital stages, and he suggests that a disturbance in the anal stage of development produces a personality who remains fixated on his inability to control his own bodily functions. Bem's premise that a positive integration of the nonspecific physiological response to otherness is the condition of a successful transition to genital sexuality locates Iago's pathology not in early childhood toilet training but at the point where subjects form mature object-cathexes. At this stage of development, when they are able to recognize others as potential sources of pleasure, they are also able to recognize cultural prejudices. Desdemona's attraction to Othello and Iago's racism and misogyny both pivot off the same point: Both Desdemona and Iago respond strongly, but in opposite ways, to exotic difference. Where Desdemona converts what Brabantio thinks should be "fear" into erotic response, Iago's racism and his misogyny reflect an inability to overcome a terror of otherness.

Othello recognizes the potential emergence of genital sexuality, as Freud does in *Three Essays on Sexuality*, as inherently in conflict with the stability of social formations. Just as Othello propels Venetian society past its potentially regressive racism when he persuades the Venetians to love him and to unite themselves through that love, in the arena of sexuality he offers a similar path of sublimation. Vowing that his marital alliance has not been formed "To please the palate of my appetite, / Nor to comply with heat" (1.3.261–62), Othello promises that even his marriage is not about sex. His ability to remain the object of a universal identification depends upon the maintenance of a general sublimation; so long as no one recognizes a homoerotic subtext in the Duke's admiring comment that "I think this tale would win my daughter, too" (170), everyone who has no direct interest in Desdemona's sexuality can continue to love Othello. Othello's identification with asexual Christian ideals reflects a commitment to a progressive narrative of civilization. As Freud distinguishes the church from the army (using Christianity as the model religion), he contends that the church adds a second layer of bonding to the structure of the army. Where the army asks only that its members put the leader in the place of the ego-ideal and identify with each other at the level of the ego, the church offers an ego-identification with the leader himself through an ethical renunciation that pervades every level of this formation. When the church requires its members to "identify themselves with Christ and to love all other Christians as Christ loved them" (*GP* 86), this formation greatly compromises the erotic life of the leader. In the more primitive formation of the army, which offers its members no identification with the leader on the level of the ego, "the leader himself need love no one else, he may be of a masterful nature, absolutely narcissistic, self-confident, and independent" (*GP* 71). But when the church asserts its "claim to have reached a higher ethical level" (*GP* 86), the leader who embodies the ego-ideal is obliged to adopt the values through which his followers identify with him.

Since the cohesion of the artificial group is fueled by the forfeiture of individual narcissism and its recovery within the group formation, the stability of the group requires the leader to value each of its members equally; as Freud puts it, "the necessary precondition" of the artificial group is that "all the members should be loved in the same way by one person, the leader" (*GP* 68). Othello recognizes this obligation when he discharges Cassio against his own inclination ("Cassio, I love thee, / But never more be officer of mine" [2.3.231–32]), but not when he promotes Cassio over Iago. Iago complains that Cassio's promotion has been made on narrow and unfair grounds, advancing an "arithmetician" (1.1.18) over a true soldier, but the play's persistent suggestions that Cassio is the potential surrogate for Othello offer a different logic behind Othello's choice. The egalitarian fiction that unites the group is as artificial as the denial of sexuality, and sexual preference is, in fact, a force that undoes the possibility of equality. When Iago complains that Cassio has "a daily beauty in his life / That makes me ugly" (5.1.19–20), Iago's lament confirms the libidinal presence that is created when the textual sign "Cassio" becomes the body and the voice of Cassio, who is able to generate an erotic current in the theatre that replicates what Iago recognizes as the sublimated undercurrent of everyday life. Iago's sensitivity to this current provides the critical perspective that can take in the full rhetorical value of the hint with which Desdemona prods Othello: "She . . . / bade me, if I had a friend that loved her, / I should but teach him how to tell my story, / And that would woo her" (1.3.162–165). Desdemona's hint mimics the structure of substitution in the Duke's imaginary identification with his daughter in response to Othello's speech, and the hypothetical "friend" is easy to name, but the back story here is murkier than in the case of Iago's hypothetical confrontation with Emilia. Othello has no reason to imply that Desdemona was threatening to move on to Cassio if Othello didn't quickly declare himself, but the proximity of the two hypothetical substitutions—the daughter for the Duke, Cassio for Othello—where there are only six lines between them, and those lines contain their own chiastic substitution ("She loved me for the dangers I had passed, / And I loved her that she did pity them" [166–67])—invites the rhetorically attentive listener to notice just how precariously the social world skims over erotic possibilities that it would be scandalous to acknowledge.

Othello can unselfconsciously report Desdemona's hint because its implications are incompatible with his idealized view of her and so, for him, those implications do not exist. Iago, who thinks that all wives, fair, foul, and black, engage in the same sexual practices, finds it entirely plausible that Desdemona would find Cassio a satisfactory alternative to

Othello. The audience's semi-conscious understanding that Iago could be right about Desdemona and Cassio constructs the condition of ideology; our knowledge is fragmented into varying degrees of recognition, and Iago reminds us that we know more than we admit: "What you know, you know" (5.2.309). The critic who takes Iago's suspicions about Desdemona most literally is Auden, who concludes that "Given a few more years of Othello and the influence of Emilia, and she might well, one feels, have taken a lover."[23] But the lover, Auden believes, would not be Cassio. Cassio, according to Auden, "is a ladies' man, not a seducer. With women of his own class, what he enjoys is socialized eroticism. . . . For physical sex he goes to prostitutes" (262). Auden's description of Cassio's interaction with Desdemona as "socialized eroticism" neatly explains Cassio's decision to continue to entreat Desdemona to be his intercessor even after Emilia assures him that Othello "loves you, / And needs no other suitor but his likings . . . / To bring you in again" (3.1.45–48). Cassio disregards Emilia's assurance that it is not necessary to involve Desdemona in his suit for reconciliation with Othello; he pleads, "Yet I beseech you, / If you think fit, or that it may be done, / Give me advantage of some brief discourse / With Desdemon alone" (48–51). Even if Cassio has no intention of seducing Desdemona, Iago realizes, it hardly matters. When Freud makes the categorical assertion that subjects are constituted by "directly sexual instincts and those that are inhibited in their aims," he goes on to explain that

> Those instincts which are inhibited in their aims always preserve some few of their original sexual aims; even an affectionate devotee, even a friend or an admirer, desires the physical proximity and the sight of the person who is now loved only in the "Pauline" sense. (*GP* 91)

Where Snow sees Othello, Desdemona, and Cassio as unwitting innocents in a schematic narrative in which "she . . . came between them . . . not as a rival object of love but as the intrusion of sexuality into the stable, 'innocent' world of male bonds,"[24] Iago believes that no social interaction is sexually innocent. Iago is actually more of an orthodox Freudian than Snow in his understanding of Cassio. When Iago sets out to manipulate Cassio, he presumes that Cassio is as helpless before his own sublimated desires as he is with alcohol; Cassio's desire for "socialized eroticism" with Desdemona is as compelling as an object-cathexis because it really is only an inhibited object-cathexis.

Iago's formula that love is "merely a lust of the blood and a permission of the will" (1.3.329), that we are nothing but bundles of directly expressed object-cathexes and cathexes that are inhibited in their aims, reflects Freud's account of diphasic sexual development, in which subjects experience two waves of object-cathexis; the first, infantile cathexes (towards the parents) are repressed and sublimated into an "affectionate" (*zärtlich*) current, and successful, mature sexuality depends upon merging that current with the directly sexual aims of the second phase of desire which forms in puber-ty.[25] Thus men look for their mothers, women for their fathers, and, in the logical development of this narrative that produces the oedipal reading of *Othello*, desire fails because of the inadequacy of the substitute object to satisfy the contradictory erotic and "affectionate" desires of both of these "currents."[26] Auden's conclusion that object-cathexis will necessarily find its outlet in illicit expression (Cassio with prostitutes, Desdemona with a lover) corresponds to Freud's analysis in "The Universal Tendency to Debasement in Love," a brief essay that recapitulates the central structural premises of *Three Essays* and foreshadows the sweeping speculations of *Civilization and its Discontents*. Freud's conclusion in "The Universal Tendency" is that "psychanaesthesia," an inability to enjoy sex, is the inevitable condi-tion of civilized people: "There are only a very few educated people," Freud judges, "in whom the two currents of affection and sensuality have become properly fused; the man almost always feels his respect for the woman act-ing as a restriction on his sexual activity, and only develops full potency when he is with a debased sexual object."[27] Othello's inadvertent analogy between his love for Desdemona and "the vices of my blood" (1.3.123) is perfectly explicable to Freud, who thinks that "Anyone who subjects him-self to a serious self-examination . . . will be sure to find that he regards the sexual act as something degrading, which defiles and pollutes not only the body" (186). Freud allows himself "an easily justifiable analogy" between these "anaesthetic men" and "the immense number of frigid women" (185) in the state of *Kultur*, but he concludes that the general frigidity of women only obtains within the marriage bond, and that women are just as capable as men of sexual fulfillment if the sensual current is indulged as a violation of social obligation. "Normal sensation" returns to women, Freud declares in "The Universal Tendency," "as soon as the condition of prohibition is re-established by a secret love affair: unfaithful to their husbands, they are able to keep a second order of faith with their lovers" (186).

The ease with which Iago can communicate a paranoia about Desde-mona's sexuality to Othello reflects Freud's melancholy conclusion in "Uni-versal Tendency" that there is an inevitable conflict between sexuality and civilization which requires the debilitation of sexuality: "it is quite impos-sible to adjust the claims of the sexual instinct to the demands of civiliza-tion. . . . the non-satisfaction that goes with civilization is the necessary consequence of certain peculiarities which the sexual instinct has assumed under the pressure of culture."[28] As *Othello* repeatedly raises the question of whether the marriage of Othello and Desdemona has been properly con-summated, the play creates a disturbing sense that there might be some-thing amiss at its erotic core, and the uncertainty of knowing whether there is a problem only heightens the difficulty of its resolution. Much has been written on the question of whether and when Othello and Desdemona are "fast married," so I will only suggest here that attempts to resolve this ques-tion—to show that marital consummation either has or has not occurred, and to argue that this either proves or disproves Othello's sexual potency— attempt to discover more certainty than the play provides. The effect of the confusing and contradictory expectations that the play repeatedly raises and reformulates is to leave the audience with a nagging sense of a question that is never properly consummated with an answer. When Othello gives no verbal answer to Iago's query "Are you fast married?" (1.2.11), the actor playing Othello has to respond in some way to this question (since even a non-response is a response), yet whatever he suggests here is reopened when Othello states that he and Desdemona have "an hour / Of love, of worldly matter . . . to spend" (1.3.297–99) together before departing for Cyprus. If Othello's greeting to Desdemona in Cyprus, "If it were now to die / 'Twere now to be most happy" and her response, "The heavens forbid / But that our loves and comforts should increase / Even as our days go grow" (2.1.186–87, 190–92) suggest, metaphorically, two different experiences of the wedding night, the subsequent information that "The purchase made, the fruits are to ensue. / That profit's yet to come 'tween me and you" and "He hath not yet made wanton the night with her, and she is sport for Jove" (2.3.9–10, 15–16) forcefully disqualify the prejourney "hour" as a sure basis that the marriage is now "fast." The uncertainty of Othello's destination when he leaves the stage after the soldiers' drunken brawl—with Montano or with Desdemona?—leaves this question pointedly open. After this series of reversals, whatever clues an audience thinks it finds in Desdemona's subsequent behaviors cannot provide an assurance that the play will not come up with another piece of contradictory evidence.

Freud suggests a causal relation between the sense of unease that hovers over Othello's sex life and his extraordinary accomplishment of having climbed from slavery to the pinnacle of Venetian society. "The Universal Tendency" is clear on this point:

> The very incapacity of the sexual instinct to yield complete satisfaction as soon as it submits to the first demands of civilization becomes the source, however, of the noblest cultural achievements [*Kulturleistungen*; GW 8.91] which are brought into being by ever more extensive sublimation of its instinctual components. . . . The irreconcilable difference between the demands of the two instincts . . . . has made men capable of ever higher achievements. (190)

This is the progressive model of civilization, built on the displacement of the generative force of object-cathexis, but it is not Freud's only account of the relation between individual desire and the social group. While "The Universal Tendency" and *Three Essays on Sexuality* consistently use the term *Kultur* to describe the social whole, in *Group Psychology and the Analysis of the Ego*, Freud uses a less favorable term for society: *die Massen*. This semantic distinction in the description of the group leads to the attribution of an entirely different value to erotic desire. Where "The

Universal Tendency" and *Three Essays* describe sexuality as a regressive tendency, "the weak spot" in "human cultural development,"[29] in "Group (or "Mass") Psychology," groups are not "noble cultural achievements"; instead, they are like children in their "weakness of intellectual ability, the lack of emotional restraint, the incapacity for moderation and delay, the inclination to exceed every limit in the expression of emotion and to work it off completely in the realm of action" (*GP* 68). It becomes the responsibility of the individual, if he "has a scrap of independence and originality," to "raise himself above them" (*GP* 78). In the final chapters of *Group Psychology*, the formation of the sexual pair bond becomes the primary vehicle of the "advance from group psychology to individual psychology" (*GP* 86).

The traits that are identified in historicist studies of *Othello* with English stereotypes of the individual psychology of people of color, gullibility and impulsiveness, are actually, Freud argues, characteristic of the group mind. *Othello* is profuse in instances of the power of group formations; from Iago's initial appeal to the white working class to Othello's promise that he will prevent Desdemona from betraying more men, the artificial group compensates itself for the relinquishment of object-cathexis with identification—a libidinal reinforcement from the other members of the group. Freud's tripartite analogy—love, the group, and hypnosis—is reflected in the forms of social power exerted over the male world of Venice by Othello and Iago. Both Othello's charismatic power over the artificial group and Iago's ability to induce preposterously irrational behavior in a series of subjects (Roderigo, Brabantio, Cassio, and Othello) illustrate the hypnotic and debilitating effect of the group formation on individual judgment. But the character of Desdemona contradicts Freud's stereotype that the artificial group produces civilized women as frigid mirrors of the male norm. Where Freud observes that the acquisition of "an intimate connection between prohibition and sexuality" in "civilized women" leads to an excessive reticence, so that "many women . . . keep even legitimate relations secret for a while,"[30] Desdemona's eagerness to "trumpet to the world" (1.3.249) her marriage to Othello flagrantly violates this principle. Nor does Desdemona's object-choice seem to conform to a Freudian pattern. Although Freud predicts that a girl is likely to "fall in love with . . . an elderly man in a position of authority" as an "echo" of her first attachment to her father,[31] Desdemona has chosen someone who is as different as possible from her own father.

In the terms of *Group Psychology*, Desdemona's flouting of social convention signals the achievement of mature, genital sexuality. Her unabashed expressions of love for Othello challenge the group's most regressive tendencies and synthesize the two libidinal currents, the "sensual" and the "affectionate," that Freud describes as integral to a successful sexual relationship. Desdemona's insistence that she sees "Othello's visage in his mind" (1.3.251) is an implicit rebuke to the laughter evoked by the racist slurs in the play's opening scenes, and her praise of Othello's "mind" and his "valiant parts" (1.3.252) blend his intellectual and erotic appeal. When Freud argues in *Group Psychology* that "Two people coming together for the purpose of sexual satisfaction are making a demonstration against the herd instinct, the group feeling" (*GP* 93), his term for the group becomes even more pejorative—not just the "mass" but "the herd," which is bound together not by an ennobling ideal but by a primitive "herd instinct": *Herdentrieb*.[32] Both Freud's oedipal account of individual psychological development and his description of the emergence of sexual love as a form of resistance to group psychology posit the same criteria for a successful sexual relation, the convergence of the "sensual" and the "affectionate" currents upon a single object, but the two analyses construe the nature of the "affectionate" current very differently. In the oedipal narrative of *Three Essays* and "The Universal Tendency," the "affectionate" current of sexuality is the residue of an infantile object-cathexis that has been repressed, idealized, and converted into an identification; when Freud calls the "affectionate current" the "older of the two"[33] in this context, he identifies it as the displaced form of the original object-cathexis for the parent. But Freud's account of the formation of the "affectionate" current of sexuality in *Group Psychology* is far less deterministic; here it is not the imperfect recovery of an infantile formation but an autonomous, mature development that precedes object-cathexis. As Freud begins his speculation on the "advance from group psychology to individual psychology," he returns to the mythology of the final chapters of *Totem and Taboo*, but he introduces a significant variation to the story he told there. Relying, as usual, on male psychology as exemplary, Freud revises his mythical account of the original group formation, where the brother horde rises up against the tyrannical father, in order to posit a single individual—whom he describes as "the first epic poet"—whose desire for personal sexual expression leads him to "free himself from the group and take over the father's part . . . in his imagination" (*GP* 87). Whether the overthrow of the father figure is a literal or an imaginative act is far from certain in *Group Psychology*, where the act of narration itself becomes the vehicle of personal liberation: "The poet who had . . . set himself free in his imagination . . . relates to the group his hero's deeds which he has invented" (*GP* 88).

While the deterministic narrative of the simple positive Oedipus complex describes mature sexuality as a convergence of a sublimated object-cathexis (for the parent) with one uninhibited in its aims, *Group Psychology* describes the sexual subject as the synthesis of an autonomous, mature object-cathexis and self-narration. The oedipal complex not only layers one object-cathexis over another; it also produces an overdetermination in the original, sublimated form of this cathexis, in which the idealization of the object (i. e., the parent) at the level of the ego-ideal and an identification with that object at the level of the ego become interdependent. When Freud provides the oedipal explanation of how object-cathexes become identifications and the sum of those identifications becomes our identity, he outlines the path from the ego-ideal to the ego: The "higher nature" in us is "the representative of our relation to our parents. When we were little children we knew these higher natures, we admired them and feared them; and later we took them into ourselves."[34] But in the non-oedipal narrative of *Group Psychology*, both the origin and the nature of the supplementary, "affectionate" current are more autonomous. Although Freud initially reaffirms in *Group Psychology* that "wherever we come across an affectionate feeling it is successor to a completely 'sensual' object-tie with the person in question or rather with that person's prototype (or *imago*)" (*GP* 90), as he continues to speculate about the mature formation of a sexual pair bond, his account of the "affectionate" current becomes relatively independent of prior erotic impulses:

> It is well known how easily erotic wishes develop out of emotional relations of a friendly character, based upon appreciation and admiration . . . between a master and a pupil, between a performer and a delighted listener. . . . In fact the growth of emotional ties of this kind, with their purposeless beginnings, provides a much frequented pathway to sexual object-choice. (*GP* 92)

This passage offers several departures from the axiomatic presentation of the construction of libidinal identity in Freud's writings on individual sexuality. In *Group Psychology*, as parents disappear from the emotional landscape, an affectionate current might claim temporal precedence over any object-cathexis. As a result, a partner is not necessarily chosen for resemblance to an idealized prototype, and the "affectionate tie," if it is a sublimation at all, is derivative of a mature, and not an infantile, object-cathexis.

Although the oedipal theory leads Freud to posit psychanaesthetic states in both civilized men and women, he sees this condition taking gender-specific forms; men characteristically overvalue women who are the objects of sexual desire, and consequently they need to debase their sexual objects in order to enjoy them, while women need only to escape their own idealization. But Freud makes no connection between the overvaluation of the sexual object and jealousy, a link that is manifest throughout *Othello*. Desdemona regularly praises Othello, but she never calls him "like one of heaven" (4.2.38). Even in the most casual instances, the vocabulary of sexual admiration in the play is entirely different for men and for women; Cassio reveres "the divine Desdemona" (2.1.74), while Desdemona only thinks that "Lodovico is a proper man" (4.3.34). The volatility with which overvaluation is converted to debasement, as in Othello's query "Was this fair paper, this most goodly book, / Made to write 'whore' upon?" (4.2.73–74), is generally considered to be a classic Freudian formation, in which one current of desire, based on the imago of the mother, is found to be incompatible with the direct expression of object-cathexis, but Freud himself offers little support for this interpretation. In his most systematic account of jealousy ("Some Neurotic Mechanisms in Jealousy, Paranoia and Homosexuality" [1922]), Freud makes a clear distinction between "normal" and delusional jealousy. He contends that some degree of jealousy is virtually universal; this formation, he argues, is rooted in the oedipal complex and rarely becomes excessive. He goes on to describe a more volatile form of jealousy that consists of the projection of a subject's own guilty desires onto a partner, but he concludes that the truly pathological form of jealousy only occurs when that projection is joined to a reaction-formation against homosexual panic. Freud explains this formation in the formula "*I* do not love him, *she* loves him."[35] Applied to *Othello*, this would suggest that the key to the play is that Othello really loves Cassio, and that he projects this desire onto Desdemona.

There has been plenty of speculation about homosexual currents in *Othello*, mostly centering on Iago's feelings towards Othello, and there is nothing illogical in the premise that Othello would believe that Desdemona loves Cassio because he himself loves Cassio; in Shakespeare's other great drama of jealousy, *The Winter's Tale*, this structure offers a plausible explanation of Leontes' accusation of Hermione and Polixenes. But shifting the erotic weight of *Othello* to an object-cathexis between Othello and Cassio exposes the arbitrariness of granting global motivational priority to object-cathexis. Auden's facile projection of the future promiscuity of Desdemona and Cassio rests upon the literal application of this orthodox Freudian principle, the universal force of object-cathexis, a premise which also informs Othello's flawed conversion of the hypothetical—the libidinal current that informs everyday life—into the literal: a sexual act between Desdemona and Cassio. But as *Othello* clearly shows that Othello's antagonist is not who he thinks it is—it is not Cassio but Iago—it exposes his deduction of the omnipresence of object-cathexis as a mistake, despite the "ocular proof" of the handkerchief. Othello's jealousy is not an inevitable effect of rival object-cathexes; it emerges from an unresolved tension between heterosexual object-cathexis and the current of libido that binds the artificial, male social group: the bond of identification. Reading *Othello* through the oedipal narrative, in which (male) subjects engage in a rule-governed competition for the possession of women, produces a social deviant (Othello) and a normal social group; the "white" members of the group are able to control the "weak spot" in their development and adhere to civilized norms, but black Othello cannot stay within the rules, since he is controlled by his "dark, impulsive id" (Snow 409). But reading *Othello* through Freud's analysis of the group formation, where (male) subjects compete not for women but for the love and admiration of each other, locates the volatility of male jealousy in the conflict between exclusive heterosexual object-cathexis and allegiance to the group tie.

While the oedipal narrative produces a clear bifurcation in the mature subject between heterosexual object-cathexis and homosocial identification, the ambiguous place of homosexuality in heteronormativity, where it is both an expression of deviance and, in its repressed form, the binding force of the social order, unsettles the stability of this opposition. Freud's usual formula for explaining homosexuality passes through the oedipal narrative, where homosexuality results from an excessive identification with the mother,[36] but in "Some Neurotic Mechanisms," Freud's hypothesis of a link between homosexual object-cathexis and jealousy suggests an entirely different etiology of homosexual object-choice. In this essay, Freud suggests that homosexuality originates in a consolidation of identification and object-cathexis when "the detachment of social feeling from object-choice has not been fully carried through" due to "an early overcoming of rivalry with men." Despite the hint that homosexuality is a form of arrested sexual development, Freud observes that homosexuals seem to be highly socialized beings: "It is well known," he pronounces, "that a good number of homosexuals are characterized by a special development of their social instinctual impulses."[37] As well they might be; Freud's oedipal account of successful, mature male heterosexuality, which involves merging a sublimated cathexis (for the mother) that has been idealized and introjected with a second object-cathexis (for a coeval) that can be directly expressed, requires a similar consolidation of a repressed and a direct cathexis.

Freud's contradictory explanations of homosexuality expose a knot in his thinking, and a fundamental question in *Othello*, about the relation between the sexual and the social. Freud moves effortlessly from the oedipal narrative, based on the primacy of object-cathexis, to the assertion that "great artificial groups" are held together by the "desexualized, sublimated homosexual love for other men" (GP 44), but his analysis of group formations opens the question of whether the group itself only reproduces or actually produces the symptoms of the oedipal complex: the repression of object-cathexis and its sublimation into an identification; the achievement, through this sublimation, of ethical disinterestedness; the idealization of an object who takes the place of the ego-ideal; and, ultimately, the categorical division of libido into object-cathexis for members of the opposite sex and asexual identification with members of one's own sex. The asymmetries that glide by in the margins of Freud's texts and that are highlighted in *Othello*, where women idealize men far less than men do women (despite Freud's assurance that women are as fixated on the imago of the father as men are on their mothers), and the role of this idealization in the production of delusional and violent jealousy, offer the terms for questioning the relation between these two formations—the oedipal complex and group formations—in Freud's work. An orthodox Freudianism posits the oedipal complex as the foundation for the psychology of the group, but it makes at least as much sense to suggest that the normative outcome of the oedipal complex, in which object-cathexis and identification are categorically separated so that the former must become unambiguously heterosexual and the latter entirely homosocial, is not the biological result of "normal" infantile development but is the requirement of a gender-polarizing social group.

The foundational premise of the oedipal complex is the natural priority of object-cathexis to identification, but the difficulty of maintaining a normative distinction between heterosexual object-choice and non-erotic, homosocial identification can be illustrated not only in Freud's arbitrary denial of any residual object-cathexis in the bond between fathers and sons but in Auden's vexed reading of Cassio's character. When Auden describes Cassio as someone who enjoys "socialized eroticism" with women of his own class and sex with prostitutes, he would seem to have described a perfectly masculinized subject with properly channeled cathexes, but this is not the case. Instead, Auden finds something disturbing in the sublimated pleasures enjoyed by a "ladies man." He thinks that Cassio's ability to socialize with women makes him a misfit with both sexes; he is not only incapable of being a "seducer" of respectable women, his drunken quarrels show that he is "ill at ease in the company of his own sex because he is unsure of his masculinity," with the result that he needs to prove that he is "as 'manly' as they are."[38] As Auden shows, the enjoyment of "socialized eroticism" is to be kept within one's own sex; if Cassio is too comfortable in the company of women, Auden worries, this might be a sign of a weak form of male identification and hence of a compromised masculinity.

Auden's difficulty in controlling the category of "socialized eroticism" mirrors Freud's difficulty in ruling out homosexual object-cathexis between the son and the father; in each case, there is a potential confusion between object-cathexis and non-sexual identification. Auden is uncertain whether Cassio's enjoyment of women's company is an acceptably sublimated object-cathexis or an immediate identification, and he realizes that this ambiguity compromises the supposedly non-erotic current of identification shared by "manly" men. This crux also troubles Freud in "Universal Tendency," where he sees the perversion of object-cathexis into homosexuality when it is combined with an excess of identification. But if identification and object-cathexis are convertible in the unconscious (as Freud's work on dreams regularly suggests) is it really possible to know the difference between the two? Freud asserts in *Group Psychology* that the distinction is clear and unproblematic: "It is easy to state in a formula the distinction between an identification with the father and the choice of the father as an object. In the first case one's father is what one would like to *be*, and in the second he is what one would like to *have*" (*GP* 47). But even if it is easy to offer a formulaic distinction between these desires in their final manifestations, Freud finds it difficult to separate them etiologically. "The Ego and the Id" is categorical in stating that identification ("what one would like to be") is only a sublimated form of object-cathexis ("what one would like to have")—except in the case of the father and the son.

The problem of distinguishing between homosexuality and identification in the oedipal narrative recurs in Freud's description of male group psychology, where homosexuality results not from an identification with the mother but from an excessive identification with male similars. It seems that whenever Freud comes to describe non-oedipal subjects (i.e., either those who do not desire women and/or those who do not identify with men), the underlying principles of the oedipal narrative lose their predictive value. The tenacity with which Freud doggedly returns to the core principle of the oedipal complex, the assertion of a knowable distinction between object-cathexis (the sexual) and identification (the non-sexual), indicates the depth of his investment in the central question that torments Othello: Othello must know whether the relation between Desdemona and Cassio is sexual or non-sexual. But as Cynthia Chase suggests, in order for something to be either sexual or not sexual, it must first have been in a prior condition of undetermined possibility: "Something *can be* sexual only insofar as it *may or may not* be."[39] Freud himself wonders, in "On Narcissism," whether "It may turn out that . . . sexual energy—libido—is only the product of a differentiation of the energy at work generally in the mind."[40] He then dismisses this speculation as unimportant because it is unanswerable ("such an assertion has no relevance. . . . we have so little cognizance, that it is as idle to dispute as to affirm it"), and he goes on to construct a theory of psychic identity premised on the irreducibility of the sexual instinct.

The maintenance of the foundational character of the oedipal complex requires supplementary theories to account for asymmetries between men and women, while the premise that the group formation of a patriarchal, gender-polarizing society produces both sexual identities and desires actually predicts those differences. In one of Freud's most notorious analyses of a supposed difference between men and women, he reluctantly concludes that women are less ethical than men, because women have not experienced the trauma of the castration complex in the same way that men have. In Freud's oedipal story, men's consciences are firmly formed when "the super-ego becomes the heir" of the oedipal complex and "Its libidinal cathexes are abandoned, desexualized and in part sublimated; its objects are incorporated into the ego, where they form the nucleus of the super-ego." Since women undergo no such trauma, "for women the level of what is ethically normal is different from what it is in men."[41] Auden's disparaging comment on the probable "influence of Emilia"[42] on Desdemona reflects a similar perception of the ethical standards of the typical woman. While Freud's assessment of women's weak superegos and of their ethical deficiencies emerges from the oedipal narrative, in *Group Psychology* he offers a very different account of the relation between the superego and ethical behavior, one in which the superego actually interferes with the development of a rational ethical faculty. As Freud praises the individual who, by virtue of "having a scrap of independence and originality" is able to raise himself above an absorption into the "herd instinct," he laments the "many individuals" in whom "the separation between the ego and the ego ideal is not very far advanced." In Freud's oedipal accounts of a conflict between instinct and civilization, civilization holds the higher ethical cards, but when the superego itself comes to be identified as an irrational force, the effect of a "herd instinct," Freud produces a more firmly tripartite distinction between libido, the ego-ideal, and the ego, and the possibility of ethical behavior comes to depend upon the establishment of a "differentiating grade in the ego" that enables it to resist the compulsions of the ego-ideal (*GP* 78–79). Both the oedipal narrative and Freud's account of group psychology produce a differentiation between object-cathexis and identification, but the two narratives produce diametrically opposed valorizations of these phenomena. In the oedipal narrative, identification is the basis of *Kultur*, and sexuality is "the weak spot" in "human cultural development," whereas in the description of group psychology, the group takes on the primitive character of *die Massen* or *die Herde*, and object-cathexis becomes a form of resistance to the lowest common denominator of the group mind.

In Freud's account of the oedipal male subject in romantic love, the overvaluation of the sexual object registers an erosion of the border between the ego and the ego-ideal, so that the object comes to occupy the role of the individual ego-ideal; in this hypnotic conflation of ego and superego, "What possesses the excellence which the ego lacks making it an ideal, is loved"[43]; "We love [the object] on account of the perfections which we have striven to reach for our own ego" (*GP* 56). This overvaluation informs the first of three passages in *Othello* that offer direct commentaries, by Othello and Emilia, on the significance of adultery. When Othello warns Desdemona that the missing handkerchief was dyed with the blood of virgins and woven by a two hundred year old sibyl with psychic gifts, he extends the hyperbolic range of his stories of exotic adventures. The hyperbole here is itself the point; adultery is given a measure of inestimable value as Othello tries to educate his young bride about the importance of marital fidelity. In Othello's second presentation on this theme, the focus of address is more oblique. Although the speech is a direct response to a question from Desdemona ("Why do you weep?"), it seems to be only indirectly addressed to her. Desdemona is referred to as if she is not present ("there where I have garnered up my heart"), and the thematic scope of the passage and its self-referentiality give it the rhetorical quality of a soliloquy:

> Had it pleased God
> To try me with affliction; had He rained
> All kinds of sores and shames on my bare head,
> Steeped me in poverty to the very lips,
> Given to captivity me and my utmost hopes,
> I should have found in some place of my soul
> A drop of patience. But, alas, to make me
> The fixed figure for the time of scorn
> To point his slow and moving finger at—

Yet could I bear that too, well, very well.
But there where I have garnered up my heart,
Where either I must live or bear no life,
The fountain from the which my current runs
Or else dries up—to be discarded thence,
Or keep it as a cistern for foul toads
To knot and gender in! (4.2.49–64).

The impression of a set speech is broken at line 58 ("Yet could I bear that too"), where the passage reverses field on what was to be a single comparative, one that would show that humiliation is worse than material deprivation. In constructing the initial image of physical suffering, Othello alludes to the most difficult part of his earlier life, "captivity," and he imagines that, having overcome that condition once, he could find the resources to endure it again. The surprising turn comes when the humiliation of cuckoldry, instead of serving as the unbearable antithesis to material sufferings, becomes one more instance of bearable suffering. Othello discovers something worse than the loss of the love of the group formation that flows through the sublimated channels of identification; the greater pain lies in the betrayal of object-cathexis. Where an orthodox Freudian analysis hears in the imagery of "the fountain from which my current runs" the oedipal "language of maternal abandonment,"[44] the image of gendering toads suggests Freud's account of jealousy in the non-oedipal narrative of *Group Psychology:* "Feelings of jealousy of the most extreme violence are summoned up in order to protect the choice of a sexual object from being encroached upon by a group tie" (*GP* 93). The intensity of the response to sexual betrayal, according to the final narrative turn of *Group Psychology,* is the result of the loss of the persona created through self-narration. As this speech reviews Othello's entire life, from his early captivity to what he imagines as his final chapters, he claims, through narration, both his adventurous youth and his courtship of Desdemona as chapters in his identity. While the specular narrative of *Othello* identifies Othello with a stereotype who inexorably enacts cultural expectations, this cultural determinacy comes up against a relentless narrativity through which Othello examines his personal history and presents it as "something striking, something that calls for explanation, not to be taken for granted, not just natural" (*BOT* 125). This narrative reflexivity is habitual for Othello, who continually assesses and accounts for himself—"Her father loved me," "Haply for I am black?," "Yet could I bear that too, well, very well"—even to point of demanding a posthumous narrative: "Say that in Aleppo once." Othello's tendency to self-narration that so annoyed Eliot and Leavis is, according to Freud, the means by which some individuals claim autonomy from the herd.[45]

The final disquisition on the significance of adultery comes from Emilia, and it is far less melodramatic than Othello's treatments of the theme.

Emilia jokingly deflects Desdemona's question "Wouldst thou do such a deed for all the world?" (4.3.62) several times before accepting its central premise, the possibility of establishing a unit of measurement for the magnitude of sexual betrayal. Emilia's assessment removes the question from the realm of the superego and its hyperbolic ideals:

> Marry, I would not do such a thing for a joint ring, nor for measures of lawn, nor for gowns, petticoats, nor caps, nor any petty exhibition; but for all the whole world? Ud's pity, who would not make her husband a cuckold to make him a monarch? I should venture purgatory for't. (4.3.71–75)

Emilia's moral flexibility seems to Auden to place her on a lower ethical plane than the "divine Desdemona," who finds it nearly impossible even to say the word "whore" (4.2.165), but this speech casts a realistic light over the central ethical concerns of the play. When Emilia advises Desdemona that infidelity matters more than jewelry, clothes, or "any petty exhibition," she identifies the currency that adultery might realistically draw. These material goods have the place of the circulating ring in *Merchant* that would not be exchanged for any worldly value except sex. Emilia acknowledges the existence of the sexual marketplace, and she concludes that, within this quotidian world, there is no material currency that is worth adultery. But when Emilia engages the hyperbolic terms of Desdemona's question—Is adultery worth "all the world"?—she accepts a broader frame of reference, one that recognizes the vast, imaginary realm of the superego. Within this imaginary world, Emilia presumes that exchanging sexual favors for "all the whole world" would mean making her husband, and not herself, its monarch. No one else in this play—not the men, and not even Desdemona, a woman in a more exalted social position—imagines infidelity as a means of advancing a partner's public career. The precise social position from which Emilia imagines this possibility is established when the Venetians arrive in Cyprus and Cassio welcomes Emilia. To her, he says "Welcome, mistress." His next lines are addressed to Iago: "Let it not gall your patience, good Iago, / That I extend my manners. 'Tis my breeding / That gives me this bold show of courtesy' (2.1.99–102). In other words, Cassio gropes Emilia a little, and then insincerely apologizes to Iago.

The lines of power in this encounter are tacit but clear. Cassio would not take similar liberties with Desdemona in front of Othello, and his fondling of Emilia marks his ascendancy over Iago as Othello's lieutenant. The subject position that is most opaque in this scene is that of the silent Emilia; what does she think of Cassio's "courtesy"? The consciousness that stands behind her silence emerges in the Willow Scene, where Emilia shows that she understands that the social world is not composed of angels and whores, and that a certain flexibility, determined by social position, is necessary for advancement. When it comes to the exact terms of Desdemona's question, Emilia concludes that while the material world offers nothing within it that makes adultery worthwhile, adultery is not more important than the entire world. In the terms of the second perlocutionary question embedded in this measurement, sexual purity is not a matter of life and death; you should not commit adultery, Emilia counsels, but neither is it worth killing someone over it.

Desdemona's observation that "Lodovico is a proper man" (4.3.34) is clearly an expression of object-cathexis, and it is Auden's expectation and Othello's fear that without the countervailing force of a properly trauma-tized superego, it will be acted upon. But this is not where Emilia locates the likelihood of adultery. She describes the conditions under which men should expect their wives to be adulterous: not when men fail to live up to impossible ideals, but when they choose to "pour our treasures into foreign laps" (4.3.86). Then women will act on their husbands' examples, identify-ing with and imitating their husbands at the level of the ego. Emilia thus articulates the gender gap that lies at the heart of the catastrophe in *Othello*: The intimate lives of subjects in a gender-polarizing society depend upon the ability of people whose attraction is driven by difference to empathize with each other. Thomas Rymer's perception of an incongruity between the triviality of the cause and the magnitude of the effect in *Othello* registers, through the empty signifier of the handkerchief, the lacuna of this final cause.[46] Othello cannot communicate with Desdemona because he cannot identify with her at the level of the ego; the play shows a world in which men's group identification leads them to see women as object-cathexes and as idealizations within the ego-ideal, but not as egos with whom they can identify through simple analogy.

The structure of empathy that allows the substitution of the self and the other is a central target of Stephen Greenblatt's reading of *Othello*. Accord-ing to Greenblatt, it is Iago's skill in imagining the inner worlds of Roderigo, Brabantio, Cassio, and Othello that makes him such an effective liar, and as for the "theorists of empathy" who imagine "a realm where subject and object can merge in [an] unproblematic accord," Greenblatt responds with a definitive principle of the New Historicism: "in *Othello* . . . all relations are embedded in power" (*RSF* 236). But the final paragraph of Greenb-latt's essay on *Othello* turns away from this principle. After a cautionary remark about the impossibility of showing that Shakespeare is doing any-thing more than "*exploring* the relations of power" in his cultural setting, Greenblatt distinguishes between the "empathy" of Iago and the "love" of Desdemona, and he gives the latter the ability to claim a "liberation from the massive power structures that determine social and psychic reality" through an "*excessive* aesthetic delight" (*RSF* 254). Greenblatt's celebra-tion of Desdemona's "purposeless pleasure," a term which seems to be a play on Coleridge's "motiveless malignity," receives no explanation beyond a footnote recommendation of further reading in Bataille, Bakhtin, Mar-cuse, Foucault, and Bersani.

The valorization of Desdemona's "love" for Othello as a transcendent value of the play is the source of a good deal of disappointment for feminist critics, for whom Desdemona's sacrifice is only a stereotypical image of the idealized woman. But beginning with the Willow Scene, *Othello* offers a subject position in Desdemona and Emilia that undermines the "massive power structures" inhabited by Iago and Othello. Emilia's speech on husbands and wives at the conclusion of the Willow Scene is a folksy, *platea* address that brings the central issue of the play down to a human scale, and it is this asymmetry of scale, based on the ability to differentiate egos from the superego, that distinguishes the play's gendered worlds. On the women's side, Emilia's and Desdemona's characters find their consistency in close naturalistic detail rather than in symbolic hyperbole. In the play's final scene, Emilia gives her own explanation of her most inexplicable behavior, her failure to tell Desdemona what happened to the handkerchief when, just before she implicates Iago, she explains that "'Tis proper I obey him, but not now" (5.2.203). Emilia's presumption of a wife's obedience is consistent with her silence before Cassio's courtesies and her assumption that Iago, but not she, could be the world's monarch. This naturalistic detail is obliterated by the heights of grandeur and foregrounded opacity of Othello's rhetoric throughout the scene. His reverence for Desdemona's inert body and its coldness contrasts with his earlier repulsion at her "hot, hot and moist" (3.4.37) hand, but that reverence dissipates when she awakes and begins to speak and move; his response to the quick Desdemona is "Peace, and be still" (5.2.48). That Desdemona finally acquiesces in the stereotype of feminine "helpless self-abnegation"[47] is a critical commonplace, but the precise phrasing of her response to Emilia's question "O, who hath done this deed?"—"Nobody, I myself" (5.2.132–33)—has a wide illocutionary range that incorporates her earlier, more assertive character. The stubborn young woman who told the Venetian Senate that anyone who saw Othello as "black" was wrong, and who repeatedly contradicted Emilia's criticisms of Othello now refuses, with her final breath, to admit to Emilia that her marriage to Othello was a mistake. Her refusal to identify her assailant echoes an earlier incident in the play when the soldiers of Venice and Cyprus, like bad children or gangsters, evade Othello's demand to be told "Who began this?" (2.3.161). Desdemona's claim that she injured herself reflects the submission of a battered wife who exonerates her husband, but it also defies the authority of Venice to judge her bond with Othello.

This nuance of naturalistic detail is spectacularly transcended in Othello's baroque imagery of a confrontation with Desdemona at the Last Judgment, where white and black bodies, immortal souls, and devils and angels all meet on the same physical plane:

> When we shall meet at count
> This look of thine will hurl my soul from heaven,
> And fiends will snatch at it.

> Cold, cold, my girl,
> Even like thy chastity. O cursed, cursed slave!
> Whip me, ye devils,
> From the possession of this heavenly sight. (5.2.280–85)

The physical presence of devils at a deathbed is derived from the *ars moriendi* tradition, where the appearances of angels and devils were imagined not only as signs of the *moriens'* fate but as actual agents trying to draw the soul upward or drag it below.[48] Othello demonstrates his loyalty to his adopted culture and religion as he correlates these supernatural figures with Desdemona's and his own skin colors; Desdemona's now inert body recovers the "cold . . . chastity" (282–83) that made her snowy, alabaster skin a "heavenly sight" (285), while Othello's self-designation as a "cursed slave" (283) functions, axiomatically, as her visual and moral opposite. But the mobility of the word "slave," which is used more often to refer to Iago than Othello in this scene, undoes the condensation of moral qualities and visual presence in blackness. Othello's epithetic "cursed slave" iterates the rhetorical efficiency of Emilia's description of him as a "blacker devil" (140) as it collapses the categories of moral character and skin color, but it even more closely echoes Montano's description of Iago as a "damned slave" (250). Othello's self-description as a "cursed slave" is fully transferred to Iago when Lodovico calls Iago first a "cursed slave" (298), and then simply a "slave" (341). Both the symbolic mobility and the theological scale of value that inhere in the racialized European conception of the "slave" inform the scenario that Othello constructs around his suicide:

> In Aleppo once,
> Where a malignant and a turbaned Turk
> Beat a Venetian and traduced the state,
> I took by th' throat the circumcised dog
> And smote him thus. (5.2.361–65)

As many commentators have noted, this passage identifies Othello both with the Turk and as his murderer, and Othello's suicide by knife both iterates the act of circumcision that marks his body as irredeemably non-Christian and hints at a castration which would serve as a penance for his sexual sins. I would only add to Lynda Boose's astute characterization of the structural form of this speech as a "strangely bifurcated discourse in which [Othello] simultaneously occupies the positions of subject and object, conqueror and transgressor, Christian and Turk"[49] that as this bifurcation produces Othello as both the sacrificial victim and the savior of the social group, it rests upon a profound confusion between the physical and the metaphysical, between the human and the divine, through which Othello offers his absolute desexing as a gesture of horizontal and vertical identification in both the ego and the superego, and as a sign of his infinite love for his brothers in Christ.

At the close of *Othello*, the English audience that may have rallied to Iago's racism at the play's opening is presented with an ethical dilemma: Is the Moor the villain of the story, the demonic murderer of an angelic white woman, or is he the victim of an irrational group prejudice? Othello himself provides the obvious answer to this question when he compares himself to a Turk, and the Turk to a circumcised dog. The opposition between this dehumanized figure and the scene's opening image of Desdemona's alabaster skin echoes the bestial imagery of miscegenation, the black ram and the white ewe, that had been hurled at Othello and Desdemona in the play's opening scene, and in doing so it calibrates the final scene's metaphysical polarity of angels and devils as a racist hierarchy. This moral overdetermination of the body resides in Shakespeare's source, but without the theological trappings; the reason that Cinthio's story about a jealous husband is a story about a Moor is that the story proleptically contains its own interpretation. For a racist European reader, a Moorish character would be likely to commit an act of sexual violence, because, this reader can assume, people of color are closer to animals and thus are likely to act on primitive instinct. Othello narrativizes—or in Brecht's term, alienates—this axiomatic racism when he asks "Haply for I am black?", a question that casts blackness as a cultural effect and not as a natural cause. Cinthio's racist narrative denies the Moor self-consciousness and reduces him to a natural, inevitable phenomenon, but when Othello asks if we see him as "black," he suggests a less obvious interpretation of his life story, one based on a different conception of what constitutes our most primitive instinct. Iago's pathological revulsion at sexuality acquires its power to drive the plot of *Othello* as it reaches out from the stage and offers an English audience the virulent pleasure of attaching that revulsion to racism. To modify Snow's formula that the problem in *Othello* is not the "impulsive id" but the "sex-hating super-ego" (409) in a way that puts race back at the center of the play, I would suggest that the catastrophe of *Othello* is brought about neither by the vicissitudes of object-cathexis nor by its repression, but by something even more primitive: *der Herdentrieb,* the herd instinct, and the pathologies of its manifestation in "our present-day white Christian culture."[50]

6   *King Lear* and the Art of Dying

I am going to make the case in this essay that the extremity of unredeemed suffering in *King Lear* represents Shakespeare's skeptical response to the postreformation softening of the genre of the *ars moriendi*, the literature that offers advice on the preparation for a good death. Where the medieval Catholic tradition had offered graphic accounts of the pains of death and ritualized procedures for confronting its terrors, postreformation guides to dying discouraged the fear of death and attempted to curb excessive lamentation for the *moriens* on the grounds that there was no reason to mourn the progress of a person of faith to a higher spiritual plane. Thomas Becon's 1558 critique of prereformation funerary practices advises "Christians" to avoid the excesses of "infidels," where the "infidels" in question are Catholics: "Let the infidels mourn for their dead: the Christians ought to rejoice, when any of the faithful be called from this vale of misery unto the glorious kingdom of God."[1] The immoderation of older mourning practices was condemned even more forcefully by Hugh Latimer in 1562 when he complained that "In the time of popery, before the gospel came amongst us, we went to buriales, with wepyng and wailing, as thoughe there were no god."[2] Latimer's complaint reflects the Calvinist perception that Catholic funerary practices were excessive not only in the amount of ritual that was performed but in the licensing of intemperate expressions of grief. Against this revisionary cultural backdrop, the relentless suffering that pervades *King Lear* represents a refusal to accept the melioristic advice of the new guides to death and mourning. As Shakespeare rewrites a familiar story of an aging king and his three daughters, one who loves him and two who are at least willing to say that they do, he gives the tale a more agonized middle and a more apocalyptic conclusion. Shakespeare's primary sources, Holinshed and *King Leir*, grant Lear a happy ending, but Shakespeare's bleaker version of the story tests the premise of whether any combination of power, preparation, and circumstance can actually lead to a fortuitous end. *Lear* asks: Is there any such thing as a good death?

Tracing the medieval roots of *Lear* has generally involved assimilating the play to the more redemptive elements of the *ars moriendi* and medieval morality traditions. Maynard Mack's classic analysis suggests that Lear "stirs memories of a far more ancient dramatic hero, variously called Mankind, Everyman, Genus Humanum," and Mack converts the Catholic valorization of redemptive suffering into a prefiguration of secular humanism when he concludes that Lear's endurance in the storm shows that "it is a greater thing to suffer than to lack the feelings and virtues that make it possible to suffer."[3] As Mack suggests, *Lear* is deeply embedded in the *ars moriendi* tradition; the play takes up the logic of *Everyman* so precisely that it is as if Lear had read *Everyman* and had tried to accommodate its warning that death means the systematic deprivation of everything that you believe belongs to you. Lear tries to bargain with death.[4] He will give up two daughters he does not like very much if he can keep the one he loves. He will give up all the authority and the responsibility of a king if he can keep the name and a few privileges. He cannot imagine the absolute scale of death's demands until Cordelia spells it out for him in the language of a parable when she says "Nothing" (1.1.86). Lear thinks that he speaks with authority when he warns Cordelia that "Nothing will come of nothing" (1.1.89), but the naturalistic context in which these words operate as a caution about the consequences of plain speaking is shadowed by the parabolic resonance of the absolute principle that Lear inadvertently articulates: "Nothing from nothing, dust to dust." While the reception history of *Lear* is divided between studies that stress the play's allegorical texture and its medieval roots versus those that focus on its naturalistic development of character psychology, the tension between the two levels of meaning that inform this exchange over "nothing" illustrates how neither an allegorical nor a naturalistic reading of *Lear* fully encompasses the play's dramatic universe. The density of *King Lear* emerges from the clash between its conflicting modes of representation; its psychological naturalism seems to promise that the material elements that make up our existence can be articulated through mimetic precision, but its allegorical breadth disdains the material world as a mere obstacle to the realization of a higher truth. This thematic tension propels the play into the "grotesque" mode of representation attributed to it by Jan Kott; as Kott argues, *Lear* offers neither tragic realism ("Regarded as a person, a character, Lear is ridiculous, naive and stupid . . . he can arouse only compassion, not pity and terror") nor parabolic illumination. Challenging the redemptive reception history of the play, Kott contends that while *Lear* adopts the schematic form of the medieval morality, its intransigent "nothings" turn "the theatre of priests" into "the theatre of clowns" (*SC*, 130, 141.)

While the allegorical tradition of *Lear* criticism has pointed to the schematic deployment of virtuous and villainous figures flanking its central protagonist, some of the most influential studies from the latter part of the twentieth century have distanced the play from the absolutist thematics and the nonrealist representational mode of the medieval theater. An affirmative realist approach to the play, initiated by Paul Alpers and continued by Stanley Cavell and Michael McCoy, argues that the locus of value in *Lear* resides in "actual human relationships" rather than universal themes.[5] Those who look for theological values in the play, Cavell contends, are "looking too high" (*DK* 46). Alpers, Cavell, and McCoy all agree that the play is not about whether Lear acquires some ultimate wisdom but is instead a psychological and ethical inquiry into whether Lear and Gloucester are finally able to see others as others "and not as a reflection of one's own personality."[6] In Cavell's development of this reading, the bond of love between Lear and Cordelia, which is most fully expressed when Lear awakens from madness, constitutes the play's central value. A more skeptical realism, advanced by Harry Berger and Howard Felperin, acknowledges the existence of the morality structure in *Lear* but contends that Shakespeare treats the conventions of the moralities as material for critique. These conventions are present, Berger contends, "as targets of critical allusion" and as "part of a more general critique of the structural limits of performance."[7] Felperin argues that Shakespeare employs a clear binary structure in which the Lear plot begins with a highly stylized opening and then "moves away from the morality vision," while the Gloucester plot begins in realism and becomes "deliberately archaic and artificial." The effect, Felperin argues, is to show the inadequacy of morality conventions, such as the sententious generalizations regularly offered by Edgar ("Ripeness is all," "The gods are just" [5.2.11, 5.3.169]), to provide protection from the "confusion of raw experience."[8]

While Berger persuasively shows how the schematic identification of characters with theological values misses the fine-grained realism that attenuates the moral distinction between Cordelia and Edgar on the one side and Goneril, Regan, and Edmund on the other, realist readings of the play greatly diminish the scope of its universal claims. Despite their thematic differences, realist studies describe the *Lear* universe as a relatively malleable world, where tragedy might be averted if parents and children could learn to communicate more honestly and openly with each other. Cavell observes that although Gloucester "recognizes the moral claim . . . to 'acknowledge' his bastard," he fails as a father to Edmund because "He does not acknowledge *him*, as a son or a person, with *his* feelings of illegitimacy" (*DK* 48). Berger notes that when Lear rejoices in being imprisoned with Cordelia, the difference in their ages means that "The sacrifices he enjoins have been, are, and will be mostly hers" (*MT* 47). Berger's readings of particular passages are often so psychologically acute and so firmly based on precise verbal detail that they are impossible to refute, but it is noteworthy that as Berger moves through what he calls Lear's "darker purpose" (where Lear constructs a scenario in which he is a victim, more sinned against than sinning) into his "darkest purpose" (where he would have to acknowledge his complicity in his family's pathology), Berger never mentions the darkest presences in the play: death and incest. Berger's *Lear* is not a world of absolute values but a network of codependent formations that structure social and family psychology, and one of the most compelling themes in Berger's analysis is that even when Lear seems to be railing at Goneril and Regan, his language consistently betrays an obsession with Cordelia that occupies the deepest level of his psyche. Berger looks at the displacement from Lear's comparison of Goneril and Regan to the storm that afflicts him ("I tax not you, you elements, with unkindness; / I never gave you kingdom, called you children" [3.2.15–16]) to his lament over the "Poor naked wretches . . . That bide the pelting of this pitiless storm" (3.4.29–30), and he argues that a sudden focus on "housing and other economic reforms . . . has comically little to do with what has been going on since the play's opening" (*MT* 38). Instead, Berger hears Lear's self-laceration over those he had exiled at the play's opening: Cordelia ("a wretch whom nature is ashamed /Almost to acknowledge" [1.1.213–14]) and Kent. But Berger never hears, in Lear's virulent misogyny or even in his denunciation of "thou simular of virtue / That are incestuous" (3.2.52–53), an implication of incest.

While Berger casts doubt on the motivations of the good children in the play by showing how effectively Cordelia and Edgar punish their fathers for not recognizing their worth, Cavell's redemptive realism celebrates the love that he believes Cordelia feels for Lear but can only imperfectly express. In Cavell's reading, Cordelia does not defy Lear in the play's opening scene but is only unable to express the depth of her love for him in such an artificial public setting. Her seeming resistance to his demands is caused by her attempts to maintain their intimacy, "to conceal her love, to lighten its full measure" (*DK* 12). But as Cavell lingers in admiration of the depth and the intensity of this bond, his prose repeatedly approaches, but never quite states, the same word that Berger avoids: incest. Cavell describes Lear and Cordelia joined in a "partnership in a mystic marriage" which raises the question of "the *nature* of his love for Cordelia," and Cavell worries that "It is too far from plain love of father for daughter. Even if we resist seeing in it the love of lovers, it is at least incompatible with the idea of her having any (other) lover" (*DK* 69–70). But Cavell does not wish to put any limits on this love, nor to see any impediments to it; he argues that "It is part of the miracle of the vision of *King Lear* to bring this before us, so that we do not care whether the *kind* of love felt between these two is forbidden according to humanity's lights" (*DK* 72). While Cavell frames his reading of *Lear* as a naturalistic study in character psychology, he nevertheless locates the heart of the play in the archetypal resonance of the formation found in Holinshed where Lear is said to have loved "specially Cordeilla the yoongest farre above the two elder."[9]

With a different degree of focalization on subtle details of rhetoric and psychology, Berger finds in the relationship between Lear and Cordelia a self-consciously manipulative daughter and a darker, self-punishing father. But Cavell's willingness to embrace the full range of the emotional engagement between Lear and Cordelia suggests that Berger does not always follow his close reading of Lear's rhetoric deeply enough into his attachment to Cordelia. When Lear's misogynist rant at Dover makes a sudden turn from a liberal indulgence towards adultery to a vehement denunciation of "the sulphurous pit" that lies below the girdle, the subtextual logic behind this shift is grounded in Lear's habitual displacement of focus from Goneril and Regan to Cordelia:

> Adultery?
> Thou shalt not die. Die for adultery? No.
> . . .
> Let copulation thrive; for Gloucester's bastard son
> Was kinder to his father than my daughters
> Got 'tween the lawful sheets.
> . . .
> Down from the waist they are Centaurs,
> Though women all above.
> But to the girdle do the gods inherit.
> Beneath is all the fiends'; there's hell, there's darkness,
> There's the sulphurous pit, burning, scalding,
> Stench, consumption! Fie, fie, fie! pah! pah!
> Give me an ounce of civet. (4.6.108–127)

When Lear's focus shifts from mankind in general to his daughters, his attitude towards sex undergoes a radical transformation. His tolerance for the natural force of copulation disappears when he reflects that Goneril's and Regan's treason towards him is located in their sexuality; despite their vows to love him more than they would their husbands, they have betrayed that promise as they have formed deeper bonds through adult sexuality. But the "sulphurous pit" that most concerns Lear is that of Cordelia, and in his desire to "have stol'n upon these sons-in-law, / Then, kill, kill, kill, kill, kill, kill" (180–81) the central target of his murderous rage is not the political faction of Albany and Cornwall but his real obsession, "the hot-blooded France" (2.4.207). Lear's mocking simile that "I will die bravely, like a smug bridegroom" (4.6.192), spoken just a few moments after both "kill, kill, kill, kill, kill, kill" and Lear's discovery that he is to be taken to his "most dear daughter" (183), is bitterly directed at the figure who has access to Cordelia's "sulphurous pit," her husband.

Not only Lear's language but the action of the play comes to reflect Lear's tortured ambivalence toward Cordelia. The bifurcation between the wife of France and the virginal daughter is, as Cavell suggests, a necessary division in Lear's mind. It is unlikely, in realist terms, that the daughter who responds to Lear's initial demand for infinite and unconditional love by saying that "I shall never marry like my sisters, / To love my father all" (*Quarto* 1.92–93; *Folio* omits second line) would return, without her husband, to offer just that in Lear's hour of need. The lack of any real explanation for the absence of the French king from the invading army (the thin pretense in the Quarto that he returns home because of "Something he left imperfect in the state" [17.3] is simply omitted in the Folio) shows that the important thing (to Lear) is that Cordelia's husband should disappear, and it does not matter why. This improbability is neither a failure of realism nor simply an expedient figure for Lear's inability to accept Cordelia's separate being. Cordelia's appearances and disappearances and her temporary displacement by the Fool raise the play to a higher level of narrative; Cordelia's departure and her return initiate and complete the stylized progression through which Lear confronts those he has failed and harmed—Goneril, Regan, Edgar, Gloucester, Kent, and Cordelia—in an allegorical sequence reminiscent of a medieval morality. This schematic structure both invokes an archaic mode of representation that advances claims of universal significance, and humanizes that mode by locating moral responsibility in personal relationships and not in abstract codes of behavior.

Lear's recognition scenes with Goneril and Regan are relatively straightforward. While Lear sees Goneril's and Regan's repudiations of the promises they made to him simply as betrayals, Berger's structure of "redistributed complicity" (*MT* 26) reminds us that Goneril and Regan have spent their entire lives as the less favored children in the Lear household. Nonetheless, the degree of moral ambiguity that informs this familial conflict does not exceed the ability of naturalist representation to contain its competing claims. Once Lear is sent into the storm, however, the use of disguise by the characters who surround him creates the non-illusionist grotesquerie described by Kott,[10] and it raises the question of the original casting of the Fool. Lear is accompanied by three figures in his descent into madness: Kent/Caius, Edgar/Poor Tom, and the Fool. In a realistic scale of representation, there are two figures in disguise and one who is clearly recognizable, but within the dramatic logic of "naive surrealism"[11] it makes far more sense to produce two characters in disguise and a third whose identity is even more opaque than that of the first two. The full grotesquerie of *Lear* depends upon the doubling of Cordelia and the Fool; both Cordelia's place in the archaic moral narrative of *Lear* and her deeply overdetermined role in Lear's psyche are intimately tied to her double representation. As this doubling supplements the disguising of Kent and Edgar, the play confronts a character whose uncertain mental state causes increasing difficulty in recognizing others with figures who deliberately change their shapes. Doubling goes one step beyond the nonrealist convention that a simple disguise will fool one's closest friends, and when both Kent and Edgar first appear in disguise, they assure the audience that they have not crossed to that higher plane. Kent's explanation comes first:

> If but as well I other accents borrow,
> That can my speech defuse, my good intent
> May carry through itself to that full issue
> For which I razed my likeness. (1.4.1–4)

While Kent's ostensible purpose is to explain why he is going into disguise, this speech, like Edgar's later explanation of why he will impersonate a mad beggar, serves to assure the audience that although the actor has discarded a prop beard and is going to speak in a different voice, he is not doubling; he is still Kent. Edgar's case is less obvious. There seems to be little indication that Lear has recognized or should recognize Poor Tom as Edgar, but a seemingly mad comment in the sheltering hovel crystallizes the ambiguity of Lear's mental condition; is Lear far wide or spot on when he tells this nearly naked beggar that "You, sir, I entertain you for one of my hundred, only I do not like the fashion of your garments. You'll say they are Persian attire; but let them be changed" (*Quarto* 13.68–70)? Lear's identification of Tom as one of his hundred followers echoes an earlier query by Regan about Edgar: "Was he not companion with the riotous knights / That tend upon my father?" (2.1.95–96). Lear's comment on Tom's attire could be madness, or it could be a private joke in which Lear indicates that he sees through Edgar's disguise, that he knows that his objection to it would be met with a faux-lunatic response ("It's Persian!"), but that he would prefer that both he and Edgar should discard their madness and return to their traditional roles. Like his later question "Hast thou given all to thy two daughters?" (3.4.49), this query could indicate a complete lack of recognition of others, or else, in a kind of foolspeak, it could be a piece of bitter humor in which Lear directs the sharper edge of a joke at himself.

The deeper resonance of Lear's difficulty in recognizing Kent and Edgar in disguise lies in his failure to meet his obligations to them as their sovereign. They have tried to protect him in his exile, but he has been unable to repay their loyalty by defending them against the humiliations inflicted by their enemies. The moment in the hovel is the closest Lear ever comes to recognizing Edgar, but the play's final scenes present a progression of tortured recognitions of Gloucester, Kent, and Cordelia. It takes nearly forty lines for Lear to answer Gloucester's question, "Dost thou know me?" (4.6.133) with the admission that "I know thee well enough; thy name is Gloucester" (171). In the interim, Lear's wild speech raises the same sort of uncertainty generated in his comment to Tom in the hovel; is Lear a raving lunatic or is he playing the bitter fool when he tells the blinded Gloucester that "I remember thine eyes well enough"? (134). By saying the most inappropriate thing possible to Gloucester, Lear paints himself as a crazy old man who cannot be held responsible for anything he says, but the following line, "Dost thou squiny at me?" (134) betrays a fear that this "darker purpose," in which Lear plays the victim, cannot stand up to close scrutiny. Lear's disparaging observation about "authority," that "a dog's obeyed in office" (153), undermines Kent's assertion (as Caius) that Lear uniquely embodied "authority" in his "countenance" (1.4.27, 24). When Lear disparages innate "authority" in speaking to Gloucester, he excuses his failure to reward Gloucester's allegiance by explaining that the fault for Gloucester's suffering lies beyond his gift.

When Lear turns from his own sorrows to admit that he does in fact recognize Gloucester, this admission unleashes a flood of homiletic clarity:

> I know thee well enough; thy name is Gloucester:
> Thou must be patient. We came crying hither;
> Thou knows't, the first time that we smell the air,
> We wail and cry. I will preach to thee. Mark.
> . . .
> When we are born, we cry that we are come
> To this great stage of fools. (4.6.171–77)

Where Felperin finds the homiletic style in *Lear* only an artificial defense against "the confusion of raw experience," in this instance the homiletic rhetoric registers the blunt force of inescapable realities, and it exposes the confusion of madness as an artificial defense against painful truths. Lear's recognition of Gloucester requires an acknowledgment of their unenviable condition; the "we" in Lear's homily is a universal subject, but it is also more concretely these two old men who took their first breaths at about the same time. Their resistance to entering this world has been justified by their disappointment as each finds that his "Nature" approaches "The very verge / Of her confine" (2.4.140–41) knowing "How sharper than a serpent's tooth it is / To have a thankless child" (1.4.265–66). Lear's darker and darkest motives, his sense of victimage and of guilt, burden the stylistic lucidity of this passage with a medieval temptation to despair.

A similar realization of moral failure informs Lear's recognition of Kent, a passage that is misleadingly glossed in virtually every modern edition of the play. This encounter interrupts Lear's grief over Cordelia's body, where Kent must become sufficiently obtrusive to deflect Lear's focus and to initiate the following exchange:

> *LEAR:*   Who are you?
>   Mine eyes are not o' the best, I'll tell you straight.
> *KENT:* If fortune brag of two she loved and hated,
>   One of them we behold.
> *LEAR:* This is a dull sight. Are you not Kent?
> *KENT:*   The same,
>   Your servant Kent. Where is your servant Caius?
> *LEAR:* He's a good fellow, I can tell you that;
>   He'll strike, and quickly too. He's dead and rotten.
> *KENT:* No, my good lord; I am the very man—
> *LEAR:*   I'll see that straight.
> *KENT:* That, from your first of difference and decay,
>   Have followed your sad steps.
> *LEAR:*   You are welcome hither.
> *KENT:* Nor no man else. (5.3.277–89)

This exchange reverses the structure of Lear's dialogues with Gloucester and Cordelia. Instead of someone asking Lear "Do you know me?", Lear now asks Kent "Who are you?" Kent's reply "Where is your servant Caius?" has the same strangely inappropriate effect as Lear's "I know thine eyes well enough"; it seems to taunt a person who is blind, or nearly so, for his infirmity. The material basis of the sight imagery that leads Lear to insist that "I'll see that straight" is lost when this line is glossed metaphorically along the lines of "I'll attend to that shortly; I'll comprehend that in a moment"; this is the Norton paraphrase, and the Arden, Signet, Longmans, and Riverside editions of the play offer similar formulas.[12] The difficulty in working out this passage seems to have resulted primarily from failing to heed the warnings issued by Alpers and Cavell about the literality of the sight imagery in the play. As Alpers argues, the imagery of sight in *Lear* is not simply a metaphor for understanding; it is used literally, and it refers to "the actual human relationships that give rise to moral obligations."[13] This obtrusive visual imagery ("Mine eyes are not o' the best," "This is a dull sight," "I'll see that straight") grounds the dialogue between Kent and Lear. Symbolically, the premise of Lear's failing eyesight reflects the loss of power that accompanies his physical decline, and it offers one possible explanation for why Lear does not recognize others. In the naturalistic economy of the play, individual misrecognitions can be attributed to this myopia, to Lear's deliberate pretense not to know someone (when he says "Your name, fair gentlewoman?" to Goneril [1.4.211]), or to his madness, which is either the organic effect of age or the result of traumatic repression. Attributing each of these misrecognitions to a material cause reduces *Lear* to a realist play, but in the moral allegory, Lear's difficulty in seeing Kent as Kent and as Caius proceeds from the same cause that prevented him from immediately recognizing Gloucester and Edgar. Lear's initial misrecognition of Kent—when he could not see Kent through the disguise of Caius—carries the thematic weight of the moralities; it shows that this world is a vale of error, where we fail to recognize what is truly valuable. Lear's literal inability to see his most loyal follower throughout the play signifies a moral failure, and their reconciliation entails the punishment of a brutally clear recognition of unfulfilled obligation.

Lear's question to Kent, "Who are you?" marks his ignorance of how much he really owes this person. He knows that Kent was loyal to him and he knows that Caius was loyal to him, but he does not know that these debts are compounded by being joined in the same person. His explanation that "Mine eyes are not o' the best," while literally true, does not take into account what the audience knows but Lear does not: that this figure can be difficult to recognize because he changes his appearance. Lear's complaint that "This is a dull sight" registers his incredulity, based on the confusion between an organic difficulty in seeing and the unlikelihood of what Lear thinks he sees. His ability to suspect "Are you not Kent?" indicates that the actor playing Kent has recovered something of the appearance he had in the play's first scene before his transformation into Caius. When Kent assures

Lear that he is, in fact, both himself and Caius, Lear's response—"I'll see that straight"—is absolutely literal. Lear wants to *see* the man standing in front of him as both Kent and Caius. It would be implausible for Kent to once again be bearded, but the addition or deletion of a costume prop—a hat or an article of clothing—and the alternations of Kent's and Caius's "accents" would produce the necessary effect. When Lear is given the ocular proof that Kent is Caius, he is confronted with how much he owes this preternaturally faithful servant. Having been banished by Lear, Kent has returned in disguise and "from your first of difference and decay / . . . followed your sad steps." What can Lear say that would be commensurate with this degree of service? His expression of gratitude is tempered by the necessity of maintaining his status as king. "You are welcome hither" preserves Lear as host and Kent as his guest, and Kent's assertion "Nor no man else" hints at where he knows the narrative is headed. Kent claims the right to be present at the king's deathbed. If anyone has earned this right, he has.

Taken separately, Lear's recognitions of Edgar, Gloucester, and Kent seem to operate primarily in naturalistic terms; seen as part of a sequence, they construct the emblematic journey of the morality hero who must discover the truths of his existence on his way to death. As Alpers argues, in *Lear* these are not "abstractly formulated moral truths" but "the actual human relationships that give rise to moral obligations."[14] The bonds between Gloucester, Kent, and Lear belong to a feudal world, and the representation of these bonds has been viewed by Marxist critics from John Danby to Hugh Grady as a protest against what Grady identifies as the forces of "reification" in emergent modernity, represented by an amoral, Machiavellian nexus of power and sex inhabited by Edmund, Goneril, and Regan.[15] But as Berger's reading of the play so powerfully shows, the moral clarity of medieval conventions is relentlessly undermined by the naturalistic vein of the play. Edgar's defeat of Edmund in single combat seems to advance the conventional narrative in which the dispossessed good son ultimately triumphs over his illegitimate usurper, but Edgar's triumphant expression of charity towards the defeated Edmund collapses under close scrutiny into some very unattractive pieces:

> Let's exchange charity.
> I am no less in blood than thou art, Edmund;
> If more, the more thou hast wronged me.
> My name is Edgar, and thy father's son.
> The gods are just, and of our pleasant vices
> Make instruments to plague us.
> The dark and vicious place where thee he got
> Cost him his eyes. (5.3.165–72)

The self-righteousness of Edgar's condemnation of his father's libertinism and of Edmund's origin has been widely noted, and the difference between

Edgar's moral exegesis of events, "The gods are just," and Edmund's amoral summary, "The wheel"—Fortune's wheel—"is come full circle" (173) is obvious. Janet Adelman has suggested that the phrase "thy father's son" only superficially marks a common ancestry; it also distinguishes Edgar as the father's proper son from Edmund as his mother's child, and it intimates that "the dark and vicious place" of Edmund's conception is not only the brothel room but yet another misogynist iteration of "the sulphurous pit."[16] The initial lines of this speech might be the most insidious: "I am no less in blood than thou art. . . . If more, the more thou hast wronged me." This profession of equality implies that Edmund had no reason to contest Edgar's standing as the elder, legitimate brother. Since Edgar suggests that he is unsure that he is any "more" than Edmund, he implies that the two brothers might have lived as equals, sharing their father's inheritance. When this implicit equality is made explicit it can be seen as obviously false—Edgar, not Edmund, was going to become the Duke of Gloucester—but the implicit fiction is necessary in order to delegitimate Edmund's actions. Edgar's suggestion that Edmund has gratuitously upset the balance of a harmonious, egalitarian world is, as Berger's reading of the play suggests, a scapegoating gesture that protects the artifice of a morally ordered society.

Berger's description of the moral landscape of *Lear* as a structure of shared complicity in which it becomes difficult to know if Edgar and Cordelia are any better than Edmund, Goneril, and Regan privileges character-and-action realism over the broad morality structure in which the play's central protagonist is flanked by a series of easily distinguishable good and evil figures, but the broad allegorical texture of *Lear* is not always simpler than its fine-grained realism. Berger's argument that the naturalist, morally ambiguous *Lear* constitutes a "general critique of the structural limits of performance" is part of his polemic on behalf of a "literary model" of reading as opposed to a "theatrical model" which, Berger argues, operates within a set of ideological constraints (*MT* 67). When Berger argues that Shakespeare "represented both the limits of performance and its ideological implications, and . . . this representation is more accessible to readers than to playgoers,"[17] he aligns reading with an ironic mode of interpretation that exposes the artificiality of theatrical conventions, while theatre becomes the site of "serious speakers" whose meanings correspond perfectly with their intentions.[18] But in the opening scene of *Lear*, moral cruxes only begin to emerge with the appearance of a broadly allegorical mode of representation; the play opens with thirty lines of naturalistic prose that seem to promise an idyllic future in which both property and affection can be evenly and effortlessly divided, and even their transmission across generations occurs without noticeable loss. According to Kent and Gloucester, Albany and Cornwall will receive scrupulously equal portions, and Edmund is no less valued than his older, legitimate brother. The rhetorical style of this section is pure realism; Kent, Gloucester, and Edmund speak casually to each other with no consciousness of audience. Everything changes with

Lear's entrance and his announcement of a "darker purpose" (1.1.34); the storyline becomes familiar and ritualistic, the language changes to verse, and Lear assumes the public role of the King. The schematic narrative of the division of the kingdom among three heirs, and the public roles played by the king and his inheritors in that ritual, put the audience in the position not simply of watching actors playing characters but of watching characters playing public roles. This ritualistic situation has an immediate impact on the weight of the spoken words. There is no reason to judge Kent to be a hypocrite when he tells someone he has known for about sixty seconds that "I must love you" (1.1.28), but the moral value of the word "love" begins to demand closer scrutiny when Lear calls for a command performance to know "Which of you shall we say doth love us most" (49). When Goneril promises that "Sir, I love you more than words can wield the matter" (53), the exchange of the word "love" between Lear and Goneril reiterates the compacted tension of power and affection in Kent's pledge that he "must love" Edmund; is it possible to love sincerely under compulsion? This paradox, which structures both the familial and the social order, seems to be effortlessly negotiated in the play's opening lines, but it quickly becomes both intractable and explosive once the play takes up the archaic and artificial story of the division of the kingdom and the love between a king and his three daughters.

The opening of *Lear* moves fluidly across the playing spaces of the upstage *locus* and the downstage *platea*. A casual obliviousness to any sense of audience places the initial exchange between Kent, Gloucester, and Edmund entirely within the *locus*, while Cordelia's first aside ("What shall Cordelia speak? Love, and be silent" [1.1.60]) is the first full use of the *platea*. The intervening exchange between Lear and Goneril blurs these artificial borders as the assumption of public roles by Lear and Goneril turns the action outwards and begins to erode the barrier between the actors and the audience. As the *locus* is transformed into a public space of performance, the characters' awareness that they are not simply conversing with each other but are playing roles before onstage interlocutors makes the offstage audience into more than eavesdroppers; as Goneril speaks, the audience joins with those onstage in evaluating her performance. As the subtle erosion of the fourth wall unifies on- and offstage space, it gives the onstage action more of a narrative than a mimetic texture. This effect can be diminished or enhanced in actual performance. The recent National Theatre production directed by Richard Eyre shows the tradeoffs involved in choosing a more modern, realist performance style. In the filmed version of this production, the camera follows reaction shots such as Albany's discreet approval of Goneril's speech and of the allotment they receive, and it registers his dismay when he realizes that the change in Lear's retirement plan means that he has not seen the last of his troublesome father-in-law.[19] This realist focus, for which Berger's close scrutiny of the interdependent personal relationships in the play could have provided the dramaturgy, requires cutting

Cordelia's asides. Their artificiality clashes with the mimetic focus on realistic character and action.

Cordelia's asides to the audience, with their implicit criticism of Goneril and Regan, assert control over audience response and demolish the optimistic, egalitarian premises of the play's opening lines. Once Cordelia speaks, it is no longer possible to believe that affection can be expressed as easily as Kent offers it to Edmund. For Cordelia, the consequences and obligations of the word "love" have actual weight; the word itself is difficult to say because "my love's / More ponderous than my tongue" (76–77). Nor can the equal distribution of property be allowed; Cordelia's assertion of moral superiority demands a choice, with no ambiguity, winner takes all. As Brecht says of the narrative quality of epic theater, the spectator is no longer simply provided with a spectacle; she is "forced to take decisions" (*BOT* 37). That these decisions must be made on a moral basis, and that this demand comes from the *platea*, recreates the functional division of space on the medieval stage. The moral starkness produced in the opening scene of *Lear* is very different from the more incremental treatment of similar thematic material in *King Leir*. In *Leir*, an audience learns to side with Cordella from a variety of sources. Before Cordella's first aside conveys her disdain for the flattery of Gonorill and Ragan, they have already condemned themselves through the vicious jealousy they express towards her, and Perillus has had a choric aside explaining that Lear is making a big mistake. In Shakespeare's *Lear*, Goneril and Regan are less obviously evil in their opening speeches; their expressions of love for Lear simply employ the same rhetoric of extravagant compliment that Kent adopts in his profession of love to Edmund. A realist, character-and-action approach to *Lear* can legitimately ask: If Goneril and Regan have spent their lives as the less favored children in Lear's household, and if they expect that this is the last they will see of him, what is the moral harm in exaggerating their love for him in this final moment? It is up to Cordelia, with no help from the surrounding circumstances of the play, to insist that a world in which the word "love" can be handled as lightly and expeditiously as it is by Goneril, Regan, and Kent is morally unacceptable.

Cordelia's insistence on a morally absolute truth that is incompatible with the compromises of everyday life is *Lear*'s deepest inheritance from the *ars moriendi* tradition. The evolution of this tradition from its medieval roots to its postreformation expression shows a significant shift in emphasis from the spiritual to the secular realm. The late medieval *Book of the Craft of Dying* is unequivocal in its demands; when it requires that "whomsoever will well and surely die, he ought to set simply and all from him all outward things and temporal, and ought all to commit to God fully," the "outward things" to be relinquished involve not only material possessions but familial affections; one of the chief impediments to a good death "that most troubleth the secular and worldly men is the over great occupation of outward things and temporal: as toward his wife, his children and his friends carnal."[20] If Lear seems not fully to have accepted the absolute asceticism of the *Craft*, at least his decision to plan for his end, rather than allowing death to overtake him, begins to fulfill the principle articulated in William Becon's mid-sixteenth century Calvinist tract *The Sick Man's Salve*: "He is a happy man and greatly blessed, which forsaketh and giveth over the world before the world forsaketh him."[21] Becon echoes the Biblical citation in Caxton's *Craft* that "The day of the death is better than the day of the birth," and he provides a supplementary Scriptural reference for this asceticism: "Such obey this commandment of St. John, 'Love not the world, nor those things that are in the world.'"[22] Later guides, though, were often less dismissive of secular and worldly obligations. By 1597, William Perkins could pronounce that "to die intestate, or to leave earthly responsibilities untended, is a sin."[23] While texts from the medieval period through Becon's *Salve* often contained a good deal of spiritual advice from the *moriens* to his wife and children, Lucinda Beiers notes that by the time of William Gouge's *Of Domesticall Duties* in 1622, "Gouge's concern with dying had little to do with the ultimate destination of the dying person's soul: He concentrated upon the obligations dying people and survivors owed each other," including "providing portions," "arranging suitable marriages and callings," and, from the children's side, "payment of parental debts."[24]

Lear's earthly responsibilities are greatly enhanced by the fact that he is not only a father but a king, and the imperative for the audience to "take decisions" on his actions is raised considerably by this public function. Realist studies and productions that have focused on the intricate psychological interaction between Lear and Cordelia as father and daughter have often understated the public dimension of the play; where historicist studies have brought out the cultural resonance of the reduction of Lear and Edgar to beggars, Berger sees Lear's concerns with the homeless as "comically" irrelevant to the central domestic narrative (*MT* 38). But Lear's behavior would resonate, in obvious ways, with some of the broadest political themes of the moment. His willingness to explicitly set out the terms of his succession compares favorably with Elizabeth's disapproval of any such talk during her reign, but his decision to divide the blessed isle in three had to awaken curiosity in the original audience about whether this division was in some way the ancient root of later divisions. The presentation of a segment of ancient national history has the effect that Marvin Carlson attributes to the ritualistic aspect of theater: "Such a performance is experienced by an individual who is also part of a group, so that social relations are built into the experience itself."[25] As an early seventeenth century London audience watches the unfolding story of someone vaguely recognizable as an ancient "ruler over the Britaines,"[26] they become aware of themselves as the legatees of this history, as Britons. The use of *platea* address, a residual performance practice, consolidates the historical community of the audience and the *platea* speaker as it erodes the theatrical fourth wall. When the Fool jokes that "This prophecy Merlin shall make; for I live before his time" (3.2.93), he highlights his access to a double temporality, that of the historical *locus* and that of the spectators. As Robert Weimann notes, the privilege of parodic anachronism is common to the fool in medieval moralities, who is apt to remind an audience that "'This must have happened long, long ago.'"[27]

A realist focus that treats Lear's manipulative and controlling tendencies solely as psychological quirks deprives him of both his political and his emblematic status. When Lear announces that he is prepared to "unburthened crawl toward death" (1.1.39), he takes on the role of the representative *moriens* far more fully and actively than his predecessor in *Leir*. Leir makes a few allusions to age and impending death, but his primary concerns lie with his management of his daughters and not with his ultimate fate. Leir's commitment to "resigne these earthly cares, / And think upon the welfare of my soul" [28] addresses his personal fate in neat, orthodox terms, while Lear's "unburthened crawl toward death" reflects the struggle that informs the more tortured expressions of the *ars moriendi*. Lear's "crawl" acknowledges the progressive physical infirmity of the *moriens*, but it also serves as a defiant caution to his children that Lear is not going to hurry his final journey for their sake. His willingness to "shake all cares and business" (1.1.37) before they are taken from him suggests a commendatory foresight, but his inability to include Cordelia among the "all" that he relinquishes shows the one unresolved cathexis that binds him to the world. In Cordelia's case, psychologically oriented critical studies and productions of *Lear* have often found her somewhat cold in her obduracy, but Cordelia's absolutism serves more than a realist function. Lear's reply to Cordelia's "Nothing" is to caution her to "mend your speech a little" (1.1.93), as if it is possible to compromise a bit and live happily ever after, but this response displays an inadequate understanding of the absolute deprivation that awaits him. Cordelia's inflexible repetition of "Nothing" tells Lear what he needs to learn: that in the journey to death, nothing really belongs to him.

When realist readings of *Lear* look for alternatives to its tragic outcome, they typically misconstrue the play's overdetermined texture of representation. In Cavell's argument that things could have turned out very differently if Lear had accepted the love that Cordelia offers him, and in Maureen Quilligan's contention that Cordelia at first properly resists Lear's incestuous advances but then is punished for eventually succumbing to those designs,[29] each takes a single overdetermined term, "love" in Cavell and "incest" in Quilligan, too literally, if the literal can be understood as the antithesis of both the hypothetical and the overdetermined. When Shakespeare weaves Holinshed's claim that Lear loved "specially Cordeilla the yoongest farre above the two elder" into his own version of the story, incest becomes not simply an aberrant erotic fantasy based on a personal object-cathexis, which could be subtracted from the plot by a moral choice; in *King Lear,* the bond between Lear and Cordelia presents cross-generational, father/daughter incest as an overdetermined temporal fantasy that structures the entire narrative. Cordelia embodies the principle for which the *ars moriendi* demands recognition, the fact that the normalcy of everyday life is illusory and temporary. As the figure who both tells Lear of his prospective annihilation and who functions as the tabooed object of desire that grounds his identity, Cordelia marks a line that cannot be crossed without the destruction of everyday life. Cordelia must be held in abeyance, kept in a premarital limbo, in order to maintain the persistence of the normal, where Lear is the head of a unified Britain and of a household of loving daughters. Both death and incest, the spectres that threaten this fragile normalcy, haunt Lear in the person of Cordelia as they reverse the relation of the natural and the unnatural by alienating the connection between truth and experience. Death seems unnatural; it seems far more natural to continue to live, but it would actually be unnatural for Lear to live indefinitely beyond his present fourscore and upward. In truth, it is natural for him to die very soon. It seems natural to Lear that Cordelia belongs to him, and is part of his being. It seems unnatural that she should leave him to in order to begin a sexual life with a stranger.

Without Cordelia, Lear begins to live a posthumous, ghostly existence, moving from temporary homes with diminishing resources to the nothing of homelessness. His need for Cordelia results in her reappearance in a displaced form, as the Fool. The textual indications of this doubling are overt and familiar, beginning with the referential blurring in Lear's demands "Where's my knave? my fool? Go you, and call my fool hither . . . You, you, sirrah, where's my daughter?" (1.4.38–39), and culminating in "my poor fool is hanged" (5.3.304). The most substantive recent arguments that the roles of Cordelia and Fool are written for a single actor are made by Stephen Booth, Richard Abrams, William Ringler, and John Southworth,[30] while the most emphatic denial comes from T. J. King, who charges that such speculation "overlooks historical evidence." King asserts that "The Fool was first played by Robert Armin,"[31] but he does not provide any actual historical evidence to this effect except to note that Armin was a member of the King's Men when the play was first performed. Most text-based studies of the play simply describe Cordelia and the Fool as distinct characters, and when this presumption is extended to commentary on theatrical practice, the objection to the doubling hypothesis is often put in categorical terms: "the parts could not have been doubled" says Kenneth Muir, while Arthur Sprague finds it "very implausible," "most unlikely."[32] But as Booth argues, these objections are ultimately aesthetic, and betray a bias towards realism. As Sprague outlines the tactics used by nineteenth century theatrical companies to conceal the fact that some actors played multiple roles, he cites both the aesthetic justification for the deception and an underlying material implication; not only was it "of real benefit to the audience to believe that Walter Plinge was a real person and not an alias," but "It was the strollers who as a direct consequence of their poverty doubled shamelessly.

Doubling was a sign of deficiency in the company practicing it."[33] Doubling Cordelia and the Fool not only underlines a functional similarity in their characters; it shamelessly invokes an archaic, preprofessional theatrical practice, and signals a displacement of the emergent model of naturalistic character development by an older style of allegorical representation and homiletic narrative.

While it is common among theatre historians to assign the role of the Fool to Armin,[34] both Ringler and Southworth propose an alternative piece of casting: Armin, who was probably in his forties in 1605 and could hardly have been referred to as "boy" seven times (1.4.91; 1.4.114; 1.5.8; 1.5.42; 3.2.66; 3.2.76; 3.4.27) and as "my pretty knave" (1.4.82), plays Edgar. In this hypothesis, instead of taking his customary role as an artificial fool, Armin plays a character who pretends to be a natural fool. Ringler and Southworth identify two plays written by Armin in which he played characters similar to Edgar (*The Two Maids of More-Clack* and *Foole upon Foole*), and Ringler suggests a number of ways in which the role of Edgar suits Armin, including the demand for multiple voices and the size of the part; the combined role of Cordelia (117 lines) and the Fool (227 lines) would be the fourth largest part in *Lear*, while Edgar/Poor Tom (395 lines) is the second largest speaking part.[35] Casting Armin as a character who pretends to be a natural fool, and replacing his usual motley with actual rags, would be another instance of a role that calls attention to its metatheatricality and thus contributes to the construction of Lear's environment as the symbolically dense site of his personal psychomachia. Some sense of the overdetermination of the figure of Cordelia and the Fool in the construction of this environment of naive surrealism can be gleaned from their fate in modern criticism. In Kott's and Cavell's classic essays on *Lear*, each rejects one side of the Cordelia/Fool dichotomy. Cordelia's name never appears in Kott's essay in which the Fool is the only one who fully grasps the total absence of humanist values in the *Lear* universe, but in Cavell's analysis, where Cordelia is "the purest arch of love," fools are condemned to be only "distortions of persons . . . among whom human relationship does not arise" (*DK* 67, 78). This densely overdetermined figure, Cordelia/Fool, demands a decision, even though s/he does not offer the moral clarity of such medieval ancestors as Good Deeds and Vice.

Even those critics who have been attracted to the interpretive possibilities generated by the initial blurring of Cordelia into the Fool have tended to restore a relatively integral Cordelia after her return from France. Abrams offers a canny reading of the Fool's first appearance in 1.4 as a "pseudoreunion" of the "Cordelia-actor" and her defender Kent which foreshadows Cordelia's true reunion with Lear in 4.7, but he wishes to limit the impact of the initial reunion on the later one: "A delicate balance could be upset," Abrams argues, "if, even for a moment, Lear, wincing to make out his daughter ('Methinks I should know you' [4.7.65]), was suspected of glimpsing her physical resemblance to the Fool." Even if Cordelia seems to Abrams to be "faded in verisimilitude"[36] in her return, Lear's recognition of her love still functions, in Abrams' reading as in Cavell's, as the emotional and ethical center of the play. Similarly, Booth's *tour de force* presentation of contradictory signals in the play's conclusion ultimately consigns anything that distracts from the audience's focus on Cordelia's death to the status of "incidental static"[37] that stretches our cognitive and affective faculties and consequently gives *Lear* a sense of magnitude. When these forays into nonrealist representation recover a realistic Cordelia in the final scenes, they reconcile themselves to the most traditional moral reading of *Lear*. In Mack's aphoristic phrasing, "we know it is better to have been Cordelia than to have been her sisters";[38] in Cavell's philosophical terms, Cordelia embodies the "coherence" of the "soul" that is able to "judge a world in which evil is successful and the good are doomed" (*DK* 81). In order to find a moral center in *Lear*, the important thing is not that virtue should be rewarded but that, through Cordelia, it is possible to distinguish good from evil. All that is necessary for this moral clarity is for Cordelia to be Cordelia.

The primary evidence that Cordelia is not always or entirely herself is the Clark Kent/Superman staging in which the Fool and Cordelia never meet onstage and the text repeatedly calls attention to this fact, and the elaborate coherence of the lines that acquire additional significance if the roles are played by a single actor. The enhanced resonance that attaches to "My poor fool is hanged" depends upon transforming the stage into a site of nonrealist representation, a process that begins with the first appearance of the Fool in 1.4. The Fool's entry comes just minutes after the actor playing Kent offers his belabored assurance that, appearances to the contrary, he is still Kent. The subsequent appearance of the Cordelia-actor as the Fool fulfills the expectation of a doubling actor that has just been raised and denied by Kent. Although the Fool is summoned by Lear, he first speaks to Kent, offering his coxcomb "For taking one's part that's out of favor" (1.4.85). The dissonance between Kent's doggedly realist insistence that he is still himself and the Cordelia/Fool figure's doubleness highlights the stakes of the choices made by these characters and the irreconcilability of the values implicit in naturalistic and allegorical modes of representation. The Fool's observation that "this fellow has banished two on's daughters and did the third a blessing against his will" (87–89) is powerfully self-referential for the Cordelia-actor; under the superficial veneer of another character, Cordelia can describe herself as a lucky survivor and Kent as a natural fool who continues to follow the politically impotent Lear. Cordelia's mocking message to Kent for "taking one's part that's out of favor" is that you're still you, still upholding Lear's old privileges, but I'm no longer me.

Having been punished for speaking the plain truth to her father in her own person, Cordelia/Fool assumes an identity though which she can speak as bluntly as she likes. When Lear reminds the Fool that his license is not unlimited, he replies with a metaphor that is available to Fools but not to princesses, comparing speech to dogpiss (96). Kent's response to the Fool's improvised song that is either brilliantly witty or nonsense—"This is nothing" (111)—gives the Fool an opening for a broader attack. The repetition of the word "nothing" returns Lear, Cordelia, and Kent, like any unhappy family, to their last unresolved argument:

> *KENT:* This is nothing, fool.
> *FOOL:* Then 'tis like the breath of an unfeed lawyer; you gave me
>   nothing for't. Can you make no use of nothing, nuncle?
> *LEAR:* Why, no, boy; nothing can be made out of nothing. (111–14)

The Fool's iteration of "nothing" becomes a provocatory taunt to Lear, reminding him of how he treated Cordelia in their last meeting. The leading question "Can you make no use of nothing, nuncle?" draws Lear into a typical Fool's trap; when Lear repeats himself ("Nothing can be made out of nothing"), he quickly realizes that the irony in his repetition of his tautological wisdom comes at his own expense. The Fool's final mock on this theme returns to its beginning; the Cordelia figure who escaped to France can now, through her surrogate, tell Lear the same thing she told Kent: "I am better than thou art now; I am a fool; thou art nothing" (1.4.168–69). Each time the word "nothing" is repeated, it acquires a resonance that goes beyond its immediate context and suggests an order of coherence that is out of the reach of the characters embedded in the realist *locus*. Where optimistic readings of *Lear* seek to attach a recognizable value to that higher order—such as love, forgiveness, or gratitude— the morality tradition does not allow for a direct progress from the plane of the everyday to the plane of redemption. Such an achievement can only be earned through suffering and the total relinquishment of the worldly values that inform everyday life.

Lear's redemption is traditionally linked to Cordelia's return, a meeting that, like Lear's dialogues with Gloucester at Dover and with Kent in the play's final scene, begins in a misrecognition: "You are a spirit, I know. Where did you die?" (4.7.49). Once again, the misrecognition registers Lear's sense of failed obligation, but the heightened stakes of this misrecognition are reflected in the allegorical trappings of the scene. Lear's perception of Cordelia as a spirit and his belief that he has been retrieved from death ("You do me wrong to take me out o' the grave" [45]) construct the deathbed scenario of the *ars moriendi*, where the dying person is surrounded by those closest to him in his final trial. Lear's proto-christian imagery, which identifies Cordelia as a "soul in bliss" and himself as "bound / Upon a wheel of fire" (46–47), hints at the medieval iconography of the deathbed as a site where angels and demons appeared and tried to draw the soul of the *moriens* to heaven or to hell. The impossibility of developing the prechristian Lear's intimations of a morally ordered afterlife into a fully Christian cosmology hints at a vexing theological issue: What is the fate of those souls who lived before the coming of the Word? Can Lear and Cordelia go to heaven? The question of the eternal fate of the "infidel" was revisited in a more immediate form for Shakespeare's audience by the event of the Reformation, when theologians like Becon and Latimer prescribed new, more muted forms of mourning that would be consistent with the principles of firmly held religious faith.

The theological conflict between the Catholic values of the medieval morality and the Calvinist impact on the postreformation English church was reflected in the changing shape of the morality play on the sixteenth century English stage. Medieval moralities were typically constructed on the model of the psychomachia of an individual soul whose fate was decided only in the last moment of his earthly existence, but the Protestant moralities of the mid-sixteenth century, bowing to the Calvinist doctrine of election, created a very different narrative structure involving dual protagonists who were clearly distinguishable in moral terms. In *The Tide Tarrieth No Man*, they are named Christianity and Greediness; in *The Trial of Treasure*, Lust and Just; in *Like Will to Like*, they are Virtuous Life and Nichol Newfangle the Vice.[39] As Phoebe Spinrad notes, suffering was incompatible with the chosen status of the elect protagonist, and so the virtuous characters suffer very little in these plays, and when they do suffer, their suffering generally takes place offstage.[40] The double plot of *Lear* adopts the dual protagonists of the mid-century Calvinist morality, but it transforms both of these figures, Lear and Gloucester, into the flawed, suffering heroes of the traditional Catholic morality. The doctrinal content of the Gloucester plot is fairly overt. The *Craft of Dying* teaches that "It is necessary to every man that will die, that in what sickness be it, short or long, that he murmur or grutch not, but suffer it patiently," and Edgar's treatment of his father adheres to these Catholic principles. In Edgar's explanation that "Why I do trifle thus with his despair / Is done to cure it" (4.6.33–34) and in his admonition to Gloucester that "Men must endure / Their going hence, even as their coming hither; / Ripeness is all" (5.2.9–11), Edgar addresses the second and third temptations of the *moriens*, despair and impatience. The lesson Gloucester must learn at Edgar's hands is that suffering is a trial sent by God, and it cannot be avoided. The precepts of the *Craft*, designed for a Catholic readership, could provide some grounds for hope even in the suffering of Gloucester and Lear. The *Craft* advises that "the infirmity before death is like as a purgatory" in that earthly trials can substitute for posthumous suffering. Consequently, our worldly pains should be seen not only as an accidental blessing but as a specifically divine intervention; sometimes "God mercifully sendeth temporal tarrying, to the end that he not go to eternal pain."[41] The Catholic valorization of suffering makes it possible to imagine that even if Lear and Gloucester existed before the coming of the true faith, their suffering could provide for their spiritual cleansing.

If Lear is to be reconciled with Cordelia, this blessing can only come about through the purgatorial suffering that Lear claims to have endured.

Lear's assertion that he is "a man / More sinned against than sinning" (3.2.57–58) is a Catholic calculation; the notion that one's sins are weighed in a balance against one's afflictions, and that salvation depends upon the latter outweighing the former, places a value on suffering that belongs to a prereformation world view that, in *Lear*, is displaced to an even more archaic English past. While the Protestant emphasis on faith rather than good works is often credited with bringing about an enhanced sense of personal interiority, this Catholic narrative in which personal suffering serves as an absolution for wrongs done to others supports the intensely solipsistic focus of Lear's psychomachia. Cordelia's expressions of pity for Lear's suffering and her commitment to forgive him for the sake of that suffering reflect, as Edgar Schell notes, a precalvinist "quality of grace,"[42] and it is not a stretch, given Lear's earlier expression of his desire to "set my rest / On her kind nursery" (1.1.123–24), to suggest that, in Lear's mind, Cordelia takes on a Marian dimension as a maternal figure of mercy. In modern criticism and performance, the quality of pity in this Catholic narrative has been smoothly assimilated to a realist, character-and-action-based narrative. Bradley's "enskied and sainted"[43] Cordelia serves as a perfect foil for a sentimentally appealing Lear, a sympathetically "foolish fond old man" (4.7.61). If Laurence Olivier's televised *Lear* shows the dangers of overdoing this sentimentality, the widely praised 1993 Royal Shakespeare Company production directed by Adrian Noble and the equally well received 2008 Globe production can serve as examples of just how much sentiment will satisfy modern theater audiences.[44]

Critics who have looked at *Lear* as a realist reading text have often noted the discrepancy between the refractory Cordelia of the opening scene and the infinitely charitable figure who returns later in the play. Cavell bridges the gap between the two by asserting that Cordelia's actions in the play's opening are misunderstood; he suggests a realist, *locus*-based staging in which Cordelia's first three responses to Lear, two "Nothings" and "Unhappy that I am, I cannot heave / My heart into my mouth. I love your majesty / According to my bond; nor more nor less" (1.1.90–92) are all spoken privately to Lear in an attempt to get him to abandon his demand for a public profession of love (*DK* 64). Transforming these lines into confidential moments with Lear rather than public pronouncements softens Cordelia's initial character, but it also dispels the allegorical resonance that sets Lear on his emblematic journey. Berger establishes a different, darker continuity in Cordelia. In Berger's reading, Cordelia understands exactly what is likely to happen to Lear when she leaves him to the mercies of Goneril and Regan. The seemingly generous exchange in the reconciliation scene, where Lear acknowledges his debt to Cordelia ("You have some cause") and she denies his culpability ("No cause, no cause" [4.7.76]) is, according to Berger, a joint contract of bad faith; Lear's admission solicits Cordelia to deny his guilt, and she complies because in doing so she erases her own role in putting Lear in jeopardy (*MT* 45–46).

When Berger's morally nuanced, psychologically complex account of this scene is compared to the modern stage history in which audiences easily indulge its melodramatic sentiment, it might seem difficult to resist Berger's larger argument that slow, solitary reading of *Lear* is the only way to resist "the response such sentiments seem to demand in performance" and hence to transcend the "structural limits of performance" (*MT* 67). But the moral clarity of this melodrama only exists in modern, realist performance terms. If Cordelia is played by the boy actor who has played the Fool during the play's middle acts and "this man" is the disguised Kent, the multiple sources of Lear's confusion when he confesses that "I fear I am not in my perfect mind. / Methinks I should know you, and know this man" (64–65) deflect empathic feeling into hermeneutic scrutiny and ethical ambiguity. Lear has been brought from the noisy and bewildering atmosphere of the storm, where both he and the audience were faced with trying to bring some coherence out of the baroque improvisations of Edgar and the Fool and the confusing appearances of one doubling and two disguised actors while primitive thunder effects banged away in the background, into this refuge of austere clarity. Lear's continuing confusion as he tries to establish the real identities of Cordelia/Fool and Kent/Caius suggests that his moral journey has not actually come to full closure. In Berger's realist reading of the scene, the impediment to moral authenticity lies in the individual psychologies of Lear and Cordelia, who prefer to remain in a state of denial about their complicity in a family pathology, but the doubts raised by the naive surrealism of the doubled actor have broader implications. A nonrealist production can convey a skepticism about the degree of moral resolution achieved in this reunion by causing an audience to doubt whether Lear and Cordelia actually meet on the plane of realism. If Lear's moral resurrection depends upon an emblematic journey in which he acknowledges his debts to those he has harmed, it is just too perfect to believe that the person he has most wronged would miraculously appear at his deathbed to deny that any such injury occurred.

The reunion between Lear and Cordelia becomes a fantastic inversion of the deathbed scene of the *ars moriendi*. Instead of the *moriens* learning to relinquish the things of this world in preparation for the next, Lear discovers that he actually gets to keep his dearest worldly possession. Lear's refusal to surrender Cordelia, which in the play's opening scene signified his selfishness and his inability to accept his mortality, is now fully gratified. When Cordelia returns as a doubling boy actor who has played a substantial male role during the middle acts of the play, she returns as a complete fantasy figure; she is not only without her husband but is also without a sulphurous pit. That the capture and removal to prison of Lear and Cordelia represents an intensification of Lear's incestuous fantasy is reflected in the difference in tone between his abashed final line in the reunion scene,

"Pray you now, forget and forgive. I am old and foolish" (85) and his far
more upbeat reaction to having been taken prisoner:

> Come, let's away to prison.
> We two alone will sing like birds i' the cage.
> When thou dost ask me blessing, I'll kneel down,
> And ask of thee forgiveness. So we'll live,
> And pray, and sing, and tell old tales, and laugh
> . . .
> and we'll wear out,
> In a walled prison, packs and sects of great ones,
> That ebb and flow by the moon. (5.3.8–19)

Once Cordelia returns, Lear no longer recognizes that he is in the final stage
of a crawl towards death; now he imagines an indefinite reprieve, in which
he transcends the shifting fortunes of worldly men. In this utopia that is
freed from time, the relation between Lear and Cordelia is, in generational
terms, thoroughly confused. Lear is at once the father who knelt to sing and
play with his youngest daughter, the erotic rival who has drawn her from
her husband, and the child who is dependent on her kind nursery; Cordelia
is the maternal, Marian figure of mercy, the lover who has abandoned her
husband, and, in perpetuity, Lear's innocent, pregendered child.

That the responsibility for separating Lear and Cordelia should fall to
Edmund activates the contradictory moral narratives that flow through the
play. In the theological melodrama, Edmund is the Vice, who shows an
inherent antipathy to Cordelia's goodness. This designation, Edmund has
eloquently protested, is entirely unfair. In his terms, he is simply the force
of nature. As the object of desire of both of the adult women in the play, he
embodies the grown-up, coeval sexuality that requires Lear to relinquish his
quasi-incestuous possession of Cordelia. Edmund's function as the natural
son is to dissolve connections between material events and moral or metaphysical meanings. His pronouncement that "The younger rises when the
old doth fall" (3.3.22) is really only an articulation of the principles that lie
behind Cordelia's refusal to accord Lear the infinite deference he believed
was due to his age, even if Edmund attributes that sentiment to Edgar as the
exemplary philosophy of the evil child. Edmund's mockery of his father's
astrological superstition resonates in the play's conclusion to divide the
two scenes that were traditionally joined in the medieval representation
of death: the deathbed and the Last Judgment.[45] Gloucester sees his own
impending death as a harbinger of the apocalypse, a symmetry revealed
in "late eclipses in the sun and moon" that portend a panoply of "ruin-
ous disorders" that "follow us disquietly to our graves" (1.2.96, 105–06),
but Edmund's derisive comment that "we make guilty of our disasters the
sun, the moon, and stars" [1.2. 110–11]) makes Gloucester's perception of
cosmic significance in his personal fate sound just a bit narcissistic. This

tension between Edmund's materialist demystification and Gloucester's metaphysical projection foreshadows Kent's and Edgar's apocalyptic commentaries on Cordelia's death. When Kent asks of the figure of the dead Cordelia, "Is this the promised end?" and Edgar solemnly echoes his query with "Or image of that horror?" (5.3.262–63), once again the question is raised of whether a particularly proximate death is the equivalent of the end of the world.

The reception history of Cordelia's death suggests that *Lear* effectively invests this moment with enough resonance to make Kent's question seem appropriate to both theatrical audiences and readers. Edmund's death is explicitly assigned a lesser sense of scale by Albany:

> *MESSENGER:* Edmund is dead, my lord.
> *ALBANY:*   That's but a trifle here. (5.3.294)

Well, maybe not to Edmund. The greater theatrical impact of Cordelia's death does not depend entirely upon its mimetic representation of a parent's loss of a child. Freud found in this moment a dense allegory that requires the generational confusion that Lear conjures in his imaginary utopic captivity. Freud suggests that the theme of a man choosing from among three women is a common story, in which the man is usually young and the third woman (the inevitable choice) is a love object; he offers the stories of Paris and Aphrodite, the prince and Cinderella, and Bassanio and Portia as examples. But this love story, Freud argues, is actually a screen narrative for a more elemental structure in which the third choice is a figure of death. The image of Lear carrying the dead Cordelia is, in Freud's reading, an inversion of the figure of the Valkyrie carrying the dead warrior from the battlefield. By making the hero of this tale an aging, dying man, Freud concludes, Shakespeare recovers the basis of the original myth.[46]

Freud's analysis suggests that the terror unleashed in the final movement of *Lear* operates in a classic Aristotelian fashion; death is presented as "the misfortune of a man like ourselves"[47] when the implicitly normative, adult male subject position, embodied in the aging Lear, is deprived of the prop that enables him to imagine himself as something other than a man in the final stage of life. Cordelia is the vehicle through which Lear sees himself in other identities: as a father, a child, a lover, and, finally, as a warrior and rescuer. These roles can only be played in narratives that involve rolling back the clock and stopping the natural progression in which "the younger rises when the old doth fall." Lear's invocations of his failed attempt to save Cordelia express his astonishment at the gap between the past identity that he recognizes as himself and the present one that is pressing upon him: "I have seen the day, with my good biting falchion / I would have made them skip: I am old now" (5.3.275–76). The multiple roles played by Cordelia in Lear's fantasies draw him into his final misrecognition: "my poor fool is hanged" (304). Lear has managed the difficult recognitions of Edgar,

Gloucester, and Kent, but this is too much. Seeing Cordelia straight would mean not only acknowledging his own mortality, but also facing up to the moral fact that the natural relationship between parents and children is a zero-sum game, and that every way in which Lear imagines ending up with more than nothing involves a theft from Cordelia. It is a mixed blessing that Cordelia means too many things to Lear to be seen with such clarity.

While Freud focuses on Lear as both the agent and the victim of tragedy, Katherine Goodland contends that the tableau of "Enter Lear with Cordelia in his armes" (*TLN* 3217) and Lear's last words (in the Folio only), "Looke on her? Looke her lips, / Looke there, looke there" (*TLN* 3283–84; 5.3.308–09), which suggest an insistent pointing at the dead Cordelia, make Cordelia's body the central figure in the closing movement of the play. While Freud suggests that it is "really" Lear who is being brought to his final rest, Goodland argues that Lear's carrying of Cordelia would strike English audiences as an inversion of an archaically resonant Catholic icon, the pieta figure from the Mystery Cycles.[48] The mutability of this image and its susceptibility to being presented in this revised form draw upon the ambiguous symbolism of Mary as the mother, the widow, and the daughter of the crucified Christ; the relation between Mary and Christ is as generationally complex as that of Lear's imaginary relation to Cordelia. The figure of Mary in the Mysteries is, as Goodland notes, a figure whose expressions of grief represent the sort of lamentation that Protestant reformers found excessive. Goodland finds in Lear's anguished accusation that "you are men of stones" (5.3.256) a "critique of the Protestant construction of death" for its repression of the legitimate claims of mourning. Mid-sixteenth century reforms had brought about the removal of the corpse from the interior of the church during the funeral service, but in Lear's demonstrative grief over Cordelia, as Goodland eloquently puts it, "The taboo corpse, banned from the English funeral service where parishioners once collectively looked upon and wept over it, is thrust upon our sights."[49]

While Goodland's focus on Cordelia offers a description of how the final scene of *Lear* generates pity, the emotion "aroused by unmerited misfortune," and Freud's attention to Lear accounts for its production of terror, which is felt for "the misfortune of a man like ourselves,"[50] Greenblatt's analysis in "Shakespeare and the Exorcists" completes the aristotelian dramatic structure. As Greenblatt's title suggests, if the demonic provokes terror, then exorcism is its purgation; the strategies of the Catholic priests who discovered and dispelled devils, and the repetition of that strategy by the reformers who identified the priests themselves as the source of the evil that needed to be expelled, returns to its original home in the theater, where the devil, and the metaphysical principle of "evil" for which he is a vehicle, are only fictional presences that can be left behind when we return to our real, nonfictional lives. Greenblatt closes "Shakespeare and the Exorcists" with a gesture of exorcism; the final words of his essay are a quotation of the last words of *King Lear,* Edgar's summary judgment (attributed to Albany in the Quarto), that "We that are young / Shall never see so much, nor live so long" (5.3.324–25), accompanied by a preemptive gloss that explains that the audience is left with "the intimation of a fullness that we can savor only in the conviction of its irremediable loss" (*SN* 128). Greenblatt thus echoes Edgar's hailing of a "we" that, while it mourns a scene of loss, can distance itself from "its" occurrence. Edgar makes explicit the criteria for being a member of this "we": "we that are young." This subject category has been repeatedly assailed throughout *Lear,* but its vulnerability has been underestimated throughout the play's critical history.

The opening couplet of Edgar's valediction ("The weight of this sad time we must obey; / Speak what we feel, not what we ought to say" [322–23]) is sometimes criticized, either for its vapidity or because Edgar, who has been a fountain of platitudes throughout the play, has no right to say it, but critics have been more comfortable with Edgar's assessment in the final couplet that "The oldest hath borne most" compared to the less dire prospects of "We that are young." The retrenchment from Albany's construction of a categorical moral hierarchy in which "All friends shall taste / The wages of their virtue, and all foes / The cup of their deserving" (5.3.301–03) seems to signal a realistic acceptance of the fact that virtue is not actually a guarantee of prosperity. But the real difference between Edgar's subject categories and Albany's binary moral opposition is that Albany has been too blatant; his tautology that identifies our friends as those who deserve to be rewarded and our foes as those who should and will be punished is too obviously partisan. It is too easy to imagine Edmund agreeing with Albany's construction of a moral universe: friends good, enemies bad. Edgar's "we" seems more inclusive, but it is no less effective at producing and legitimating two morally polarized sets of subjects. This moral division, reflected in Mack's aphoristic observation that "we know it is better to have been Cordelia than to have been her sisters,"[51] is endorsed across a wide critical spectrum. David Bevington phrases this opposition in traditional humanist terms when he argues that *Lear* shows that "We can choose . . . to be as like Cordelia, Kent, and Edgar as we are able, and as unlike Goneril, Regan, and Edmund as our strength permits," and Hugh Grady's Marxist echo offers even more liberating possibilities: "Shakespeare in *King Lear* affirms . . . the freedom to be Edmund or Edgar; Cornwall or Albany; the Fool or Oswald; Regan, Goneril, or Cordelia."[52] But as Edmund (or Harry Berger) might observe, Edmund could never have chosen to be Edgar, and it seems unlikely that Goneril or Regan could have chosen to be their father's favorite child. As Shakespeare inherited the story from Holinshed, Lear "had by his wife three daughters, without other issue, whose names were Gonorilla, Regan, and Cordeilla, which daughters he greatly loved, but specially Cordeilla the yoongest farre above the two elder."[53] In one narrative that runs through *Lear,* good and evil people are opposed in melodramatic conflict in the fashion of the mid-sixteenth century morality *Like Will to Like,* where

"The virtuous do not the virtuous' company mislike. / But the vicious do the virtuous' company eschew: / And like will unto like, this is most true."[54] In a parallel world constructed of the same words, figures of privilege defend their privileges and vilify as "evil" those who contest the prevailing order. As Edgar's final aphorism shows, the division of the world into good people (friends) and evil ones (foes) begins in the imagining of an unsituated subject, a fantasy figure whose only attribute is to be "young." Edgar's optimistic belief that it is better to be young than to be old is, from the perspective of the *ars moriendi*, less cynical but ultimately no less deluded than his brother's observation that "the younger riseth when the old doth fall." That critics who feel themselves hailed by this subject category ("we that are young") should find it simply a matter of choice to align oneself on the side of the angels is a wonderfully efficient ideological effect.

Greenblatt's description of *Lear* as an iteration of a "larger cultural text" (*SN* 95) in which "the force of evil" is invoked and contained in theatrical ritual employs the rhetorical strategy that Greenblatt attributes to Harsnett: the "force of evil" is "half accusation, half metaphor" (*SN* 98) when Greenblatt writes that "The force of evil in the play is larger than any local habitation or name" (*SN* 127). Greenblatt avoids the literalminded superstitiousness that would identify Edmund with a metaphysical property called "evil," but at the same time he allows for the power of that force to account for the suffering that informs the reception history of *Lear* as a play that is experienced as both uniquely painful and as "large," achieving what Aristotle calls "a certain magnitude."[55] The conclusion of "Shakespeare and the Exorcists" offers a clean break with the fictions of metaphysical superstition as it brings a curtain down on the play; offering a tableau of "Edmund, Goneril, Regan, Cornwall, Gloucester, Cordelia, Lear: all dead as earth," a summary judgment of how "we" feel about this outcome, and an unadorned citation of the final lines of the play as the last words of his own essay, Greenblatt constructs the fourth wall between our modern, material reality and the theatrical fiction of the past as clearly as Edgar distinguishes "we that are young" from the trials of the old.

Lear offers two reasons to doubt that this distinction between us (young) and them (terrible suffering) can be maintained: death and incest. In the Lear story as Shakespeare inherits it and as Nahum Tate revises it, the happy ending that allows Cordelia to inherit the kingdom while Lear lives on as a contented elder statesman depends upon erasing the implications that Shakespeare drew from Holinshed's account of Lear's love for "Cordeilla the yoongest farre above the two elder." Lear's fantasies about Cordelia (as mother, lover, and eternal child) are his ways of engaging in all of the evasions of death that are envisioned in the *ars moriendi*. Edgar's offer to imagine ourselves within a subject category ("we that are young") that will never be subject to the sufferings we have just witnessed ("shall never see so much") echoes the attempts of mid-sixteenth century reformers to persuade English subjects to hold the dead at a distance and to have no fear of their own deaths. *The Craft of Dying* hails a broader subject position than "we who are young"; it offers "innstruccion . . . to hem that schullen dye."[56] The reason to gather the community around the deathbed, as Theophilus tells the dying Epaphroditus in *The Sick Man's Salve*, is that "In you, as in a clear mirror, we behold ourselves, and see what should become of us hereafter."[57] Edgar's premise that the "young" can be separated from the "oldest" as cleanly as good from evil and friends from foes follows upon his attempt to persuade Lear, as he has repeatedly encouraged Gloucester, to remain one of us; he conjures the dying or dead Lear, "Look up, my lord" (5.3.311). It falls to Kent to correct him and to play the necessary role of a "true friend, devout and commendable, which in his last end assist him truly,"[58] who allows Lear to pass from "the rack of this tough world" (5.3.313). The medieval stage did not provide a spectacle upon which a curtain could be drawn; it was, in Kott's words, "a theatre with actors, but without an audience. No one watches the performance, for everybody is taking part" (*SC* 139). As Kent's parabolic last words, "I have a journey, sir, shortly to go; / My master calls me, I must not say no" (320–21) anticipate his own death, he accepts the universal address contained in the final sentence of Caxton's translation of the *Craft*: "And therefore to every person that well and surely will die, is of necessity that he learn to die."[59] If *King Lear* is any guide, this is not going to be easy.

When Kott describes *Lear* as an "ironic, clownish morality play on human fate" (*SC* 153), he distances the play from an aristotelian fulfillment in catharsis in favor of a style of performativity that is both medieval and presentist. Yet even in Kott's "grotesque" reading, the play's unwelcome truths can too easily be identified with what has become its emblematic line: "I am a man more sinned against than sinning." A thematics of suffering informs Kott's account of the central figures of *Lear* as victims of existential forces: the "grotesque," the "absolute" (*SC* 130, 133). Kott's existential fatalism provides a compelling explication of the themes that, as R. A. Foakes has shown in a detailed reception history, vaulted *Lear* past *Hamlet* into the role of Shakespeare's masterpiece in the nineteen-fifties.[60] Foakes attributes this shift of critical fortunes to the temper of the times, when the apocalyptic potential of nuclear holocaust and the Stalinist shadow of dictatorial self-aggrandizement gave the bleakness of *Lear* a contemporary gloss. Both Foakes and Kott allude regularly to the Bomb as the defining specter of the zeitgeist that produced Peter Brook's *Lear*, thus defining their cultural moment in Cold War, rather than in postwar, terms. But Brook's *Lear* also shares that cultural moment with the Milgram experiment, an intellectual exercise that asked not about the random absurdity of suffering but about the deliberate production of it. When Brook eliminated the servant who tries to prevent Gloucester's blinding, his depiction of unchecked cruelty affirmed the bleakest results of Milgram's work.

As Harry Berger has so eloquently shown, a moral reckoning that allows Lear to remain a victim underestimates the play's psychological and moral complexity; it reaches into Lear's "darker purpose" but not into his darkest one, and it allows Lear to avoid recognizing his culpability for the suffering he has caused. Berger's account of Lear's and Cordelia's darkest purposes begins to open up Shakespeare's own exploration not only of suffering but of cruelty, but Berger's character-and-action approach to the play leads him to conclude that this ethically nuanced world can only be realized through the naturalist representation of individual character. In order to reimagine the saintly Cordelia as someone who is really not much better than her sisters, it seems necessary to understand the wider dimension to her character through a modern conception of individuated personality rather than through a medieval representation of moral types. The paradox here is that while the moral nuances of *Lear* seem to us to emerge from a modern, naturalistic conception of character, it is actually the legacy of the archaic, medieval mode of representation of the moralities to redirect the full range of the play's moral demands towards the audience. It is not the fate of Everyman to discover that he is the victim of implacable existential forces; Everyman is meant to learn that he is responsible for his own moral fate, and we are meant to learn that we are in the same moral jeopardy as Everyman. This sense of universal moral jeopardy begins to reemerge at the far end of Berger's naturalist structure of "redistributed complicity" (*MT* 26) if we weigh Regan's blinding of Gloucester against Cordelia's willingness to walk away from her father knowing what his life is likely to be like in the care of Goneril and Regan. If we place these acts on a continuum of cruelty, it can become difficult to judge whether the sisters are more alike or different, to know whether their difference can be ascribed to character or to circumstance, or to be certain where we would fall on this continuum.

The sentimental reading of *Lear*, which seems to offer a reassuring moral gulf between Regan and Cordelia, depends upon an aesthetic of empathy that allows us not only to identify with the privileged subjects of Cordelia, Edgar, and Lear, but also to believe that this "viewpoint of the dominators" (*BOT* 109) represents a different moral space than that of Goneril, Regan, and Edmund. This sentimentality recovers the moral clarity of the Reformation disavowal of "infidels" whose "wepynge and wailing" signified a failure to recognize a moral order in the "promised end." It also diminishes the immediacy of *Lear* and relegates it to the safety of a temporary, fictional disruption of "real life." But when *Lear* contests the differences between "we that are young" and the rest of us, between the living and the dead and between the privileged and the dispossessed, it recovers the presentism of the medieval theater as it demolishes the borders we construct between our moral fictions and the actions that make up our real lives.

Notes

NOTES TO THE INTRODUCTION

1. Jan Kott, *Shakespeare Our Contemporary*, trans. Boreslaw Taborski (Garden City, NY: Anchor Books, 1966), 137; J. L. Styan, *The Shakespeare Revolution: Criticism and Performance in the Twentieth Century* (Cambridge: Cambridge University Press, 1977), 233; *Brecht on Theatre: The Development of an Aesthetic*, trans. and ed. John Willett (New York: Hill and Wang, 1964), 225.
2. David Kastan, *Shakespeare After Theory* (New York: Routledge, 1999), 16–17.
3. Stephen Greenblatt, *Shakespearean Negotiations: The Circulation of Social Energy in Renaissance England* (Berkeley: University of California Press, 1988), 95.
4. Paul de Man, *Allegories of Reading: Figural Language in Rousseau, Nietzsche, Rilke, and Proust* (New Haven: Yale University Press, 1979), 3.
5. Greenblatt, *Shakespearean Negotiations*, 65; *Learning to Curse: Essays in Early Modern Culture* (New York: Routledge, 1990), 147; Kastan, *Shakespeare After Theory*, 18.
6. Georg Lukacs, *The Meaning of Contemporary Realism*, trans. John and Necke Mander (London: Merlin Press, 1973 [orig. pub. 1957]), 43.
7. Douglas Bruster, *Shakespeare and the Question of Culture* (Houndmills: Palgrave Macmillan, 2003), 23.
8. Georg Lukacs, *Theory of the Novel*, trans. Anna Bostock (Cambridge, MA: MIT Press, 1971 [orig. pub. 1920]).
9. The opposition between allegory and symbol is a central theme of Benjamin's *Origin of German Tragic Drama* (London: New Left Books, 1977). Benjamin makes the distinction between "trace" and "aura" in *Aesthetics and Politics: Debates between Ernst Bloch, Georg Lukacs, Bertolt Brecht, Walter Benjamin, and Theodor Adorno*, ed. Ronald Taylor (London: New Left Books, 1977), 135.
10. This is Brecht's term, cited by Margot Heinemann in "How Brecht Read Shakespeare," in *Political Shakespeare: Essays in Cultural Materialism*, 2nd edition, ed. Jonathan Dollimore and Alan Sinfield (Ithaca: Cornell University Press, 1984), 233.
11. William Wimsatt and Monroe Beardsley, "The Intentional Fallacy," in *The Verbal Icon* (Lexington: University of Kentucky Press, 1946); Roland Barthes, "The Death of the Author," in *Image-Music-Text*, trans. Stephen Heath (New York: Hill and Wang, 1977), 142–48.
12. Jacques Derrida, *Limited Inc.*, trans. Jeffrey Mehlman, Samuel Weber, and Alan Bass (Evanston, IL: Northwestern University Press, 1988), 56.

13. Paul de Man, "The Intentional Structure of the Romantic Image," in *The Rhetoric of Romanticism* (New York: Columbia University Press, 1984), 4; "Form and Intent in the American New Criticism," in *Blindness and Insight*, 2nd ed. (Minneapolis: University of Minnesota Press, 1983), 28.
14. Stephen Greenblatt, *Renaissance Self-Fashioning: From More to Shakespeare* (Chicago: University of Chicago Press, 1980), 256.
15. Hugh Grady, *Presentist Shakespeares* (London: Routledge, 2007), 4.
16. Evelyn Gajowski defends this interpretive strategy in her Introduction to *Presentism, Gender and Sexuality in Shakespeare* (Houndmills: Palgrave Macmillan, 2009), 10.

NOTES TO CHAPTER 1

1. "Alienation-effect" has become the standard English translation of Brecht's term *Verfremdungseffekt*, first used in the essay "Alienation Effects in Chinese Acting" (*BOT* 91–99). John Willett suggests that the term is based on Viktor Shklovskji's "Priem Ostrannenija," or "device for making strange" (99).
2. Aristotle, *Aristotle's Poetics*, trans. S. H. Butcher (New York: Liberal Arts Press, 1948), 6.
3. Immanuel Kant, *Critique of Judgment,* trans. J. H. Bernard (New York: Hafner Press, 1951), 101.
4. Karl Marx, *The German Ideology*, ed. C. J. Arthur (New York: International Publishers, 1988), 123.
5. Lukacs, *The Meaning of Contemporary Realism*, 43.
6. Walter Cohen, "Political Criticism of Shakespeare," in *Shakespeare Reproduced: The Text in History and Ideology*, ed. Jean E. Howard and Marion F. O'Connor (New York and London: Methuen, 1987), 33–34.
7. William Wimsatt and Monroe Beardsley, "The Intentional Fallacy," 10.
8. Karen Newman, *Fashioning Femininity and English Renaissance Drama* (Chicago: University of Chicago Press, 1991), 93.
9. Jacques Derrida, "Typewriter Ribbon: Limited Ink (2) ('within such limits')," in *Material Events: Paul de Man and the Afterlife of Theory,* ed. Tom Cohen, Barbara Cohen, Andrzej Warminski, and J. Hillis Miller (Minneapolis: University of Minnesota Press, 2001), 336, 278.
10. Immanuel Kant, *Critique of Judgment*, 111; Paul de Man, *Aesthetic Ideology*, ed. Andrzej Warminski (Minneapolis: University of Minnesota Press, 1996), 80.
11. Paul de Man, *The Rhetoric of Romanticism*, 260.
12. Jacques Derrida, "Typewriter," 279.
13. For example, in *Speech Acts in Literature* (Stanford: Stanford University Press, 2001), J. Hillis Miller constructs an unproblematic continuity from Wimsatt and Beardsley's "The Intentional Fallacy" through the work of Derrida and de Man (92–94, 105–06), despite de Man's critique of the treatment of intentionality by the New Critics in "Form and Intent in the American New Criticism" and in "The Intentional Structure of the Romantic Image." In Miller's treatment of Derrida, he tracks Derrida's dissection of the performative sleight of hand that effaces rhetorical agency in the American Declaration of Independence as Derrida demonstrates that the document "creates the conventions it needs in order to be efficacious" (112), but the same terms are inadequate to Miller's description of Derrida's own deconstructive work, where Miller is forced to fall back on intentionalist constructions (e.g., "Derrida has . . . so cleverly set up these opening sentences" [117]) in order to describe Derrida's rhetorical strategies.

14. J. L. Austin, *How To Do Things With Words*, ed. J. O. Urmson and Marina Sbisa (Cambridge, MA: Harvard University Press, 1975), 22.
15. John Searle, "Reiterating the Differences: A Reply to Derrida," *Glyph: Johns Hopkins Textual Studies* 1 (1977): 205.
16. Jacques Derrida, "Typewriter," 281.
17. Catherine Belsey, *Why Shakespeare?* (Houndmills: Palgrave Macmillan, 2007), 168; Marjorie Garber, *A Manifesto for Literary Studies* (Seattle: University of Washington Press, 2003), 12, 66.
18. Jane Gallop, "The Historicization of Literary Studies and the Fate of Close Reading," in *Profession 2007* (New York: Modern Language Association of America, 2007), 182; Ellen Rooney, "Form and Contentment," *Modern Language Quarterly* 61 (2000): 20.
19. Barbara Hodgdon, *A Companion to Shakespeare and Performance* (Malden, MA: Blackwell Publishing, 2003), 4.
20. Robin Headlam Wells, *Shakespeare on Masculinity* (Cambridge: Cambridge University Press, 2000), 218.
21. Judy Kronenfeld, *King Lear and the Naked Garment of Truth* (Durham, NC: Duke University Press, 1998), 21; "'So Distribution Should Undo Excess, and Each Man Have Enough': Shakespeare's *King Lear*—Anabaptist Egalitarianism, Anglican Charity, Both, Neither?" *ELH* 59 (1992): 776.
22. Hugh Grady, *Shakespeare's Universal Wolf: Studies in Early Modern Reification* (Oxford: Clarendon Press, 1996), 67
23. Karen Newman, *Fashioning Femininity*, 92.
24. Marx criticizes the "reactionary character" of all "so-called *objective* historiography" in *The German Ideology* (60). Greenblatt describes how the political backdrop to his studies during the Vietnam War taught him that "neutrality was itself a political position, a decision to support the official policies in both the state and the academy" (*LTC*, 167).
25. Paul de Man, *Aesthetic Ideology*, 186.
26. Louis Althusser, "Ideology and Ideological State Apparatuses," in *Lenin and Philosophy and Other Essays,* trans. Ben Brewster (New York: Monthly Review Press, 1971), 172.
27. Leah Marcus, "The Two Texts of *Othello* and Early Modern Constructions of Race," in *Textual Performances: The Modern Reproduction of Shakespeare's Drama,* ed. Lukas Erne and Margaret Jane Kidnie (Cambridge: Cambridge University Press, 2004), 30.
28. Cited in Celia Daileader, *Racism, Misogyny and the Othello Myth* (Cambridge: Cambridge University Press, 2005), 214.
29. Margot Heinemann, "How Brecht Read Shakespeare," 233.
30. Sher played Iago in Gregory Doran's 2004 production of *Othello* at Trafalgar Studios in London.
31. The term is used by Brecht in *Brecht On Theatre* (17), and by Derrida in "Typewriter" (281).
32. Christopher John Farley, "Dave Speaks," *Time* (14 May 2005), 5–6.
33. Marx, *German Ideology,* 53.
34. J. L. Styan, *Shakespearean Revolution,* 233.
35. Brecht describes the use of screens as an alienation device in *Brecht on Theatre*, 44, 77, 85, 143.
36. Charles Spencer, "A tale for our time summons the blood," *The Daily Telegraph* (14 May 2003), accessed May 1, 2011, https://www.nationaltheatre.org.uk/?lid=3109&dspl=reviews; Mark Steyn, "Henry goes to Baghdad," *The New Criterion* (1 September 2003); accessed May 1, 2011, http://www.newcriterion.com/articles.cfm/Henry-goes-to-Baghdad-1692.

37. Robert Weimann, *Shakespeare and the Popular Tradition in the Theater: Studies in the Social Dimension of Dramatic Form and Function*, ed. Robert Schwartz (Baltimore: Johns Hopkins University Press, 1978), 260.

38. W. B. Worthen, *Shakespeare and the Authority of Performance* (Cambridge: Cambridge University Press, 1997), 3–4; James Bulman, *Shakespeare, Theory and Performance* (London: Routledge, 1997), 1–2.

39. Barbara Hodgdon, *A Companion to Shakespeare and Performance*, 2.

40. Worthen, *Shakespeare and the Authority of Performance*, 3; *Shakespeare and the Force of Modern Performance* (Cambridge: Cambridge University Press, 2003), 16; Bulman, *Shakespeare, Theory and Performance*, 1.

41. Hodgdon, *A Companion to Shakespeare and Performance*, 2, 4–5.

42. Worthen, *Shakespeare and the Force of Modern Performance*, 9; "Staging 'Shakespeare': Acting, Authority, and the Rhetoric of Performance," in Bulman, *Shakespeare, Theory and Performance*, 13; *Shakespeare and the Force of Modern Performance*, 22.

43. Worthen, *Shakespeare and the Force of Modern Performance Force*, 74, "Staging," 24.

44. Derrida, "Typewriter," 279.

45. Hugh Grady, "Shakespeare Studies 2005: A Situated Overview," *Shakespeare* 1 (2005): 113–14.

46. Douglas Bruster, *Shakespeare and the Question of Culture*, 23.

47. Terence Hawkes, *Shakespeare in the Present* (London: Routledge, 2002), 3.

48. Marx, *German Ideology*, 60, 141; Grady, "Overview," 112.

49. Ewan Fernie, "Action! *Henry V*," in *Presentist Shakespeares*, ed. Hugh Grady and Terence Hawkes, 98.

50. Fernie, "Action! *Henry V*," 98; "Terrible Action: Recent Criticism and Questions of Agency," *Shakespeare* 2 (2006): 105.

51. Fernie, "Action! *Henry V*," 115.

52. Laura Mandell, "Introduction" in "Romanticism and Contemporary Culture," *Romantic Circles Praxis* 6 (2002); accessed May 1, 2011, http://www.rc.umd.edu/praxis/contemporary/mandell/issue_intro.html

53. Clifford Geertz, *The Interpretation of Cultures* (New York: Basic Books, 1973), 448.

54. Richard Halpern, *Shakespeare Among the Moderns* (Ithaca: Cornell University Press, 1997), 4.

55. Walter Benjamin, *Illuminations: Essays and Reflections*, trans. Harry Zohn (New York: Schocken, 1969), 154.

NOTES TO CHAPTER 2

1. The description of the Bogdanov production can be found in Graham Holderness's *The Taming of the Shrew: Shakespeare in Performance* (Manchester: Manchester University Press, 1989). The account of Edwards' production is my own.

2. Elizabeth Schafer, *Ms-Directing Shakespeare: Women Direct Shakespeare* (New York: St. Martin's Press, 2000), 71; Graham Holderness, *The Taming of the Shrew*, 96.

3. Holderness, *Taming*, 97–98.

4. In Chapter 1 (pp. 21–25), I discuss Derrida's critique of John Searle's unproblematic use of the terms "real life" and "serious discourse" in contradistinction to theatrical performance.

5. Holderness, *Taming*, 113–14.

6. Holderness, *Taming*, 113.

7. Pamela Allen Brown, "'Fie, what a foolish duty call you this?' *Taming of the Shrew*, Women's Jest, and the Divided Audience," in *A Companion to Shakespeare's Works, Volume 3, The Comedies,* ed. Jean E. Howard and Richard Dutton (Oxford: Blackwell, 2003), 291, 303.

8. Lynda Boose, "Scolding Brides and Bridling Scolds: Taming the Woman's Unruly Member," *Shakespeare* Quarterly 42 (1991): 184.

9. Holderness, *Taming*, 103, 116.

10. John Rainolds, *Th'overthrow of stage-plays* (Middleburg: Richard Schilders, 1599), 18. [UMI EEBO Reel STC / 349:16]

11. Alan Dessen and Leslie Thomson, *A Dictionary of Stage Directions in English Drama*, 1580–1642 (Cambridge: Cambridge University Press, 1999), 124.

12. Michael Shapiro, *Gender in Play on the Elizabethan Stage: Boy Heroines and Female Pages* (Ann Arbor: University of Michigan Press, 1996), 121, 138, 146.

13. John Fletcher, *The Woman's Prize, or The Tamer Tamed*, ed. George B. Ferguson (London: Mouton, 1966).

14. Louis Montrose, "'The Place of a Brother' in *As You Like It*: Social Process and Comic Form," Shakespeare Quarterly 32 (1981): 28–54.

15. Valerie Traub, *Desire and Anxiety:*Circulations of Sexuality in Shakespearean Drama (New York: Routledge, 1992), 118.

16. Valerie Traub, *The Renaissance of Lesbianism in Early Modern England* (Cambridge: Cambridge University Press, 2002), 13, 310.

17. W. B. Worthen, *Shakespeare and the Authority of Performance*, 13.

18. W. B. Worthen, "Staging 'Shakespeare': Acting, Authority, and the Rhetoric of Performance," 16.

19. W. B. Worthen, *Shakespeare and the Force of Modern* Performance, 18, 22.

20. Worthen, *Shakespeare and the Force of Modern Performance*, 13; contrary to Derrida's *"il n'y a pas de hors-texte,"* in *Of Grammatology*, trans. Gayatri Spivak (Baltimore: Johns Hopkins University Press, 1974), 158.

21. My critique of Worthen's systematic substitution of a canonical reception history of "Shakespeare" for the original intention of the playwright William Shakespeare is prefigured in the confrontation between Barthes and de Man at the 1966 Johns Hopkins conference that brought Barthes, Derrida, and Lacan to the US. In the discussion that followed Barthes' paper, de Man objected that Barthes was "simply wrong" in his underestimation of the degree of self-consciousness in pre-1900 literature, and he charged Barthes with having constructed "a historical myth of progress to justify a method which is not yet able to justify itself by its results." Barthes pretty much conceded de Man's point, saying that "I never succeed in defining literary history independently of what time has added to it. . . . For me, Romanticism includes everything that has been said about Romanticism. . . . However, in telling you this, I am not excusing anything; I am simply explaining and that does not suffice." In *The Structuralist Controversy: The Languages of Criticism and the Sciences of Man*, ed. Richard Macksey and Eugenio Donato (Baltimore: The Johns Hopkins University Press, 1971), 150–51.

22. Adrian Turpin, "Celia, you're breaking my heart," *Independent of London* (6 December 1996); accessed May 1, 2011, http://www.independent.co.uk/arts-entertainment/theatre-celia-youre-breaking-my-heart-1336664.html

23. Joseph Roach, *Cities of the Dead: Circum-Atlantic Performance* (New York: Columbia University Press, 1996), 2.

24. Derrida, "Typewriter," 278.

25. Anne Barton provides a Preface to Arlidge's book in which she judges that Arlidge's argument about the original circumstances of performance is

"considerably more persuasive than Leslie Hotson's argument in 1954 for a first performance at court" (*Shakespeare and the Prince of Love* [London: Giles de la Mare, 2000], viii). Ralph Berry finds that "Mr Arlidge builds up a very strong case based on circumstantial evidence" and offers a "persuasive thesis" (94) that the February 1602 performance in Middle Temple was a first, commissioned performance ("Shakespeare at the Middle Temple," *Contemporary Review* 278:1621 [2001]: 93–97). Peter Parolin's verdict is that Arlidge "may fail to prove conclusively that 2 February 1602 was *Twelfth Night's* premiere, but he makes a good case that we need to understand the Inns of Court as an important context for the play" (*Sixteenth Century Journal*, 33:1 [2002]: 268–69).

26. Bruce Smith, *Homosexual Desire in Shakespeare's England: A Cultural Poetics* (Chicago: University of Chicago Press, 1994), 72–73.
27. Philip Finkelpearl, *John Marston of the Middle Temple: An Elizabethan Dramatist in His Social Setting* (Cambridge, MA: Harvard University Press, 1969), 6–7; J. Bruce Williamson, *The History of the Temple, London* (New York: Dutton, 1924), 221.
28. Williamson, *History of the Temple*, 122–23, 299–300.
29. Williamson, *History of the Temple*, 178.
30. Finkelpearl, *John Marston of the Middle Temple*, 70–71
31. Barnabe Riche, "Riche His Farewell to Militarie Profession," Appendix One in *Twelfth Night: The Arden Shakespeare*, ed. J. M. Lothian and T. W. Craik, (London: Thomson Learning, 2005), 159.
32. Stephen Orgel, *Impersonations: The Performance of Gender in Shakespeare's England* (Cambridge: Cambridge University Press, 1996), 58.
33. Anthony Arlidge, *Shakespeare and the Prince of Love*, 54.
34. Alan Bray, "Homosexuality and the Signs of Male Friendship," *History Workshop Journal* 29 (1990): 2; *Homosexuality in Renaissance England* (London: Gay Men's Press, 1982), 16.
35. Orgel, *Impersonations*, 59.
36. Judith Butler, *Bodies that Matter* (New York: Routledge, 1993), 226.
37. Edward Coke, *The Third Part of the Institutes of the Laws of England*, 3rd ed. (London: J. Fleshner, 1660 [orig. pub. 1628]), 58.
38. Bruce Smith, *Homosexual Desire in Shakespeare's England*, 16.
39. Michel Foucault, *The History of Sexuality. Volume 1: An Introduction*, trans. Robert Hurley (New York: Vintage, 1980), 43.
40. Christina Malcolmson, "'What You Will': Social Mobility and Gender in *Twelfth Night*," in *The Matter of Difference: Materialist Feminist Criticism of Shakespeare*, ed. Valerie Wayne (Ithaca: Cornell University Press, 1991), 45.
41. Wilfrid R. Prest, *The Inns of Court Under Elizabeth and the Early Stuarts 1590–1640* (London: Longman, 1972), 92; Arlidge, *Shakespeare and the Prince of Love*, 103; Finkelpearl, *John Marston of the Middle Temple*, 65.
42. Prest, *The Inns of Court*, 209–11; Arlidge, *Shakespeare and the Prince of Love*, 21–26.
43. Arlidge, *Shakespeare and the Prince of Love*, 102.
44. Christopher Whitfield, "Some of Shakespeare's Contemporaries at the Middle Temple," *Notes and Queries* 13 (1966): 122–125; 283–87; 363–69; 443–48.

NOTES TO CHAPTER 3

1. Stephen Greenblatt, "Marlowe, Marx and Anti-Semitism," *Critical Inquiry* 5 (1978): 294.
2. Alan Sinfield, *Cultural Politics—Queer Reading* (Philadelphia: University of Pennsylvania Press, 1994), 6.

3. Janet Adelman, *Blood Relations: Christian and Jew in* The Merchant of Venice (Chicago: University of Chicago Press, 2008); M. Lindsay Kaplan, "Jessica's Mother: Medieval Constructions of Jewish Race and Gender in *The Merchant of Venice*," *Shakespeare Quarterly* 58 (2007): 1–30. My disagreements with Adelman and Kaplan involve their attribution of a weak form of intentionality to *Merchant* in its treatment of race. Adelman concludes her book with the contention that Antonio is "the epitome of the relationship that the play unwittingly discloses between Christian and Jew. For the play cannot know its own fear and guilt about Christianity's relation to the Jews" (133). This assertion of the impossibility of intention—this "cannot"—is a critical imperative that enables a diagnostic vocabulary, but this alleged failure is grounded in the critical narrative and not in the illocutionary logic of the text. While Kaplan argues that the terms that differentiate Jessica's conversion from Shylock's intransigent Jewishness are a historically specific inheritance from medieval theological formations, Jessica's greater ease in crossing racial lines is not a unique, or even unusual, historical formation. If Jessica's situation is compared to the position of "creole" women of color in New Orleans in the late eighteenth and nineteenth centuries, the similarity between these early modern and modern formations shows, in each case, that both race and gender operate as useful categories that serve the interests of a dominant social group (i.e., white Christian men).

4. James Shapiro, *Shakespeare and the Jews* (New York: Columbia University Press, 1986), 185.

5. All Biblical quotes are from the *Geneva Bible*; facsimile of 1560 edition (Madison: University of Wisconsin Press, 1969).

6. Thomas Aquinas, *Summa Theologica* (Notre Dame, IN: Ave Maria Press, 1981), 3:1513.

7. William Longman, *The History of the Life and Times of Edward III* (New York: B. Franklin, 1969), 2:262; Alwyn Ruddock, *Italian Merchants and Shipping in Southampton* (Southampton: Southampton University Press, 1951), 163–65.

8. Martin Holmes, "Evil May-Day, 1517: The Story of a Riot," *History Today* 16 (1965): 642–50.

9. R. B. Wernham and J. C. Walker, *England under Elizabeth* 1558–1603 (New York: Longman, Green, 1932), 219.

10. The cultural and economic contours of "Gentile mercantilism" have been variously defined in that reception history. Walter Cohen and Michael Ferber find very different class politics in *Merchant*; where Cohen sees the play valorizing an "absolutism [that] served the interests of the neofeudal aristocracy against those of all other classes, in the epoch of western Europe's transition from feudalism to capitalism," Ferber offers the contrary thesis that "it is precisely the ideological conjunction of heroic adventure and bourgeois merchant adventuring" that Shakespeare "frankly celebrate[s]." Walter Cohen, "*The Merchant of Venice* and the Possibilities of Historical Criticism," *ELH* 49 (1982): 783; Michael Ferber, "The Ideology of *The Merchant of Venice*," *English Literary Renaissance* 20 (1990): 462.

11. William Camden, *The historie of the most renowned and victorious princesse Elizabeth, late Queene of England* (London: Benjamin Fisher, 1630), 4:59. Charles Edelman questions the reliability of Camden's account of the execution in "The Strange Case of Dr Lopez and Mr Shakespeare," *Archiv für das Studium der neueren Sprachen und Literaturen* 240.1 (2003): 108–12, but he offers no new documentation on behalf of this objection.

12. Edward Coke, *The Third Part of the Institutes of the Laws of England*, 3rd ed. (London: J. Fleshner, 1660 [orig. pub. 1628]), 58.

13. Thomas Wilson, *A Discourse upon Usury*, ed. and intro. R. H. Tawney (New York, A. M. Kelly, 1963 [orig. pub. 1572]), 205

14. Bruce Smith, *Homosexual Desire in Shakespeare's England*, 18.

15. James Shapiro, *Shakespeare and the Jews*; Alan Bray, *Homosexuality in Renaissance England*.

16. Accounts of the Perez affair and of Francis Bacon's pursuit of the Attorney General's position are intertwined in Anthony Bacon's papers, compiled in Thomas Birch's *Memoirs of the Reign of Queen Elizabeth* (New York: AMS Press, 1970 [orig. pub. 1754]), 1:160. This has led to speculation among historians about the connection between the two matters. See Paul Johnson, *Elizabeth I: A Study in Power and Intellect* (New York: Holt, Rhinehart and Winston, 1974), 371; Perez Zagorin, *Francis Bacon* (Princeton: Princeton University Press, 1998), 13; and Lisa Jardine and Alan Stewart, *Hostage to Fortune: The Troubled Life of Francis Bacon* (New York: Hill & Wang, 1999), 161.

17. Zagorin, *Frances Bacon*, 13.

18. *The Works of Francis Bacon*, ed. James Spedding et al. (New York: Garrett, 1968), 8:322–23.

19. *The Works of Francis Bacon*, 8:278.

20. Jonathan Goldberg, *Sodometries: Renaissance Texts, Modern Sexualities* (Stanford: Stanford University Press, 1992), 142.

21. Joseph Pequigney, "The Two Antonios and Same-Sex Love in *Twelfth Night* and *The Merchant of Venice*," *English Literary Renaissance* 22 (1992): 202, 215.

22. Seymour Kleinberg, "*The Merchant of Venice*: The Homosexual as Anti-Semite in Nascent Capitalism," in *Literary Visions of Homosexuality*, ed. Stuart Kellogg (New York: Haworth Press, 1983), 120.

23. Alan Bray, *Homosexuality in Renaissance England*, 10, 15, 8.

24. For the role of the concept of "blood purity" in producing "racial antisemitism," see Jerome Friedman, "Jewish Conversion, the Spanish Pure Blood Laws and Reformation: A Revisionist View of Racial and Religious Antisemitism," *Sixteenth-Century Journal* 18 (1987): 3-29, and Norman Roth, *Conversos, the Inquisition and the Expulsion of the Jews from Spain* (Madison: University of Wisconsin Press, 1995), 229–37.

25. John D. Rea, "Shylock and the Processus Belial," *Philological Quarterly* 8 (1929): 311.

26. Hyam Maccoby, *The Sacred Executioner: Human Sacrifice and the Legacy of Guilt.* (London: Thames and Hudson, 1982), 154–62.

27. William Tyndale, "A Prologe in to the thirde boke of Moses, called Leviticus." *The Pentateuch* (Antwerp: Hans Luft, 1530. [unpaginated]).

28. For the history of this fantasy, see James Shapiro, *Shakespeare and the Jews*, 113–30.

29. Michael Ferber, "The Ideology of *The Merchant of Venice*," *English Literary Renaissance* 20 (1990): 463.

30. Cecil Roth, *A History of the Jews in England* (Oxford: Clarendon Press, 1964), 79.

31. Norman Roth, *Conversos, the Inquisition and the Expulsion of the Jews from Spain*, 223.

32. Brian Pullan, *The Jews of Europe and the Inquisition of Venice* (Oxford: Blackwell, 1983), 125, 308.

33. Hermann Strack, *The Jew and Human Sacrifice* (London: Benjamin Blom, 1971), 34.

34. James Shapiro, *Shakespeare and the Jews*, 110.

35. Martin Holmes, "Evil May-Day, 1517," 642, 648.

36. In *The Jews in the History of England, 1485–1850* (Oxford: Oxford University Press, 1994), David Katz expresses confidence in Lopez's guilt (49–106), but Elizabeth not only resisted Essex's initial prosecution of Lopez, she brought him out of imprisonment in the Tower to attend her in an illness after his conviction. She also delayed his execution to the point that her counselors warned of "dishonour and scandal" to the Crown if it were not soon carried out (*Calendar of State Papers, Domestic Series* 1591–94 [Nedeln, Liechtenstein Kraus Reprint Ltd., 1967], 3:460). These events are nicely summarized by Margaret Hotine in "The Politics of Anti-Semitism: *The Jew of Malta* and *The Merchant of Venice*," *Notes and Queries* 38 (1991): 35–38.

37. Hyam Maccoby, *The Sacred Executioner*, 161.

38. The equation of the finger-ring and the vagina is discussed by Gordon Williams in *A Dictionary of Sexual Language and Imagery in Shakespearean and Stuart Literature* (London: Athlone, 1994), 3:1158–60. The story of Hans Carvel's ring, told by Rabelais and others, is recorded in a series of fifteenth and sixteenth century texts and appears in *Mery Tales, Wittie Questions and Quicke Answeres, Very pleasant to be Readde* (1567) in the following form: "A man that was right iolous on his wyfe, dremed on a night, as he laie a bed with hir and slepte, that the dyuell appeared vnto him and sayed: wouldest thou not be glad, that should put the in suertee of thy wyfe? yes saied he. Holde (saied the diuell) as longe as thou haste this rynge vpon thy fyngere no manne shall make thee cuckolde. The man was glad therof, and whan he awaked he founde his fynger in his wyves tayle." *Mery Tales, Wittie Questions and Quicke Answeres, Very pleasant to be Readde, Imprinted in Fleetestreeate, by H. Vyykes, 1567.* [ProQuest EEBO Reel 2229: 20a]

39. Thomas Wilson, *A Discourse upon Usury*, 379.

40. Michael Billington, "Exit, pursued by boos," *The Guardian* (1 June 1998): 13. The Globe seems determined to present *Merchant* as light comedy. The play was revived there in 2007 in a production that Lyn Gardner called "The jolliest *Merchant* I have ever seen" (*Guardian*, 30 June 2007), accessed May 1, 2011, http://www.guardian.co.uk/stage/2007/jun/30/theatre. Alistair Smith wrote of the same production that "One would struggle to find a lighter, funnier version," but he also acknowledged that the production was "something of a guilty pleasure" when "some of the evening's largest laughs come from jokes which in a modern context might be termed racist" (*The Stage*, 29 June 2007); accessed May 1, 2011, http://www.thestage.co.uk/reviews/review.php/17292/the-merchant-of-venice

41. Toby Lelyveld, *Shylock on the Stage* (Cleveland: Western Reserve University Press, 1960), 27, 31. This contradiction reappears in modern accounts of Macklin's performance; Bernard Grebanier follows Gentleman in concluding that Macklin "presented Shylock as a detestable monster" (*The Truth About Shylock* [New York: Random House, 1962], 326), while Matthew Kinservik, like Boaden, believes that Macklin's Shylock was a "fiercely dignified character," "A Sinister Macbeth: The Macklin Production of 1773," *Harvard Library Bulletin* 6 (1995): 56.

42. William Appleton, *Charles Macklin: An Actor's Life* (Cambridge, MA: Harvard University Press, 1960), 46.

43. Philip H. Highfill, Kalman A. Burnim, and Edward A. Langhans, *A Biographical Dictionary of Actors, Actresses, Musicians, Dancers, Managers & Other Stage Personnel in London, 1660–1800* (Carbondale, Southern Illinois University Press [1973–]), Volume 10: 2, 4.

44. Brian Pullan, *The Jews of Europe and the Inquisition of Venice*, 75.

45. Toby Lelyveld, *Shylock on the Stage*, 31.

NOTES TO CHAPTER 4

1. This structural pattern is discussed by Casey Dué in *Homeric Variations on a Lament by Briseis* (Lanham, MD: Rowman and Littlefield, 2002) and by Mihoko Suzuki in *Metamorphoses of Helen: Authority, Difference and the Epic* (Ithaca: Cornell University Press, 1989). Shakespeare surely knew George Chapman's English translation of *Seven Books of the Iliads of Homer* (1598), and he may also have read Latin translations. Shakespeare's access to Chapman's *Iliad* and other source texts is nicely summarized by David Bevington in his Arden edition of the play (Surrey: Thomas Nelson, 1998).
2. Robert Henryson, *Testament of Cresseid*, ed. Denton Fox (London: Nelson, 1968).
3. Rene Girard, "The Politics of Desire in *Troilus and Cressida*," in *Shakespeare and the Question of Theory*, ed. Patricia Parker and Geoffrey Hartman (New York: Methuen, 1985), 193.
4. Linda Charnes, "'So Unsecret to Ourselves': Notorious Identity and the Material Subject in *Troilus and Cressida*," *Shakespeare Quarterly* 40 (1989): 424; Carol Cook, "Unbodied Figures of Desire," *Theatre Journal* 38 (1986): 42; Valerie Traub, *Desire and Anxiety:Circulations of Sexuality in Shakespearean Drama* (New York: Routledge, 1992), 83; Girard 72.
5. Jacques Lacan, *Feminine Sexuality*, trans. Jacqueline Rose, ed. Juliet Mitchell and Jacqueline Rose (New York: W. W. Norton, 1985), 170.
6. Denis De Rougemont, *Love in the Western World*, trans. Montgomery Belgion (New York: Pantheon, 1956).
7. *Andreas Capellanus on Love*, trans. G. Walsh (London: Duckworth, 1982), 156, 185.
8. Rene Girard, "The Politics of Desire in *Troilus and Cressida*," 188–89.
9. Mihoko Suzuki, *Metamorphoses of Helen,* 219; Linda Charnes, "'So Unsecret to Ourselves," 423.
10. Geoffrey Chaucer, *Troilus and Criseyde*, ed. Barry Windeatt (London: Penguin, 2003), 5.1576–82.
11. Linda Charnes, "'So Unsecret to Ourselves," 438.
12. Denis de Rougemont, *Love in the Western World*, 109.
13. George Peele, "The Tale of Troy" in *The Life and Minor Works of George Peele*, ed. David H. Horne (New Haven: Yale University Press, 1952), 197.
14. Sigmund Freud, *Totem and Taboo*, trans. A. A. Brill (New York: Vintage, 1986), 182–86.
15. Jacques Lacan, *Ecrits: A Selection*, trans. Alan Sheridan (New York: W. W. Norton, 1977), 4.
16. Lacan, *Ecrits*, 19.
17. Julia Kristeva, *Tales of Love*, trans. Leon S. Roudiez (New York: Columbia University Press, 1987), 30.
18. The critical controversy over the "strange fellow" is documented in the New Variorum *Troilus and Cressida*, ed. Harold N. Hillebrand (Philadelphia: J. B. Lippincottt, 1953), 411–15.
19. The Quarto has "giver"; the Norton adopts the Folio's "givers."
20. Julia Kristeva, *Tales of Love*, 222.
21. Jacques Lacan, *Feminine Sexuality,* 153.
22. Julia Kristeva, *Tales of Love*, 227.
23. Alexandre Kojeve, *Lectures on the Phenomenology of Spirit*, assembled by Raymond Queneau, trans. James H. Nichols, Jr., ed. Allan Bloom (New York: Basic Books, 1969), 7.
24. Alexandre Kojeve, *Lectures*, 19.
25. Jacques Lacan, *Feminine Sexuality,* 141.
26. Andreas Capellanus, *On Love,* 223.

27. Several such cases appear in Capellanus, e.g., 205–07, 254–55, 258–59.
28. Denis De Rougemont, *Love in the Western World,* 114.
29. Jacques Lacan, *Feminine Sexuality,* 144–45.
30. Andreas Capellanus, *On Love,* 221.
31. Andreas Capellanus, *On Love,* 35.
32. Peter Dronke, *Medieval Latin and the Rise of European Love-Lyric* (Oxford: Clarendon Press, 1968), 48.
33. Andreas Capellanus, *On Love,* 225.
34. Francesco Petrarch, *The Secret,* trans. and ed. Carol E. Quillen (Boston: Bedford/St. Martin's Press, 2003), 91.
35. Julia Kristeva, *Powers of Horror,* trans. Leon S. Roudiez (New York: Columbia University Press, 1982), 5.
36. Jacques Lacan, *The Four Fundamental Concepts of Psychoanalysis,* trans. Alan Sheridan, ed. Jacques-Alain Miller (New York: Norton, 1991), 103.
37. Cited in David Bevington, in "Introduction" to *Troilus and Cressida: The Arden Shakespeare,* 90.
38. Both Quarto and Folio are generally held to be corrupt in this passage. Both give the words "Nay, do not snatch it from me" to Diomedes (5.2.83; *TLN* 3068). I follow the Oxford and Norton editors in giving the line to Cressida, due primarily to the continuity with the next line ("He that takes that doth take my heart withal"). I do not agree with the placement of the stage direction inserted by the Oxford and Norton editors immediately before this, which has Diomedes take the sleeve at this point. The Norton and Oxford follow the Folio "DIOMEDES: As I kiss thee" with the stage direction "[*He snatches the sleeve*]" in the middle of line 83. Since Cressida says at line 87 "You shall not have it," I think this indicates that she continues to hold the sleeve at least through 5.2.87.
39. Jan Kott, *Shakespeare Our Contemporary,* 82.
40. Andreas Capellanus, *On Love,* 185.
41. Jacques Lacan, *Feminine Sexuality,* 156.
42. Jacques Lacan, *Feminine Sexuality,* 157–58.
43. Michael Coveney; cited in Bevington, "Introduction," 108.
44. Julia Kristeva, *Powers of Horror,* 53.
45. Denis de Rougemont, *Love in the Western World,* 51.
46. Julia Kristeva, *Powers of Horror,* 162.

NOTES TO CHAPTER 5

1. Janet Adelman, *Suffocating Mothers: Fantasies of Maternal Origin in Shakespeare's Plays, Hamlet to The Tempest* (New York: Routledge, 1992), 73.
2. G. K. Hunter, "*Othello* and Colour Prejudice," in *Dramatic Identities and Cultural Tradition: Studies in Shakespeare and His Contemporaries* (Liverpool: Liverpool University Press, 1978), 31–59.
3. Ania Loomba, "'Delicious traffick': Racial and Religious Difference on Early Modern Stages," in *Shakespeare and Race,* ed. Catherine M. S. Alexander and Stanley Wells (Cambridge: Cambridge University Press, 2000), 209; Eric Griffin, "Un-Sainting James: or, *Othello* and the 'Spanish Spirits' of Shakespeare's Globe," *Representations* 62 (1998): 52–99; Julia Reinhard Lupton, "*Othello* Circumcised: Shakespeare and the Pauline Discourse of Nations," *Representations* 57 (1997): 73–89.
4. Edward Snow, "Sexual Anxiety and the Male Order of Things in *Othello,*" *English Literary Renaissance* 10 (1980): 409. Other essays that locate the central problematic in *Othello* in Iago and sexual repression, rather than

in race or illicit sexuality, are Lynda Boose, "Othello's Handkerchief, 'The Recognizance and Pledge of Love," *English Literary Renaissance* 5 (1975): 360–74; Stephen Greenblatt, "The Improvisation of Power" in *Renaissance Self-Fashioning*, 222–54; and Stanley Cavell, "Othello and the Stake of the Other" in *Disowning Knowledge In Seven Plays of Shakespeare* (Cambridge: Cambridge University Press, 1987).

5. As Kim Hall notes, disagreement on this question informs the earliest recorded responses to the play. Thomas Rymer's objection in 1693 that Shakespeare violated rules of nature by making a black man both a military leader and an object of sexual attraction in a European setting was contradicted by Charles Gildon in 1694, who wrote that "'Tis granted, a *Negro* here does seldom rise above a Trumpeter, nor often perhaps higher at *Venice*. But that proceeds from the Vice of Mankind, which is the Poet's Duty . . . to correct, and to represent things as they should be, not as they are. . . . The Poet has therefore well chosen a polite People to cast off this customary Barbarity of confining Nations, without regard to their Virtue and Merits, to slavery and contempt for the meer Accident of their Complexion" (74). Kim Hall, "*Othello* and the Problem of Blackness" in *A Companion to Shakespeare's Works: Volume One, The Tragedies*, ed. Richard Dutton and Jean E. Howard (Oxford: Blackwell, 2005): 357–74; Thomas Rymer, *A Short View of Tragedy*, in *The Critical Works of Thomas Rymer*, ed. Curt A. Zimansky (New Haven: Yale University Press, 1956), 227–70; Charles Gildon, "Some Reflections on Mr. Rymer's Short View of Tragedy and an Attempt at a Vindication of Shakespeare," in *Shakespeare, The Critical Heritage: Volume 2, 1693–1733*, ed. Brian Vickers (London: Routledge, 1974), 63–85.

6. Sigmund Freud, *Three Essays on the Theory of Sexuality*, trans. James Strachey (New York: Basic Books, 1962), 15. "Civilization" is Strachey's translation of Freud's *Kultur*.

7. *Group Psychology and the Analysis of the Ego*, trans. and ed. James Strachey (New York: W.W. Norton, 1989). Strachey's use of the word "group" has become the standard English translation for Freud's text *Massenpsychologie und Ich-Analyse*. The title is rendered more literally by Jim Underwood as *Mass Psychology* (London: Penguin, 2004).

8. Freud, *Gesammelte Werke: Chronologisch Geordnet*, ed. Anna Freud, E. Bibring, W. Hoffer, E. Kris and O. Isakower (London: Imago, 1942–50), 13: 157. Henceforth cited as *GW*.

9. Giraldi Cinthio, "The Moor of Venice" from *Gli Hecatommithi* ("Hundred Tales") in *Othello: A Norton Critical Edition*, ed. Edward Pechter (New York: W. W. Norton, 2004), 151–61.

10. The Norton editors give "*black*: dark-haired or dark-complexioned," and the Norton Third Edition deletes the comment in the Second Edition that "the latter meaning has special relevance in *Othello*." This "special relevance" is also diminished to various degrees by other editors, including Edward Pechter in the Norton Critical Edition (New York: Norton, 2004), where he gives "black: dark-complexioned or dark-haired—hence unattractive," David Bevington in HarperCollins (New York: HarperCollins, 1992), who gives "black: dark-complexioned, brunette," and by Alvin Kernan in the Signet (New York: Penguin, 1986) and Frank Kermode in the Riverside (Boston: Houghton Mifflin, 1974), who simply say "black: brunette." Since Iago's comparison of the "fair" and the "black" echoes the Duke's assessment of Othello as "more fair than black," it is difficult to deny the "special relevance" of the word "black" in this usage.

11. For an incisive discussion of how race functions as an alibi throughout *Othello*, providing a "*substitute* idiom for something that cannot *properly*

be registered in language" (111), see Madhavi Menon, *Wanton Words: Rhetoric and Sexuality in English Renaissance Drama* (Toronto: University of Toronto Press, 2004).

12. Arthur Kirsch, "The Polarization of Erotic Love in *Othello*," *Modern Language Review* 73 (1978): 738; Adelman, *Suffocating Mothers*, 66.

13. Sigmund Freud, "The Ego and the Id," trans. Joan Riviere, in *The Standard Edition of the Complete Psychological Works of Sigmund Freud* (London: Hogarth Press, 1953–74), 19:32.

14. Edward Pechter, *Othello and Interpretive Traditions* (Iowa City: Iowa University Press, 1999), 110.

15. Pechter, *Othello and Interpretive Traditions*, 117, 149.

16. Freud, "The Ego and the Id," 29.

17. Freud, "The Ego and the Id," 31.

18. Freud, *Three Essays*, 12.

19. Daryl Bem, "Exotic Becomes Erotic: A Developmental Theory of Sexual Development," *Psychological Review* 103 (1996): 322.

20. Cited in Emily Bartels in "Too Many Blackamoors: Deportation, Discrimination and Elizabeth I," *Studies in English Literature* 46 (2006): 316.

21. Emily Bartels, "Too Many Blackamoors."

22. Sigmund Freud, "Instincts and Their Vicissitudes," trans. C. M. Baines, in *The Standard Edition of the Complete Psychological Works of Sigmund Freud*, 14:139.

23. W. H. Auden, "The Joker in the Pack," in *The Dyer's Hand and Other Essays* (New York: Random House, 1962), 269.

24. Edward Snow, "Sexual Anxiety and the Male Order of Things in *Othello*," 393.

25. This process is described both in *Three Essays* (66) and in *Group Psychology* (55). In each case, Freud uses the term *zärtlich* to describe the nonsexual form of cathexis (*GW* 5:101; 13:123).

26. Freud, *Three Essays*, 94.

27. Sigmund Freud, "On the Universal Tendency to Debasement in the Sphere of Love (Contributions to the Psychology of Love II)," trans. Alan Tyson, in *The Standard Edition of the Complete Psychological Works of Sigmund Freud*, 11:185.

28. Freud, "Universal Tendency," 190; both "civilization" and "culture" are *Kultur* [*GW* 8:91]).

29. Freud, *Three Essays* 15; "cultural development" is *Kulturentwicklung* [*GW* 5.48]).

30. Freud, "Universal Tendency," 187, 186.

31. Freud, *Three Essays*, 94.

32. Freud, *Gesammelte Werke* 13:157; "group feeling" is *"Massengefühl"*.

33. Freud, "Universal Tendency," 180.

34. Freud, "The Ego and the Id," 36.

35. Sigmund Freud, "Some Neurotic Mechanisms in Jealousy, Paranoia and Homosexuality," trans. James Strachey, in *The Standard Edition of the Complete Psychological Works of Sigmund Freud*, 18:221–34 (orig. pub. 1922), 39.

36. "Leonardo da Vinci and a Memory of His Childhood," trans. Alan Tyson, in *The Standard Edition of the Complete Psychological Works of Sigmund Freud*, 11:59–137; *Three Essays*, 11.

37. Freud, "Some Neurotic Mechanisms," 232.

38. W. H. Auden, "The Joker in the Pack," 261.

39. Cynthia Chase, "Desire and Identification in Lacan and Kristeva," in *Feminism and Psychoanalysis*, eds. Richard Feldstein and Judith Roof (Ithaca: Cornell University Press, 1989), 83.

40. Freud, "On Narcissism," 79.
41. Sigmund Freud, "Some Psychical Consequences of the Anatomical Distinction Between the Sexes," trans. James Strachey, in *The Standard Edition of the Complete Psychological Works of Sigmund Freud*, 19:257.
42. W. H. Auden, "The Joker in the Pack," 269.
43. Freud, "On Narcissism," 101; "excellence" is *Vorzüge* (*GW* 10:169); "perfections" are *Vollkommenheiten* (*GW* 13: 124).
44. Janet Adelman, *Suffocating Mothers, 66.*
45. T. S. Eliot "Shakespeare and the Stoicism of Seneca" in *Selected Essays* (London: Faber and Faber, 1932), 126–40; F. R. Leavis, "Diabolic Intellect and the Noble Hero; or, the Sentimentalist's Othello" in *The Common Pursuit* (Penguin: Harmondsworth, 1952), 136–59.
46. Thomas Rymer, *A Short View of Tragedy.*
47. Janet Adelman, *Suffocating Mothers*, 74.
48. Bettie Anne Doebler, "Othello's Angels: The Ars Moriendi," *ELH* 34 (1967): 156.
49. Lynda Boose, "'The Getting of a Lawful Race': Racial Discourse in Early Modern England and the Unrepresentable Black Woman," in *Women, "Race," and Writing in the Early Modern Period*, ed. Margo Hendricks and Patricia Parker (London: Routledge, 1994), 40.
50. Sigmund Freud, "The Future of an Illusion," trans. W. D. Robson-Scott, in *The Standard Edition of the Complete Psychological Works of Sigmund Freud*, 21:20.

NOTES TO CHAPTER 6

1. Thomas Becon, *The Sick Man's Salve,* in *Prayers and Other Pieces of Thomas Becon S.T.* (Cambridge: Cambridge University Press, 1844 [orig. pub. 1558]), 120.
2. Hugh Latimer, *Certayn godly Sermons, made upon the lords Prayer* (London, John Day, 1562); cited in Katharine Goodland, *Female Mourning in Medieval and Renaissance English Drama: From the Raising of Lazarus to King Lear* (Aldershot, England: Ashgate, 2006), 203.
3. Maynard Mack, *King Lear in Our Time* (Berkeley: University of California Press, 1965), 57, 117. In a recent essay, Michael O'Connell argues that *Lear* "pushes morality traditions back beyond the bourgeois [i. e., Puritan] moralities" of the mid-sixteenth century in order to "lead us back to the dramatic traditions of the fifteenth century" ("*King Lear* and the Summons of Death," in *Shakespeare and the Middle Ages,* ed. Curtis Perry and John Watkins [Oxford: Oxford University Press, 2009], 206). I agree with O'Connell's argument that *Lear* recapitulates in significant ways the story of the Summons of Death in *Everyman,* but not with his judgment that *Lear* is "about the acquisition of self-knowledge and wisdom" (214).
4. The idea that Lear bargains with death is discussed by Susan Snyder in "King Lear and the Psychology of Dying," *Shakespeare Quarterly* 33 (1982): 449–60 and by David Bevington in "'Is This the Promised End?': Death and Dying in *King Lear.*" *Proceedings of the American Philosophical Society* 133 (1989): 404–415.
5. Richard Alpers, "King Lear and the Theory of the 'Sight Pattern,'" in *A Defense of Reading: A Reader's Approach to Literary Criticism*, ed. Reuben A. Brower (New York: E. Dutton, 1962), 135; Stanley Cavell, *Disowning Knowledge in Seven Plays of Shakespeare* (Cambridge: Cambridge University

Press, 1987); and Richard C. McCoy, "'Look upon Me, Sir': Relationships in King Lear," *Representations* 81 (2003): 46–60.

6. Alpers, "King Lear and the Theory of the 'Sight Pattern,'" 145.
7. Harry Berger, *Making Trifles of Terrors: Redistributing Complicities in Shakespeare* (Stanford: Stanford University Press, 1997), 67.
8. Howard Felperin, *Shakespearean Representation: Mimesis and Modernity in Elizabethan Tragedy* (Princeton: Princeton University Press, 1977), 98, 95, 101.
9. Raphael Holinshed, *Holinshed's Chronicles of England, Scotland and Ireland* (London: J. Johnson et al., 1807), 1: 147.
10. "Shakespeare makes use of all the means of anti-illusionist theatre to create a . . . . landscape which is only a blind man's illusion." Jan Kott, *Shakespeare Our Contemporary*, 144.
11. Margot Heinemann, "How Brecht Read Shakespeare," 233.
12. Perhaps the closest reader of this passage is Stephen Booth, who lists the following challenges to straightforward referentiality: "'This is a dull sight' has no clear, fixed referent" and only a "syntactically improbable antecedent provided by 'Mine eyes are not o' the best,'" "the reference of 'Nor no man else' is unfixed and multiple," and this line too is only "an inaccurate and still syntactically random continuation from 'followed your sad steps.'" Booth applauds Kenneth Muir's "brave editorial effort" in the Arden edition to explain "Nor no man else," in which some of Muir's hypotheses are "This may mean 'No, neither I, nor any man, is welcome.' . . . But I think it probably . . . means simply 'I am really him and no one else.'" As for "I'll see that straight," when Booth presumes that Lear uses "'see' to mean 'understand,'" he follows a consistent editorial tradition that underestimates the literality of what Alpers calls the "sight pattern" in the play (King Lear, Macbeth, *Indefinition, and Tragedy* [New Haven: Yale University Press, 1983], 30–32).
13. Alpers, "King Lear and the Theory of the 'Sight Pattern,'" 135. Alpers describes how sight imagery signifies the political and personal relations between Kent and Lear in the play's opening scene when Lear banishes Kent by pronouncing, "Out of my sight!" and Kent protests by continuing the figure of seeing: " See better, Lear, and let me still remain / The true blank of thine eye (1.1.158–59). As Alpers explains, when Kent asks Lear to "see better," he is not asking Lear to learn to revalue Cordelia. The "blank" is the center of a target, which is where Kent wants to remain: in the center of Lear's field of vision. Presuming that "the king's sight is an active emanation that sheds grace and favor," Kent feels "to be out of it is, in effect, not to exist" (134–35).
14. Alpers, 134–135.
15. Hugh Grady, *Shakespeare's Universal Wolf: Studies in Early Modern Reification* (Oxford: Clarendon Press, 1996), 149.
16. Janet Adelman, *Suffocating Mothers*, 106.
17. Harry Berger, *Imaginary Audition: Shakespeare on Stage and Page* (Berkeley: University of California Press, 1989), xiii–xiv.
18. For a discussion of the dispute between Derrida and John Searle about "serious discourse" and theatrical performance, see Chapter 1, pp. 21–25.
19. *King Lear*, directed by Richard Eyre. DVD. (WGBH Boston, 1998).
20. William Caxton, trans., "The Book of the Craft of Dying," in *The Book of The Craft of Dying and Other Early English Tracts Concerning Death*, ed. Francis M. M. Comper (NY: Arno Press, 1977), 64. I have quoted from this modern spelling edition of William Caxton's condensed version of the text from 1490 except for one passage in the *The Boke of Crafte of Dyinge* that is not included in Caxton's translation, where I have cited the English version

that was originally (and wrongly, according to his nineteenth century editor Carl Horstman) attributed to Richard Rolle (see fn. 56).

21. Thomas Becon, *The Sick Man's Salve*, 130.
22. Caxton, "The Book of the Craft of Dying," 57; Becon, *The Sick Man's Salve*, 130.
23. Nancy Lee Beaty, *The Craft of Dying: A Study in the Literary Tradition of the Ars Moriendi in England* (New Haven: Yale University Press, 1970), 118.
24. Lucinda McCray Beiers, "The Good Death in Seventeenth-Century England," in *Death, Ritual and Bereavement*, ed. Ralph Houlbrooke (London: Routledge, 1989), 50.
25. Marvin Carlson, *Performance: A Critical Introduction* (London: Routledge, 1996), 198.
26. Holinshed, *Holinshed's Chronicles of England, Scotland and Ireland*, 1:446.
27. Robert Weimann, *Shakespeare and the Popular Tradition in the Theater*, 78.
28. Anon., *The History of King Leir* (London, Oxford University Press, 1907), 1.1.27–28.
29. Maureen Quilligan, *Incest and Agency in Elizabeth's England* (Philadelphia: University of Pennsylvania Press, 2005).
30. Stephen Booth, "Speculations on Doubling in Shakespeare's Plays," in *King Lear, Macbeth, Indefinition, and Tragedy*; Richard Abrams, "The Double Casting of Cordelia and Lear's Fool: A Theatrical View," *Texas Studies in Literature and Language*, 27 (Winter 1985): 354–368; William A. Ringler, "Shakespeare and His Actors: Some Remarks on King Lear," in *Lear from Study to Stage: Essays in Criticism*, ed. James Ogden and Arthur H. Scouten (London: Associated University Presses, 1997), 123–34; John Southworth, *Fools and Jesters at the English Court* (Thrupp, Gloucestershire: Sutton, 1998).
31. T. J. King, *Casting Shakespeare's Plays: London Actors and Their Roles, 1590–1642* (Cambridge: Cambridge University Press, 1992), 270.
32. Kenneth Muir, ed. *King Lear: The Arden Shakespeare* (London: Methuen, 1980), 205; Arthur Colby Sprague, *The Doubling of Parts in Shakespeare's Plays* (London: Society for Theatre Research, 1966), 33–34.
33. Sprague, *Doubling*, 12.
34. Thomas Baldwin first assigned the role of the Fool to Armin in *The Organization and Personnel of the Shakespeare Company* (Princeton: Princeton University Press, 1927). Andrew Gurr thinks that Armin was "probably . . . Lear's Fool," but he notes that Southworth and others disagree (*The Shakespeare Company 1594–1642* [Cambridge: Cambridge University Press, 2004], 218).
35. I am using the line counts from the database for the new Penguin edition, ed. Jonathan Bate (available at www.shakespeareswords.com), accessed May 1, 2010.
36. Richard Abrams, "The Double Casting of Cordelia and Lear's Fool," 360, 364.
37. Stephen Booth, King Lear, Macbeth, *Indefinition, and Tragedy*, 54.
38. Maynard Mack, *King Lear in Our Time*, 117.
39. See David Bevington, *From Mankind to Marlowe: Growth of Structure in the Popular Drama of Tudor England* (Cambridge, MA: Harvard University Press, 1962), 152–70.
40. Phoebe Spinrad, *The Summons of Death on the Medieval and Renaissance English Stage* (Columbus: Ohio State University Press, 1987), 93.
41. Caxton, "The Book of the Craft of Dying," 62–63.

42. Edgar Schell, *Strangers and Pilgrims: From* The Castle of Perseverance *to* King Lear (Chicago: University of Chicago Press, 1983), 187.
43. A. C. Bradley, *Shakespearean Tragedy: Lectures on* Hamlet, Othello, King Lear*, and* Macbeth (London: Macmillan, 1964 [orig. pub. 1904]), 262.
44. Benedict Nightingale exemplifies the critical response to the 1993 RSC production when he credits Stephens' performance with "emotional authenticity" and finds that there was "a quiet humility to his reconciliation with Cordelia, a touching excitement to their joint exit to prison" ("Some Recent Productions," in *Lear from Study to Stage*, 242). My sense of that RSC production (directed by Adrian Noble) is closer to that of Carol Rutter in "Eel Pie and Ugly Sisters" (in *Lear from Study to Stage*) and Pascale Aebischer in *Shakespeare's Violated Bodies: Stage and Screen Performance* (Cambridge: Cambridge University Press, 2004) than to the journalistic consensus represented by Nightingale. Rutter notes the dissatisfaction of the actresses who played Goneril and Regan with the framing of their characters (220), while Aebischer calls the production "a prime example of the privileging of Lear and the violence this privileging is predicated upon" (151). Both Paul Taylor in the *Independent* and Lyn Gardner in the *Guardian* called David Calder's performance in the similarly sentimental 2008 Globe production "magnificent." (http://www.guardian.co.uk/stage/2008/may/05/theatre; http://www.independent.co.uk/arts-entertainment/theatre-dance/reviews/king-lear-shakespeares-globe-london-821521.html); accessed May 1, 2011.
45. Philippe Aries, *The Hour of Our Death*, trans. Helen Weaver (Knopf: New York, 1981), 107.
46. Sigmund Freud, "The Theme of the Three Caskets," trans. James Strachey, in *The Standard Edition of the Complete Psychological Works of Sigmund Freud*, 13:289–301.
47. Aristotle, *Poetics*, 16.
48. Catharine Goodland, *Female Mourning in Medieval and Renaissance English Drama*, 201–19. Rowland Wymer describes the potential sources of Shakespeare's familiarity with the Mystery Cycles in "Shakespeare and the Mystery Cycles," *English Literary Renaissance* 34 (2004): 265–85, an account supported by Michael O'Connell in "*King Lear* and the Summons of Death" (199–200; see footnote 3). John Murphy documents the inclusion of *King Lear* in the repertory of a Catholic touring company in 1609–10 in *Darkness and Devils: Exorcism and King Lear* (Athens: Ohio University Press, 1984), 103–15. Richard Wilson notes the adoption of *Lear* by this company, and he suggests that the cuts to the Folio *Lear* indicate Shakespeare's decision to distance himself from the martyrdom of activist Catholic resistance (*Secret Shakespeare: Studies in Theatre, Religion and Resistance* [Manchester: Manchester University Press, 2004], 283–90).
49. Goodland, *Female Mourning*, 218–19.
50. Aristotle, *Poetics*, 16. I would suggest that the division that Janet Adelman sees the play fostering in feminist critics through the competing claims of the characters of Cordelia and Lear (*Suffocating Mothers*, 125) is structured on this division between pity and terror. While the body of Cordelia evokes pity, terror is experienced through an identification with Lear as he embodies the adult male subject position that is posited by the play as the normative, universal identity (Aristotle's "a man like ourselves") moving into the final stage of life.
51. Maynard Mack, *King Lear in Our Time*, 117.
52. David Bevington, "'Is This the Promised End?'" 41; Hugh Grady, *Shakespeare's Universal Wolf*, 180.
53. Holinshed, *Chronicles of England, Scotland and Ireland*, 1:447.

54. Ulpian Fulwell, *Like Will to Like,* in *The Dramatic Writings of Ulpian Fulwell,* ed. John S. Farmer (London: Early English Drama Society, 1966), "Prologue" 4–6.
55. Aristotle, *Poetics,* 8.
56. *The Boke of crafte of dyinge,* in volume 2 of *Yorkshire Writers: Richard Rolle of Hampole and his Followers,* ed. Carl Horstmann (London: Swan Sonnenschein, 1896; orig. pub. circa 1400), 414.
57. Thomas Becon, *The Sick Man's Salve,* 185.
58. Caxton, "The Book of the Craft of Dying," 87.
59. Caxton, 88.
60. R. A. Foakes, *Hamlet versus Lear: Cultural Politics and Shakespeare's Art* (Cambridge: Cambridge University Press, 1993).

Performance Bibliography

King Lear. Directed by Peter Brook. DVD. Columbia-Tristar. 1970.

King Lear. Directed by Michael Elliot. DVD. Granada. 1983.

King Lear. Directed by Adrian Noble. Stratford and London. 1993.

King Lear. Directed by Richard Eyre. National Theatre, London. 1997.

King Lear. Directed by Richard Eyre. DVD. WGBH Boston. 1998.

King Lear. Directed by Dominic Dromgoole. Shakespeare's Globe. London. 2008.

The Merchant of Venice. Directed by Richard Olivier. Shakespeare's Globe, London. 1998.

The Merchant of Venice. Directed by Trevor Nunn. National Theatre, London. 1999.

Othello. Directed by Gregory Doran. Trafalgar Studios, London. 2004.

The Taming of the Shrew. Directed by Michael Bogdanov. Stratford. 1978.

The Taming of the Shrew. Directed by Gale Edwards. Barbican Theatre, London. 1996.

The Taming of the Shrew. Directed by Jonathan Miller. DVD. BBC Video. 1980.

The Taming of the Shrew. Directed by Franco Zeffirelli. DVD. Paramount Pictures/ Home Video. 1966.

Twelfth Night. Directed by Tim Carroll. Shakespeare's Globe, London. 2003.

Twelfth Night. Directed by Trevor Nunn. DVD. Fine Line Features. 1996.

Wicked Bastard of Venus. Written and directed by Julie-Anne Robinson. Southwark Theatre, London. 1993.

Index